Economic Development

Economic Development

A Regional, Institutional, and Historical Approach

Richard Grabowski
Sharmistha Self
Michael P. Shields

M.E.Sharpe
Armonk, New York
London, England

Library of Congress Cataloging-in-Publication Data

Grabowski, Richard, 1949–
  Economic development : a regional, institutional, and historical approach/
Richard Grabowski, Sharmistha Self, Michael P. Shields.
     p. cm.
  Includes bibliographical references and index.
  ISBN-13: 978-0-7656-1752-1 (cloth: alk. paper); ISBN-10: 0-7656-1752-8 (cloth: alk. paper)
  ISBN-13: 978-0-7656-1753-8 (pbk.: alk. paper); ISBN-10: 0-7656-1753-6 (pbk.: alk. paper)
  1. Economic development. I. Self, Sharmistha, 1963– II. Shields, Michael P., 1945–
III. Title.

HD75.G712 2007
338.9–dc22
                                                                                    2006010854

To Nikki, Adam, and Andy.
Richard Grabowski

To my mother and my father, Indrani and S.C. Lahiri.
Sharmistha Self

To my daughters, Kathryn and Carolyn,
may they and their generation live in a peaceful world
where economic development becomes the norm and not the exception.
Michael P. Shields

Contents

Tables, Figures, and Maps

Tables

Figures

Maps

Preface

Most comprehensive books on economic development follow a similar methodology. A series of topics are covered: capital, population growth, education, international trade, international finance, and the like. Within each chapter, there is generally a theoretical presentation, which is then illustrated through reference to a number of country-specific examples. Recently, several books have taken a growth theory perspective, but the methodology has been similar.

These books are based on the underlying assumption that development can be understood in terms of economic models adjusted to be relevant to the circumstances facing a particular economy. Less-developed countries are seen as facing low levels of physical and human capital, incomplete markets, and poor institutions. This standard approach is incomplete in that it does not address how these conditions arose. This book provides an alternative treatment of economic development that incorporates regional and historical differences into its treatment of development.

This book is innovative in a variety of ways. First, a regional approach is taken. That is, the economic development of a particular region is analyzed, with the theory being developed within the regional context. This, in turn, leads to the second innovative aspect of the book: an emphasis on institutional structure, with different regions illustrating diverse institutional structures. In order to do this, the history of the particular region becomes important, and this emphasis on history represents the third innovative aspect of the book. Fourth, every chapter ends with a reflection on what has been learned from the particular region's experience. This reflection ties together the basic message—the reasons behind the successes and failures as they apply to that region. This is meant to help readers understand why, in spite of theoretical similarities and some similarities in economic policies, different regions faced different outcomes. The book ends with a general reflection on what has been learned from all the different experiences and different regions that have been covered in the book. The chapters make use of theoretical concepts to tell the story of development. We have also made sure that readers will not lose sight of the development story due to the mathematical models used herein. In doing so, we hope to have achieved our purpose of having a larger and more inclusive readership. We do not wish to exclude those who are interested in economic models; however, where applicable, these have been included in appendixes.

There are a number of advantages to such an approach. While the theoretical models utilized in most development books are not difficult, readers are often put off by the theory, and this poses a stumbling block. In this book, the economic experiences of each region are analyzed and the theory is used to make sense of the experience. A second advantage of this approach is that there are ideas and themes that recur among the regional chapters. These themes provide a cohesive perspective, as indeed among the regional diversity there are a number of fundamental and recurring theoretical connections and rhythms. A third advantage of this approach is that the uniformities and regularities discussed above are often reflected in diverse institutional forms. For example, protection for income streams flowing from investment is essential for economic development. However, the institutional provisions of such protection can come in a variety of forms. One need only think of property rights protection in China relative to Japan and the United States.

This book is aimed at the student of economic development without a background in economics. It could be used in undergraduate-level courses in economic development, political economy, comparative systems, world economic systems, and international relations. A sophisticated reader can understand this material without having any previous coursework in economics. While a course in the principles of economics (micro or macro) might be desirable, it is possible to use this book as a textbook for students without this background.

Acknowledgments

The writing of this manuscript took place over several years. Some of the material was used to teach undergraduate courses in economic development. The students in these classes made numerous useful comments, which ultimately improved the quality of the work. In addition, we would like to thank Steven Reynolds, who read parts of the manuscript and gave us valuable feedback. Also, we would like to thank Nancy Mallett, who typed the manuscript and its many revisions.

Economic Development

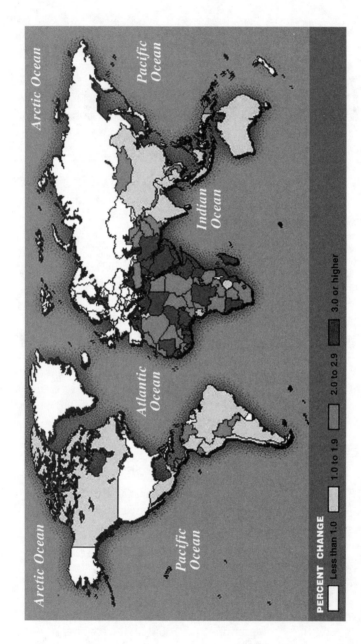

World population growth rates

1

Introduction to Economic Development

One can rationally presume that all countries want to achieve a decent standard of living for their people through improved material well-being. However, sixty years following World War II, when the plight of the poor was brought to the forefront, and economists, policy makers, and rich nations leapt forward with solutions, there are still many countries that have high rates of poverty. The gap between rich and poor has widened in many. Growth remedies—scores of them—have failed. Even as recent as 1999, nearly two-thirds of the world's population lived in countries where the average income was about one-tenth of the United States's level. William Easterly (2002) referred to economists' endeavors to solve the poverty puzzle as an "elusive quest." According to him, this quest has remained elusive due to the failure to apply economic principles to practical policy work. Timothy Yeager (1999) argues that the main reason behind failed growth experiments is not the lack of well-functioning markets (along with the absence of excessive government regulations), which has traditionally been offered as the cure to the problem, but the absence of a correct institutional framework.

Various sources have been identified as explanations for the different growth experiences of countries. These are varied and wide ranging, such as differences in human capital, natural resource endowments, population density, degree of openness, market structures, government policies, technology, geography, integration (trade), and institutional differences. Some of these factors are exogenous (i.e., caused by factors outside the economy) while others are not. Certain factors, such as technology, were presumed to be exogenous, but have since been found to be endogenously determined (i.e., caused by factors within the economy) or "embodied." Other factors, such as institutions, were presumed to be a by-product of growth. However, this perception has changed and appropriate institutions are now thought of as an essential precondition for growth (North and Thomas 1973). One thing that is being recognized from failed and successful growth experiments is that a single explanation or a specific set of explanations does not fit all. What works for one country may not work for another. Why is it that some countries increased the size of the production pie, but only a few actually enjoyed this increase? Alternatively, in some countries, the bigger pie was evenly distributed, and in yet others the pie did not increase at all. Why is it that some economies can produce relatively more efficient institutions than others can? How did Indonesia, prior to the Asian crisis, manage to grow so rapidly in spite of weak institutions and distorted policies? How did some Southeast Asian countries manage to find their footing and begin the process of recovery soon after the East Asian financial crisis of 1997, while a much stronger and more developed economy such as Japan remained crippled? How did China grow in spite of the absence of private-property rights? Why did countries such as India do poorly until the 1980s and then show remarkable growth, while Brazil and Venezuela did well until the 1980s and poorly thereafter? This book is written with these different growth experiences in mind. It looks at different parts of the developing world and seeks to explain what worked where and what went wrong.

In the following chapters, an attempt is made to identify and analyze which of these explanations are pertinent to which parts of the world, and why. In order to do so, different parts of the world are targeted and an attempt is made to dig deeper into their development stories, instead of looking at set explanations and matching them to a "case study" as is commonly done. In this book, regional and country experiences create the development story; they present the puzzles that economists and policy makers try to solve. The pieces (explanations) look different in each case. Even if they appear similar, they fit (application) differently in each case. Each puzzle comes with its own backdrop (history) and rules (institutions), so that each puzzle/picture is unique. The trick is not just in finding the right pieces, but the pieces that are right for the relevant puzzle. The theme that remains central and common through the discussions is the emphasis on the historical experiences of countries. The belief is that the development paths countries have taken and may yet follow are informed by its history. It is in understanding history that the information is gained that provides the key to the future and to understanding the present.

Growth Versus Development

What Is Economic Growth? What Is Economic Development?

The evolution of the concept of economic development started in the 1930s, when economists began realizing that most of humankind did not live in advanced capitalist countries. This thinking/reexamination was sparked by Colin Clark's 1939 study, the first study to make quantitatively evident the gulf between European countries and the rest of the world. Clark's work was responsible for initiating interest in the concept of development, but the interest in growth thereafter went through a lull, to be rekindled by Robert Solow's neoclassical growth theory, in 1956, which is based on diminishing-returns technology. In the 1970s, interest shifted from growth theory to monetary theories, business cycles, and rational-expectation theories. In the early 1980s, interest in real factors gained in importance over monetary factors. In the late 1980s, "new" growth theory, which emphasized the role of human capital in the growth process, rekindled interest in growth theory. Paul Romer and Robert Lucas's work on increasing returns to scale and endogenous growth marked a new era of interest in growth. Growth literature in the 1990s and early 2000s has refocused on the concept of total factor productivity, embodied or endogenously determined technology, the direction of causality between human capital and growth, and the role of institutions.

The existing literature shows that the concept of economic development is often confused with economic growth. It is difficult to distinguish between theories of development and theories of growth. Economic growth is the rise in national or per capita income or product typically measured by gross domestic product (GDP) or gross national product (GNP). An increase in per capita GDP, while characteristic of economic growth, does not necessarily lead to an increased standard of living if the growth is not evenly distributed. Economic development is a much broader concept than economic growth, though the two have been and continue to be used interchangeably in economic literature. One can think of economic growth as a precondition or a necessary condition for economic development. Countries that are typically poor are also typically less developed, though a rich country does not necessarily have to be a developed country. Consider some of the oil-rich Middle Eastern countries that have experienced large increases in per capita GDP, yet lag far behind in areas of development.

As mentioned, with the end of the World War II and the recovery of the West, the world was made aware of the huge economic and social differences between the developed West and the rest of the world. With the information revolution, the world has seemingly become a smaller place and access to goods and services has become cheaper and more easily accomplished. One can think of these closer links in information as helping the world get "more connected," which facilitates the faster flow of help and services. However, the information revolution has ostracized those parts of the world that have yet to become involved. In many ways, people there, along with their needs, have become even more remote. Table 1.1 presents some basic economic indicators for selected countries for 1998. These show that gaps in economic and social indicators continue to exist.

Following Clark's study, several economists started analyzing economic development as an independent subject. One such noted economist was Simon Kuznets (1966). The concept of modern economic growth was applied by Kuznets to refer to the current economic experience as contrasted with merchant capitalism or feudalism. Today we understand economic development to combine (1) self-sustaining growth; (2) structural changes in patterns of production; (3) technological upgrading; (4) social, political, and institutional modernization; and (5) widespread improvement in human conditions (Adelman 2000). When Kuznets was referring to modern economic growth, he was referring to the first of the three characteristics of development thus cited. The latter two were added by economists such as T.W. Schultz (1962) and Dudley Seers (1969). Shultz introduced the concept of human capital as a necessary ingredient for growth. This introduced education and training as important prerequisites for growth. According to Seers, development was a social phenomenon that involved more than growth in per capita output. Seers believed that development meant the elimination of poverty, unemployment, and inequality. This led to a reviewing of structural issues such as education, health, population growth, urbanization, agricultural reform, and so forth on their own merits and not as small pieces to the growth puzzle.

Table 1.1

Basic Economic Indicators, 1999

	GDP per capita[a]	Population density[b]	Population[c]	Education[d]
Argentina	8,073	13.3	36.1	3
Bangladesh	358	989	127	60
Botswana	3,854	2.8	1.58	25
China	769	134	1,253	17
Canada	21,752	3.3	30.2	0
Ethiopia	113	62.7	62.8	63
France	29,049	106	58.4	0
Germany	31,712	230	82	0
India	450	335	997	44
Mexico	3,626	50.6	96.6	9
Saudi Arabia	6,607	9.4	20.2	25
South Africa	3,930	34.5	42.1	15
Haiti	370	283	7.8	52
Brazil	4,482	19.9	168	15
United Kingdom	21,105	247	59.3	0
United States	31,073	30	278	0

Source: World Bank (2002).

[a] GDP per capita is GDP divided by midyear population. Data are in constant 1995 U.S. dollars.

[b] Population density is midyear population divided by land area in square kilometers.

[c] Total population is based on the *de facto* definition of population (in millions).

[d] Adult illiteracy rate (percentage of the population over fifteen years of age who cannot read and write).

Commonly Used Measures of Development

As mentioned above, economic development was traditionally equated with economic growth, which is typically measured by per capita GDP. GDP is the market value of all final goods and services produced in an economy in a year. However, given the acceptance of economic development as an independent concept, different variables and indexes have been used by economists to define and measure development.

Economic development is a broad and inclusive term; it is easily conceptualized but difficult to measure and/or quantify. Other than per capita GDP, economists have traditionally used some measure of health (life expectancy, infant mortality, incidence of disease, HIV/AIDS cases, immunization, etc.) or education (enrollment rates, average years of education, youth and/or adult literacy rate) or other economic conditions (poverty rate, inequality of income distribution, child labor, unemployment rate) to proxy for development.

Some research institutions have recently developed indexes to serve as more inclusive measures of development. The World Bank introduced the idea of "redistribution with growth" (RWG). RWG's basic idea is that governmental policies should shape development in such a way that low-income producers realize an increase in earning opportunities and receive resources to take advantage of them simultaneously. Another approach to measuring economic development is the "basic human needs" (BHN) approach, which aims at providing the poor with several basic commodities and services. Much of the appeal of BHN lies in its connections with the concept of human capital. Many factors that improve human capital can also improve the quality of human resources.

Efforts at quantifying and identifying proxies for these measures have led to several different indexes. Some of these measures are skewed toward the health aspect of development, while others are skewed toward social or socioeconomic aspects of development. An explanation of these individual indexes will clarify to the reader the aspect of development being targeted. Some examples of these are the DALY (disability-adjusted life years), QALY (quality-adjusted life years), DALE (disability-adjusted life expectancy), and HALE (healthy life expectancy) by the World Health Organization; the HDI (human development index), the GDI (gender development index), and HPI (human poverty index) of the United Nations Development Programme (UNDP); and the World Bank's World Development Indicators (WDI), which comprises a host of different indicators, such as variables to measure quality of life, human capital, progress toward development, and so on.

DALY measures the burden of disease in a population by combining "years of life lost" and "years lived with disability." The QALY is a single health-state measure combining quantity and quality of life. It is a generic measure that sums years spent in different states of health using weights (on a scale of 0 [dead] to 1 [perfectly healthy]) for each health state. DALE years are a measure of years lived minus an estimated percentage for each year lived in incomplete health. The number of years lost are arranged according to the main pressures of food, water, vector-borne diseases, poverty, and lifestyle. HALE is based on life expectancy (LEX), but includes an adjustment for time spent in poor health. This indicator measures the equivalent number of years in full health that a newborn child can expect to live based on the current mortality rates and prevalence distribution of health states in the population. The HDI measures the average achievement of a country in basic human capabilities. The HDI is a composite of three basic components of human development: longevity, knowledge, and standard of living. Longevity is measured by life expectancy. Knowledge is measured by a combination of adult literacy (two-thirds weight) and mean years of schooling (one-third weight). Standard of living is measured by purchasing power based on real GDP per capita adjusted for the local cost of living (i.e., purchasing power parity, or PPP). The HPI focuses directly on the number of people living in deprivation, presenting a very different picture from average national achievement. Deprivation in longevity is measured by the percentage of newborns not expected to survive to age forty. Deprivations in knowledge are measured by the percentage of adults who are illiterate. Deprivations in a decent standard of living are measured by three variables: the percentage of people without access to safe water, the percentage of people without access to health services, and the percentage of moderately and severely underweight children below the age of five. The GDI uses the same variables as the HDI. The difference is that the GDI adjusts the average achievement of each country in life expectancy, literacy, gross enrollment, and income in accordance with the disparity in achievement between men and women. The WDI, released annually, provides both cross-country data as well as time-series data for different country classifications. Some examples of their tables are those assessing vulnerability, enhancing security, disease prevention (i.e., coverage and quality), and women in development, to name a few.

Why Is GDP Still Used?

It was mentioned at the very beginning of our discussion of economic growth and economic development that economists often use some measure of income, such as GDP or per capita GDP, to measure a country's development. This might seem confusing given that there are so many other measures and given that growth has a much narrower application compared with development. Economists claim that development is a much broader concept, and yet they continue to use per capita GDP and its growth rate when assessing whether or not a country has shown signs of development. They confuse prosperity with development even when it is known that one need not necessarily lead to the other.

There are several reasons why GDP or related measures continue

Figure 1.1 **Correlation Between Per Capita GDP and Life Expectancy, 2000**

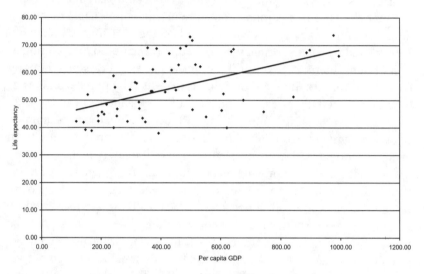

to be widely used as a measure of development. One is that there is a clear-cut meaning and acceptance among economists regarding economic growth and its measurement. When it comes to development, there are many different ways it can be measured, especially given the focus of the researcher. There is no particular measure that has been universally accepted and used. This explains why there are so many different measures commonly used in the literature. Another reason for using GDP is data availability. GDP data are available for most countries of the world and over a broad time spectrum. The same cannot be said of measures of development. Yet another reason for this confusion arises from the fact that early economic-development theory was an extension of conventional economic theory that synonymously used the terms development, growth, or industrialization. Last but not least, in spite of development economists' criticisms about using GDP as a measure of development, one finds empirically that GDP is very highly correlated with other measures of development. The measures used by the UNDP (HDI, GDI, HPI) are closely linked to GDP in construction. However, even the other measures—whether a particular variable such as life expectancy or infant mortality, or an index such as HALE—are also found to be very closely correlated with GDP. Figures 1.1, 1.2, 1.3, and 1.4 testify to the high correlation between per capita GDP and other measures of development.

Figure 1.2   **Correlation Between Per Capita GDP and Infant Mortality, 2000**

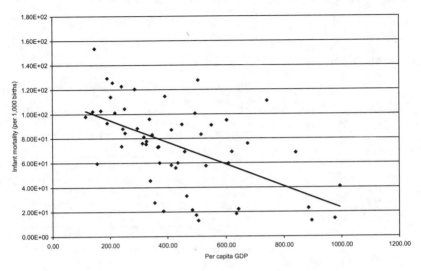

Figure 1.3   **Correlation Between Per Capita GDP and HALE, 2000**

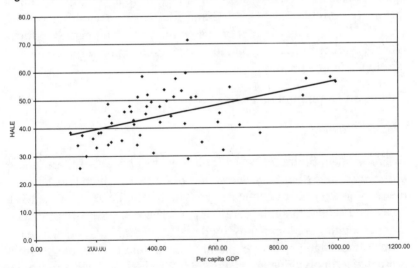

The countries in the sample are low- and middle-to-low-income countries identified by the World Bank, and the data pertain to 2000.

The figures represent scatter plots with fitted regression lines, in each case a particular variable measuring development has been regressed

Figure 1.4 **Correlation Between Per Capita GDP and HDI, 2000**

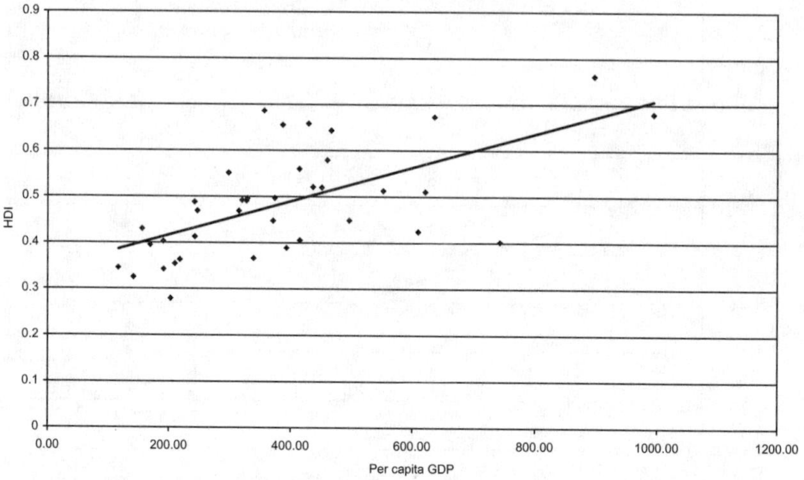

Source: World Bank (2002).

against per capita GDP. These show clearly that per capita GDP is positively correlated with HALE and life expectancy, and negatively correlated with infant mortality. Thus, in spite of its narrower focus, GDP or a related measure continues to be used to proxy for the level of development of a country.

History of Development Theory

Classical School

In 1776, Adam Smith ([1776] 1936) published his treatise, *An Inquiry into Nature and Causes of the Wealth of Nations*, which was taken by many to be a theory of economic growth. Smith, however, was clearly concerned with economic development. The classical school of economic thought, predominantly modeled after Smith, is largely geared toward understanding and explaining economic development. Smith presented a supply driven model of growth, where output was related to labor, land, and capital. Thus, economic growth, which is the increase in output, was related to population growth, investment, land growth, and increases in productivity. According to Smith, society was dependent on the economy's ability to sustain its increasing workforce. Investment was dependent on the rate of savings. Land growth was dependent on the ability to acquire more land (through conquest) or on the increase in the productivity of existing land. He also believed in the division or specialization of labor as a key factor in economic growth, enhanced by improved machinery and international trade. Smith argued that increased specialization would increase productivity and reduce per-unit costs, leading to increasing returns. However, he also thought that, in spite of increasing returns, such an economy would ultimately stagnate, wherein capital accumulation and population growth will approach zero. This will be brought about by the shrinking profits and savings of capitalists due to the higher wages that will have to be paid to laborers. Smith, however, set an optimistic tone, believing that this stagnation would not occur for several hundred years.

Smith believed that the extension of markets was the key to economic growth largely through the role that market extension played in creating greater specialization. Smith emphasized specialization as leading to greater productivity. One of the most famous passages in his book involved a pin factory and the way in which a greater division of labor—several workers specializing in one task of the many performed in making a pin—could dramatically increase productivity even without more capital being employed. To Smith, increased division of labor leads to higher worker productivity and, hence, to greater prosperity. Markets are the key because Smith believed the division of labor was limited by the completeness and the extent of markets. In other words, economic growth was occurring because markets were expanding.

Smith, a Scottish political economist and philosopher, argued that the mercantilist system was holding back England by limiting its market and, hence, limiting the division of labor. The mercantilist system, while it promoted the expansion of markets beyond the more limited markets of feudalism, restricted and regulated markets in many ways that Smith found objectionable. It limited international trade through regulations that impeded free access to foreign markets. These restrictions were particularly onerous to the North American colonies. Exports from the colonies to other parts of Europe had to first be shipped to England and then transshipped to their final destination rather than shipped directly. Domestically, so-called Corn Laws subsidized English agriculture (particularly grain) while taxing imports. Smith argued for free trade, since it would promote the greatest possible specialization in that the world is the largest possible market.

David Ricardo ([1817] 1965) modified Smith's model by introducing diminishing returns to land cultivation. Diminishing returns implies that as you apply more of a variable input (labor) to a fixed input (land), the productivity of each additional worker will eventually decline as long as technology is fixed. He claimed that land was of variable quality and finite. Thus, as an economy grows, population grows relative to land, and the productivity of the labor on the land will decline. Food, the output of land, will become relatively scarce, pushing up the price. Wages will need to rise if workers are to survive. As land becomes scarce, rental rates will rise. Both of these forces will cut into and reduce the profits of investors. Thus the expansion of the economy will grind to a halt as investment declines. According to Ricardo, the only way stagnation could be averted, at least temporarily, would be through the trade and imports of cheap food or wage goods. This would lower wages and thus prevent profits from contracting. Ultimately, however, the economy would have to come to a halt since the world is finite, and thus the law of diminishing returns would still operate in the long term. After a period of time, prices would start rising and profits would decline, setting in motion, once again, the law of diminishing returns.

The essential doctrines of John Stuart Mill (1848) differed little, if at all, from those of Ricardo. The theory of wages, for example, was formulated quite in the spirit of Ricardo. However, Mill did not see economics as the "dismal science" (so charged for its pessimistic predictions) many of his contemporaries did. He, like Smith, believed in the doctrine of *laissez-faire*, but he also recognized the possibility of modifying the system. He displayed a leaning to the socialist ideal, growing closer as his life advanced. He believed that we should sacrifice economic growth for the sake of the environment and limit population to fend off the risk of starvation.

This vision concerning population control was in direct contrast with Thomas Malthus's ([1798] 1959) prediction about population growth, which he said if left unchecked would lower economic growth and cause misery for mankind. Malthus placed the population question as being central to the future happiness of mankind. The population question concerns what determines population growth and how population size is related to per capita income. He believed that a race between population and our ability to produce would determine the future of civilization. Malthus stressed that population could easily outpace production. He stressed the potential for population to double every twenty-five years.

Malthus considered two forces that check population growth. Positive, or direct, checks include malnutrition, war, famine, and high infant mortality. Preventative checks include late marriage and celibacy. The population will eventually stabilize whatever the nature of the checks to population. However, what is important is which checks predominate. Differences in the relative strengths of these checks determine differences in population levels.

How can preventative checks be strengthened? A better way of asking this question is to ask why people would postpone having children. Answering this query should not be difficult to a college student. Most college students have decided to postpone marriage in order to further their education. You are investing in yourself by going to college. The cost of this investment is partly the income you could otherwise earn if you were not attending school and partly the sacrifice of the early joys of marriage or parenthood.

While few people sought higher education in Malthus's day, there were other opportunities for people to invest in themselves by postponing family formation or remaining unwed. The apprenticeship system was one such opportunity emphasized by Malthus. At a very young age, an apprentice would work for a master craftsman in return for board and room. He would gradually learn the trade, become a journeyman, and finally become a master craftsman. Only once he established his own trade would he marry.

This postponement of marriage in order to obtain a better life made society more prosperous for two reasons: it reduced the population, and workers became more productive because of the apprenticeship training.

Malthus contended that the Industrial Revolution was increasing birth rates because it was destroying the apprenticeship system and other preventative checks. Unless new preventative checks could be found, overpopulation would ruin civilization. Malthus advocated that educational opportunities should be provided for everyone. If this occurred, people might remain in school and postpone marriage. It would also make workers more productive, while reducing birth rates.

Marx and Engels ([1848] 1967) argued that market-based capitalism was the most dynamic force in the world. Originating in Western Europe, this economic system was based on capital accumulation, the spread of markets, and the exploitation of labor. This latter idea was based on the notion that labor is the source of all value in the production process, but labor is only recompensed part of that value, in the form of wages; the rest goes to the owner of the capital as profit (unearned according to

Marx and Engels). Profit, reinvested, is what drives the system forward. Capitalists seeking new sources of profit would spread out from Europe into the rest of the world. The spread of capital accumulation, markets, and exploitation would overwhelm all traditional societies (i.e., the developing world). These traditional societies would quickly be transformed into industrial, capitalist societies.

Although capitalism was extremely dynamic and would transform the world, there was a problem. According to Marx and Engels, the social, political, cultural, and spiritual aspects of society were determined by the mode of production. Under the capitalist mode of production, profit comes from the exploitation of human labor. However, the accumulation of capital and new technology displaces labor; that is, capitalism becomes increasingly capital intensive. As this occurs, this implies that there are fewer laborers to exploit in each firm, thus threatening the source of profit. Capitalists would thus be forced to increase the extent to which they exploit their remaining labor. The mechanization process creates an army of unemployed, a phenomenon that helps the capitalist class in pushing wages downward and intensifying the hours worked by labor.

The end result of this process is class conflict, crisis, and ultimately the collapse of capitalism. Conflict occurs between the owners of capital and the laborers as the position of the latter worsens. As the army of the unemployed grows and capital is concentrated in the hands of fewer and fewer capitalists, the intensity of the conflict poses a crisis for capitalism. Class war erupts, the workers take control of the capital (i.e., industry), and the capitalist class is eliminated as a force of history. Thus a new system emerges, socialism, where the means of production are controlled by the workers.

Modern Marxist views (Frank 1967) have dramatically revised Marx and Engles' analysis. These more recent theories have been labeled dependency theory. Where Marx and Engles saw capitalism as a dynamic force (transforming poor, traditional countries into capitalist, industrial nations), dependency theories view capitalism as a stifling force. That is, the expansion of capitalism in the center (the industrialized nations) retards the ability of the periphery (the poor, developing nations) to grow. The wealth of the center is based on the poverty of the periphery. Poor countries are created by the growth of the center.

The process by which the periphery can be impoverished is explained in many different ways. However, the common elements in the various explanations involve the extraction of profit from the periphery and the transfer of this to the center. Thus, the former lacks the resources to invest and develop its own economy. In these models, Marx and Engles's concern with the exploitation of labor by the owners of capital is replaced by an emphasis on the exploitation of the periphery by the center. Dependency theory maintains that true development cannot occur in the periphery until the exploitative link between the center and periphery, which operates through the international system of trade and investment, is broken. Nations of the periphery must pursue an inward-oriented development process if they are to raise the living standard of their peoples.

Tradition and Development

The classical theories discussed above assumed that there was a certain homogeneous character to societies. That is, society, in rich or poor countries, was not fundamentally dissimilar. However, a number of theorists have argued that tradition—the practices of the past that are handed down from generation to generation or are taught by society's dominant institutions—may pose particular problems for economic growth and development.

Max Weber ([1905] 1958) addressed this issue in his book *The Protestant Ethic and the Spirit of Capitalism*. He attempted to explain the shift of people's actions from traditional to rational-choice mechanisms. He wanted to search and find the reasons that motivated people in the West to abandon their traditional religious values in favor of a life targeted at acquiring material wealth. He reasoned that it was the "Protestant ethic" that made people relinquish their traditional values/orientation and encouraged them to apply themselves rationally to their work and to their savings and investment decisions. The Protestant ethic provided them with religious sanctions to acquire wealth. Wealth indicated that an individual might be one of God's elect (as per Calvinism), predestined for salvation, and it was this wealth-seeking behavior that ultimately paved the path to capitalism.

Joseph A. Schumpeter (1939, 1942, 1991) argued that growth was supply driven by the factors of production, with entrepreneurial innovation the most important of these. He believed in a "raw instinct" that drove entrepreneurs. He saw development as being driven by discontinuous changes in the economic environment fuelled by cycles of innovation. Schumpeter did not believe in diminishing returns to innovation. The only reason profits declined was competition. The decline in profits induces those with entrepreneurial skills to innovate and restart the process. In the long term, however, the process breaks down, not due to diminishing returns, but due to sociocultural changes. As countries develop, and their institutional characteristics change, the structural makeup of society changes. For instance, a high growth of firms might replace innovative and competitive entrepreneurs with bureaucratic managers, or lead to the transformation to an economy that depended on large-scale production to reap the benefits of economies of scale while abandoning the need to continuously innovate.

Adapting Schumpeter's model to the problems of developing countries involves an extension to the notion of tradition to incorporate bureaucratic behavior. Bureaucratic structures create rules by which individuals within an organization respond to particular situations. These rules are transmitted from a central autonomy and handed down to new generations of employers. These sorts of rules tend to be rigid and inflexible, and hence, difficult to change. In other words, bureaucratic structures and the rules they create often pose barriers to new, innovative behavior. They operate as traditions or traditional behavioral forms. If policy making within less-developed countries is dominated by traditional, bureaucratic structures, then, according to Schumpeter, innovative activity is likely to be stifled.

In the years following, various different ideas concerning development slowly evolved. These ranged from Liebenstein's (1957) theory of critical minimum effort to Boeke's (1953) and Lewis's (1954) concepts of dualism, and from Rostow's (1960) stages of development to Gerschenkron's (1962) reinterpretation of stages of development implying convergence.

From Leibenstein's perspective, there are two kinds of forces simultaneously at work in an economy: forces that shock and forces that stabilize (i.e., tradition). Whether or not an economy will break out of its traditional framework depended on whether shocks to the economy brought about by technological innovations could produce permanent change or would be suffocated by stabilizing forces brought about by low levels of education, increasing population growth, and traditional aspects of society. He believed that a critical minimum effort brought about by a major technological breakthrough or increased investment was needed to either dispel the forces of stabilization or turn them into contributors for growth. The acceptance of this change by the general population was a key factor in steering a country toward growth and recovery.

The concept of the dual economy was first associated with the Dutch economist J.H. Boeke. He examined the difference between the modern urban economies along rational capitalist lines, versus the more traditional, rural economy in the colonial Netherlands Indies. In the latter, capitalism coexisted with precapitalist social values. The modern sector was an enclave economy next to the traditional economy. The relationship between the two sectors was comparatively more beneficial to the colonizers as opposed to the indigenous population. The modern economy was more outward oriented, while the common people were making ends meet in traditional agricultural activities.

Another model based on the theory of dualism was Lewis's model of labor surplus. He divides a developing economy into the capitalist, or developed, sector, and the traditional, or subsistence, sector. There is a surplus of labor in the traditional sector, by which it is meant that there is a substantial portion of laborers in the traditional sector who make no significant contribution to the output of the sector. They are retained on the basis of tradition. For example, certain relatives may make little contribution to the family farm or firm, but they are retained because they are members of the extended family. Development, according to Lewis, is generated in the developed sector through the investment of profits generated by a transfer of resources out of the traditional sector. These profits are made possible partly because wages are kept low. This transfer of laborers out of the traditional sector is not harmful for the traditional sector because of the surplus labor that this sector had to support was a drain on their resources. After the surplus labor is absorbed, there is an upward pressure on wages and an incentive on the part of the employers in the modern sector to substitute capital for labor.

Among the theories associated with stages of development, perhaps the best known is Rostow's (1960) contribution. He believed that every society starts off as traditional in nature. It needs to create what he called "preconditions for takeoff" to be able to break out of the trap of traditionality. These would include investments by entrepreneurs, specialization and widening of markets, social overhead capital buildup, and increased monetization. These aggregately would provide the necessary ingredients for the "takeoff" stage, which would be characterized by marked increases in key economic variables. The economy then enters the "drive to maturity" phase, with a relatively steady rate of growth, and eventually into the "age of high mass consumption."

Alexander Gerschenkron (1962) added a new and unique interpretation to the theory of stages of development. His theory implied that latecomers to development would grow faster and "catch-up" or overtake the developed countries by taking advantage of advanced technology. He argued that the difference in the paths of political regimes that countries across the world faced was due to differences in the timing of industrialization and extent of backwardness. According to him, an economy's growth path was dependent both on its initial economic conditions as well as policy choices made by government. Backwardness has its advantages because late developers can grow relatively faster through increased financial and industrial concentration based on borrowed technology. Thus they can close the gap with rich countries. Institutional characteristics play an important role in this development process. Additionally, late developers are more likely to experience greater state intervention in decision making.

Models of Industrialization

In the aftermath of World War II, and with the recognition of the need for a large part of the world to develop, many different theories were put forward as remedies. One such theory revolved around industrialization as the appropriate intermediate goal to achieve development. There were several "stylized" beliefs of the day that promoted this line of thinking (Krueger 1997). First, there was the notion that developing countries were primarily producers of primary commodities, and, second, that if they adopted free trade then their comparative advantage would keep them forever trapped in producing primary commodities. There was also the notion that both price and income elasticities for primary goods were low, and hence the developing countries could not substantially increase their incomes through the exports of these goods. Moreover, following Lewis's theory, it was believed that labor was in excess supply, earning less than their marginal product, while capital, which was critical to production, was the only scarce factor of production. Additionally, it was believed that labor was quite "traditional" in the sense that it was slow to respond, if at all, to price incentives. Given these beliefs/premises, the logical conclusion was that, if countries needed to develop, they had to industrialize by accumulating more capital, which would lead to increased investment in manufacturing industries. The two main theories of industrialization were the "big push" and "unbalanced growth" theories.

The big-push theory was proposed by Rosenstein-Rodan in 1943. According to him, an economy could not succeed by taking small steps toward development. It needed a "big push" in order for the process of industrialization to evolve. There is an assumption of an increased role of the state in this theory. Ragnar Nurkse (1953) proposed a similar idea, which he called "balanced growth." This theory posited that a whole range of mutually supportive investments led to development. The main difference behind big push and balanced growth was Nurkse's recognition of the agricultural sector (which was ignored by Rosenstein-Rodan) as a required partner for growth along with the industrial sector. Another formula for industrialization was introduced by Albert O. Hirschman, also in 1958. This was called the "unbalanced growth" theory, and proposed, as its name suggests, an unbalanced growth path to lead to the creation of linkages that would summon other industries into existence. Linkages could be either backward linkages, which is the proportion of one industry's inputs purchased from other industries, or forward linkages, which is the proportion of an industry's outputs purchased by other industries. These linkages could arise out of initial investments, which could either create excess capacity or excess supply (i.e., potential for forward linkages) or create a shortage or excess demand (i.e., potential for backward linkage). Supporters of this theory saw this as a means for reducing government's role in the development process. It would merely initiate change and allow the private sector to respond via the operation of the linkages.

Neoclassical Growth and Convergence

The neoclassical theory grew out of pioneering work done by Robert Solow in the late 1950s. Solow's work regenerated a surge of interest in growth theory. The model was preceded by separate but similar growth models presented by Harrod (1939) and Domar (1946) and came to be known as the Harrod-Domar growth model. According to this model, which was based on a fixed-coefficient production function (wherein the isoquants are L-shaped, showing that capital and labor can combine only in a fixed ratio to produce output), capital accumulation and savings were the two main ingredients necessary for an economy to grow.

In order to explain the model, the symbol Δ is used to represent "change in." The first important component of the model is called the marginal "capital-to-output ratio" (v), which indicates how much capital is required to produce one additional unit of output, and can be written as Equation (1.1):

$$v = \frac{\Delta K}{\Delta Y} = \frac{K}{Y}, \tag{1.1}$$

where K is the stock of physical capital and Y is the output. Note that it is assumed that the marginal and average capital-to-output ratios are the same. This is a measure of the productivity of capital and is assumed to be fixed (i.e., exogenous).

The second component of the model is the rate of savings (s). Thus, Equation (1.2) can be written as:

$$s = \frac{\Delta K}{Y}, \tag{1.2}$$

and is assumed to be fixed (exogenous). Thus s represents new capital created (ΔK) as a share of total output or income.

Using these two components, one can now derive an expression for both the rate of growth of output $\left(\frac{\Delta Y}{Y}\right)$ and the rate of growth of capital $\left(\frac{\Delta K}{K}\right)$ as follows in Equations (1.3) and (1.4):

$$\frac{s}{v} = \frac{\Delta K/Y}{\Delta K/\Delta Y} = \frac{\Delta Y}{Y} \tag{1.3}$$

and

$$\frac{s}{v} = \frac{\Delta K/Y}{K/Y} = \frac{\Delta K}{K}. \tag{1.4}$$

These two expressions indicate that the rate of growth of output and capital are determined by s and v, the latter representing the productivity of capital. As an example, if the savings rate is 0.05 and the capital-to-output ratio is one-half, then the growth of output and capital will be 0.10 (i.e., 10 percent).

The third component of the theory is the rate of growth of population (n), which is assumed to be fixed (exogenous). With this third component, one can now derive an expression for the rate of growth of output per person, expressed as Equation (1.5):

$$\frac{s}{v} - n. \tag{1.5}$$

There are three possible situations in this model. The discussion that follows will presume that the economy is in a steady state, expressed as Equation (1.6):

$$\frac{s}{v} - n = 0. \tag{1.6}$$

In this situation, output, capital, and the level of population are all growing at the same rate. Thus per capita output and the capital-to-labor ratio remain unchanged (i.e., stationary).

What are the implications of the model? If a country is in a steady state and wants to increase per capita income, this could happen three ways. First, if the savings rate of society rises, $s' > s$, then output would grow faster than the population and per capita output would rise, as in Equation (1.7):

$$\frac{s'}{v} - n > 0. \tag{1.7}$$

Starting in the steady state, there is a second way to raise per capita income, by lowering n, the population growth rate, to $n' < n$. This will once again allow output and capital to grow faster than the population, as expressed in Equation (1.8):

$$\frac{s}{v} - n' > 0. \tag{1.8}$$

Starting once again from the steady state, the third way to increase per capita income is the introduction of a new technology that raises the productivity of capital such that $v' < v$. This results in Equation (1.9):

$$\frac{s}{v'} - n > 0. \tag{1.9}$$

Thus, according to the Harrod-Domar growth model, it is possible to cause permanent, continuous improvements in per capita income by raising savings, reducing population growth, or introducing a new technology.

The Harrod-Domar growth model was quite influential in the minds of not only economists, but also policy makers in national governments and international agencies. However, the analysis in this model was soon challenged by Robert Solow (1956), Trevor Swan (1956), and James E. Meade (1961). According to Solow's model, the fixed-coefficient production function used by the Harrod-Domar model is inappropriate. Solow substitutes a production relationship in which it is assumed that capital can be substituted for labor and vice versa. This introduces something that was missing in the Harrod-Domar model: the law of diminishing returns. In this case, v, the productivity of capital, becomes variable.

The implications that follow from this are made easy to see by referring back to Equation (1.7). The Harrod-Domar model argued that an increase in s to s' would permanently raise the growth of per capita income; Equation (1.7) becomes positive. Solow, however, argued that this effect would be temporary. If $\frac{s'}{v} - n > 0$, this implies that capital is growing relative to labor, the capital-to-labor ratio is rising. If technology does not change, then the law of diminishing returns sets in and the productivity of capital falls, and v goes up. As this continues, v will eventually reach v', as in Equation (1.10):

$$\frac{s'}{v'} - n = 0, \qquad (1.10)$$

per capita income stops rising. The conclusion, then, is that a rise in savings can only temporarily cause per capita income to grow. Eventually, the law of diminishing returns stops the growth.

The same sort of analysis applies to reducing the population growth rate. Equation (1.8) implies that this will cause per capita income to rise endlessly. However, Equation (1.8) also implies that capital will rise faster than labor, and thus the law of diminishing returns will set in, the productivity of capital will fall, and v will rise, giving Equation (1.11):

$$\frac{s}{v'} = n'. \qquad (1.11)$$

Thus, reducing population growth can, in the short run, raise per capita income, but this will be brought to a stop.

One could respond to the above arguments by saying that the law of diminishing returns could be offset if s keeps rising and/or n keeps falling, allowing Equations (1.7) and (1.8) to continue to hold, that is, capital and output to continue rising faster than labor. However, there are binding limits to this since the highest value that s could be is one, and the lowest value n could be is zero. Ultimately the law of diminishing returns always wins and the growth rate of per capita income cannot be permanently increased.

With technological change, however, the above is not true. Technological change lowers v, resulting in a situation represented by Equation (1.9). Once again, capital and output will grow faster than labor and the law of diminishing returns will set in, thus raising v. However, if technological change is rapid enough it can keep v from rising, it can prevent the return to the steady state, and per capita income will permanently rise. Whereas there are limits to the extent that a rising s and falling n can offset the law of diminishing returns, there is no limit on technological change offsetting the law of diminishing returns.

In summary, the Solow model indicates that raising s and lowering n can raise per capita income, but this can only lead to growth in the short run. Only technological innovation can lead to growth in per capita income in the long term. Within this context, what does the neoclassical model have to say about poor countries catching up with rich countries—will there be a process of absolute convergence? If poor countries are able to achieve rates of saving, population growth rates, and technologies similar to those achieved among the rich countries, then absolute convergence would, according to the neoclassical model, occur. Both countries would have the same steady state, and poor countries would achieve the same per capita income levels and growth rates as the rich. However, for most poor countries, savings rates, population growth rates, and technologies are quite different. Thus, the steady state for poor countries will be different from those of the rich. Poor countries will have steady states at lower levels of per capita income (and growth) than the rich countries.

Using Maddison's (1991) data and starting in 1870, Baumol (1986) carried out an empirical analysis of convergence theory for sixteen industrial countries. He showed that convergence theory did hold for the poorer countries in this group. He found evidence of absolute convergence to be especially strong for the post–World War II period. However, it was pointed out by DeLong (1988) that the countries in this sample were the relatively richer countries and for them convergence theory did hold. However, history has shown that convergence theory does not hold for a number of the poorer countries of the world. In fact, there is evidence that shows that incomes of developing countries in the last century have fallen far behind those of developed countries both proportionately and absolutely (Pritchett 1997).

New Growth/Endogenous Growth

The concept of human capital as an instrument of growth, over and above capital and labor, was initiated with Romer (1986). (Parts of this section are based on Foss 1997.) This model introduced human capital as an integral part of the development process, which was ignored in Solow's neoclassical model. One of the main problems with the neoclassical model was the apparent inconsistency between the theoretical and empirical estimates of the model regarding capital's share in output and its marginal productivity. Romer showed that the introduction of human capital into the production function changed its characteristic into one with increasing returns. This overturned the neoclassical conclusions, which were based on diminishing-returns technology. This was the main contribution of new growth theory to the literature on economic growth. Moreover, Mankiw, Romer, and Weil (1992) showed that introducing human capital as an input into the production function greatly improved the model's predictive powers. Following Romer's 1986 paper, three different themes emerged within the new growth framework. The first theme was the introduction of human capital into the production function by Maniw, Romer, and Weil (1992) in what was called the augmented Solow model. The second theme was the introduction of knowledge accumulation either directly via human capital or indirectly via research and development (Lucas 1988; Romer 1990). The third theme was based on the competition for patents and was introduced by Aghion and Howitt (1992).

A simple formulation that is applicable to all branches of new growth theory can be given by an aggregate production function of the form $Y = F(K, L, H, A)$, where H is human capital, K is physical capital, L is labor, and A is technology. There are two important differences between this production function and the neoclassical one: here human capital and physical capital enter as two distinct factors of production, and A is no longer constant.

In Romer's 1986 paper, A is a function of the stock of knowledge from R&D, with the assumption that there is a spillover or "externality" effect of private research on the stock of knowledge in society. Knowledge, in this model, is assumed to be an input in production that has increasing marginal productivity. According to this model, firms are productive when other firms in the economy are more productive. These knowledge/productive externalities offset the diminishing returns that the other inputs might face.

In Lucas's 1988 paper, H enters as an input into the production function (the augmented Solow model) and also has an externality effect. The externality effect is that the amount of human capital in the economy affects individual firm's productivity even though it is not taken into account in individual profit-maximizing decisions. According to this model, there is the potential for increasing returns to all factors as long as the externality effect of human capital is positive. Lucas's conclusions were similar to Romer's, though Lucas's model had predictions for long-run growth being a function of physical and human capital even if the external effects of human capital are presumed to be nil.

Romer (1990) introduced a new modeling strategy within the tenets of new growth theory, which is referred to as "endogenous growth theory." This model focused on the determinants of technology itself. In this model, H is represented by education and on-the-job training. Technology, or A, is assumed to be endogenous and nonrival, and the other inputs have their usual connotations. The research sector uses the existing knowledge and human capital and produces under increasing returns to scale. Each new product that emerges adds to the existing pool of knowledge, and in that sense, the marginal productivity of human capital in the research sector increases over time. Romer showed that the overall growth rate is determined by the amount of human capital stock employed in research; as this stock grows, so does the economy.

Changes in Recent Development Thinking

When one thinks of the twentieth century, one's attention is caught by the term globalization, which was a product of the late nineteenth and twentieth centuries. Globalization breaks down barriers and connects the world. With globalization, it is no longer possible to view theories, policies and their consequences, and ideas in isolation since actions and policies undertaken by one country are not isolated to that country but affect the rest of the world through externality effects. Along with globalization, the twentieth century also introduced economists, policy makers, and indeed the world to the practical applications of the idea of a mixed economy. The twentieth century also has forced people to consider what an "open economy" means. When one looks at the more recent trends in development thinking (mid-to-late twentieth century to the present), the areas that dominate the growth literature are the role of trade, the state, and institutions as pieces that collectively and collaboratively fit together to allow the development story to be comprehended. The role of the state and trade are integral parts in the understanding of the function of institutions. The following discussion will focus on institutions, trade, and the state, and will show how all these ideas/concepts are thoroughly integrated. The objective of the following discussion is to convey this sense of integration.

Institutions have grown in importance in the growth literature over the past decade. To answer the question "what are institutions," a simple answer would be that institutions are the "rules of the game" in society

(Yeager 1999, 9). These can be economic, social, or political in nature. The development literature has recognized that institutions are important for initiating and maintaining economic growth. An institutional framework has three basic components: formal rules, informal rules, and enforcement mechanisms. Formal rules are the written rules of society, informal rules are the unwritten rules, and enforcement mechanism is the degree to which these rules are enforced or imbibed by society. A country's degree of enforcement and success of enforcement along with the time required for changing the informal rules probably explains a large portion of the reason why countries vary in economic performance.

Rodrik (2003) highlights some important characteristics about institutions, which are arrived at cumulatively through different country experiences. First, the quality of the institutions is key; second, trade, or a government's trade policy, while important, is relatively less important than the institutional setup; third, geography is not as binding a constraint as it is often portrayed since good institutions can overcome these constraints; fourth, acquiring good institutions sometimes requires leaps of faith while paying attention to local circumstances; and fifth, initial growth does not require extensive institutional reform. Small steps taken at regular intervals can go a long way. Last but not least, only by strengthening the institutions can a country fight adverse conditions and sustain economic growth.

Economists have asked whether trade can cause growth (Frankel and Romer 1999). They have found that the causal relation one would conventionally expect is not significant. Even if one ignores causality as too strong a relation, even a positive relation between the two is much debated. While Rivera-Batiz and Romer (1991) showed the positive linkage between international trade and economic growth, theoretical studies such as Grossman and Helpman's (1991) showed that the relation between international trade and economic growth is highly ambiguous. The same conclusion is reached when examining the effects of trade policies on growth (Rodriguez and Rodrik 1999). In spite of the ambiguity regarding the trade and growth relationship, there is evidence of trade's relation with institutions. There is evidence of trade leading to better institutions (Wei 2000) and better institutions leading to more trade (Anderson and Marcouiller 1999). Moreover, it has been shown that there is a potential cause-and-effect relation between good institutions and economic growth. Thus, the causal relation between trade and growth may not be direct, but indirect via more economically conducive institutions.

The development literature commonly associates the concept of trade with globalization, a term that indeed has become an integral part of twenti-eth-century growth empirics. Harris (1993) identifies three main symptoms of globalization: growth in trade, foreign direct investment, and global corporations; change in the structure of wages and income distribution; and the growth and internationalization of services. Today, globalization is a much-discussed phenomenon, but that was not the case if one looks back only a few decades to the 1950s. The 1950s were dominated by theories in support of import-substitution policies as a means to promote industrialization. These policies appeared to work for a number of different countries, such as those in Latin America, the Middle East, and for some countries in Africa and Asia, until around the mid-1970s.

A number of almost simultaneous events, both practical and theoretical, in the late 1960s and early 1970s dispelled the myths associated with the success of import-substitution strategies. On the theoretical front, research by Bhagwati and Ramaswamy (1963), Bhagwati (1969), and others showed that import-substitution policies practiced through the imposition of different trade restrictions were not beneficial for developing countries. On the practical side, there were the oil shocks of 1973 and 1979, sharp drops in median growth rates in the developing world, worldwide reces-sion in the beginning of the 1980s, and the collapse of the Bretton Woods system of international monetary management. Around the same time, the growth experiences of Taiwan and South Korea drew the world's at-tention. These countries' trade practices were based on policies of export promotion as opposed to import substitution. These countries were also among those that resumed their growth rates following the "debt crisis" of the 1980s, unlike some Latin American countries that were crippled by external shocks and could not service their debts.

One explanation of why some countries could resume their growth paths following the debt crisis of the 1980s while others could not is given by Rodrik (2000). He argues that while there are obvious macroeconomic implications of crisis, it is the deep underlying social conflict that needs to be corrected in order to bring a country back to where it was before crisis. Some societies have poor institutions of conflict management and are thus unable to handle shocks. The failure of conflict management can be used as the explanation for the 1997 East Asian financial crises as well. The idea that more authoritative governments would be able to prevent and contain the crisis has proven to be incorrect in the countries hit by this crisis. A country like Indonesia, which was run by an autarchy, was devastated by the crisis, while countries like Thailand and South Korea, which had more democratic institutions, adjusted much better. Thus, it was the over reliance on short-term capital flows and the lack of democratic institutions to handle conflict that was responsible for the Asian crisis. Now that the crisis is over, Rodrik's explanation makes sense when one realizes that the Asian crisis was essentially a short-lived currency crisis, symptomatic of a financial panic, and not one resulting from the failure of basic macroeconomic factors. This explains, to a large extent, why most of the Southeast Asian countries resumed growth once the crisis passed.

The situation in Japan was different. The timing of when the "bubble burst" in Japan was not due to the collapse of the yen. Crisis in the stock and property markets began the economic slowdown. This was made worse by the Japanese government's rigid and somewhat contractionary monetary and fiscal policy, which kept growth stagnant, with falling consumption and investment spending leading to a dangerous deflationary situation. However, Japan's situation, being one of the key markets in the region, poses a danger to the rest of Asia.

Recently, much attention has been directed at the role of the state and how this ties in with the explanations above. History has shown that some political systems are capable of producing institutions that are more efficient while others are not. Ideologies involving the role of the state have gone from one extreme to the other in the past few decades. The role of the government or state has risen to the forefront of interest following the "miracle" growth witnessed in East and Southeast Asia, followed by the Asian crisis. In these countries, the role of the government was far more active than prescribed by the so-called Washington Consensus. The Washington Consensus had been embraced by Latin American countries, as well as in Eastern Europe. According to its dictates, the state was made less of a player in decision making, with the private sector moving to center stage. Experiences such as the failure of price reforms in Russia and the growth experiences of Latin American countries suggested this formula did not work. At the same time, the experiences of the late 1990s in Southeast and East Asia showed that authoritative government could not prevent the Asian crisis, which was widely blamed on "crony capitalism." These experiences led toward a more balanced view in the late twentieth century, one of better cohesion between state and markets. In other words, a more "mixed economy" type of approach became increasingly popular along with the realization that different sets of rules worked in different countries.

The important message that should emerge from the discussion is that perspectives have changed over time, mainly fashioned by experience. An understanding of how the views on the role of the state have changed can be gauged by studying the World Bank's views expressed through its annual *World Development Report*. The World Bank is one of the world's largest sources of developmental assistance. Its primary focus is on helping the poorest people and the poorest countries. Up until the 1980s, the World Bank spoke highly of the importance of markets in achieving economic development. The role of national governments was limited to that of a corrector of market failures and for maintaining domestic macroeconomic stability. In fact, the bank championed the growth experiences of the newly industrialized economies (NIEs) of East Asia as those rising out of free and deregulated markets. A more realistic look at the NIEs of East Asia, however, revealed to the world that governments played a much more important role in their development than was being claimed by the bank. This led to the formulation of the concept of the "governed state" by Robert Wade (1990). Consequently, in the *World Development Report 1997*, the World Bank appeared to be reconciled with the realities of the growth experiences of the NIEs, as it expressed a renewed interest in the "state's capability" in achieving development.

Today it is recognized that both markets and governments are important in order to create a functional and growth-enhancing institutional framework. Rodrik (2000) identifies five functions of the state beneficial to market efficiency. These are protection of property rights, market regulation, macroeconomic stabilization, social insurance, and conflict management. Governments are necessary for markets to be able to function properly, though that is not their only function. While one cannot ignore how important markets are for promoting growth through competition, governments have to be in place to provide incentives for markets to operate freely and to prosper without allowing the demands of special-interest groups to bias either markets or government policies. The higher the degree of cohesion between markets and governments, the more efficient the institutions and the greater the chances for efficient allocation of resources for development.

What Lessons Have We Learned and Where Do We Go From Here?

At the end of each chapter of the book there will be a section that summarizes what has been learned. In this introductory chapter, an attempt has

been made to look at and examine what others have said about the process
of economic growth and development. These theories will be used in
the following chapters to understand the experiences of various regions
of the world. This is not to say there will be no new theories introduced
in the ensuing chapters, but these will be built on the analytical base
provided in this chapter. Thus, one can view this chapter as representing
the initial box of tools that will be used to analyze the experiences of
Europe, East Asia, Sub-Saharan Africa, South Asia, Latin America, and
the Middle East. As the book unfolds, the toolbox will be expanded.

Before proceeding to an analysis of the experience of various
regions, one should keep in mind that one of the biggest mistakes
of development theorists has been the attempt to fit different country experiences to theories after the fact. Even within a particular
country's experiences, the explanations have varied between phases
of historical, institutional, and economic development. In order to
understand the true meaning and implications of development the
economist and policy maker have to understand the full context of
the problem. The success stories and failures have shown that one of
the main lessons is that it is not possible to analyze the growth and
development experiences of different countries using set explanations.
Moreover, it is difficult to isolate particular theories as explanations.
Another important empirical lesson the world has learned is that markets and states are complementary to each other in forming efficient
institutions. Improving the efficiency of one essentially improves the
efficiency of the other. Understanding this relationship has probably
been the key to success of many countries.

Key Terms	
Institutions	Dualism
GDP	Tradition
HDI	Unbalanced Growth
Specialization	Balanced Growth
Mercantilism	Neoclassical Growth
Positive Checks	Convergence
Preventative Checks	Harrod-Domar Growth Theory
Class Conflict	Endogenous/New Growth Theory
Protestant Ethic	Glooalization

References

Adelman, Irma. 2000. "Fifty Years of Economic Development: What Have We Learned?" Paper presented at the World Bank ABCDE Conference in Paris, June.

Aghion, Philippe, and Peter Howitt. 1992. "A Model of Growth Through Creative Destruction." *Econometrica* 60: 322–51.

Anderson, James E., and Douglas Marcouiller. 1999. "Trade, Insecurity, and Home Bias: An Empirical Investigation." NBER Working Paper 7000. Cambridge, MA: National Bureau of Economic Research.

Baumol, William J. 1986. "Productivity Growth, Convergence, and Welfare: What the Long Run Data Show." *American Economic Review* 76 (5): 1072–85.

Bhagwati, Jagdish N. 1969. "On the Equivalence of Tariffs and Quotas." In *Trade, Tariffs, and Growth*, ed. Jagdish Bhagwati, 248–65. Cambridge, MA: MIT Press.

Bhagwati, Jagdish N., and V.K. Ramaswamy. 1963. "Domestic Distortions, Tariffs, and the Theory of Optimum Subsidy." *Journal of Political Economy* 71 (1): 44–50.

Boeke, J.H. 1953. *Economics and Economic Policy in Dual Societies*. New York: AMS Press.

Clark, Colin G. 1939. *Conditions of Economic Progress*. London: Macmillan.

DeLong, Bradford J. 1988. "Productivity Growth, Convergence, and Welfare: Comment." *American Economic Review* 78 (5): 1138–54.

Domar, Evsey. 1946. "Capital Expansion, Rate of Growth and Employment." *Econometrica* 14: 137–47.

Easterly, William. 2002. *The Elusive Quest for Growth: Economists' Adventures and Misadventures in the Tropics*. Cambridge, MA: MIT Press.

Foss, Nicholas J. 1997. "The New Growth Theory: Some Intellectual Growth Accounting." Paper prepared for a DRUID conference, Department of Industrial Economics and Strategy, Copenhagen Business School, Copenhagen, Denmark.

Frank, Andre Gunder. 1967. *Capitalism and Underdevelopment in Latin America*. New York: Monthly Review Press.

Frankel, Jeffrey A., and David Romer. 1999. "Does Trade Cause Growth?" *The American Economic Review* 89 (3): 379–99.

Gerschenkron, Alexander. 1962. *Economic Backwardness in Historical Perspective*. Cambridge, MA: Harvard University Press.

Grossman, G.M., and E. Helpman. 1991. *Innovation and Growth in the Global Economy*. Cambridge, MA, and London: The MIT Press.

Harris, Richard G. 1993. "Globalization, Trade, and Income." *The Canadian Journal of Economics* 26 (4): 755–76.

Harrod, R.F. 1939. "An Essay in Dynamic Theory." *The Economic Journal* 49 (193): 14–33.

Hirschman, Albert O. 1958. *The Strategy of Economic Development*. New Haven, CT: Yale University Press.

Krueger, Anne O. 1997. "Trade Policy and Economic Development: How We Learn." *American Economic Review* 87 (1): 1–22.

Kuznets, Simon. 1966. *Modern Economic Growth: Rate, Structure, and Spread*. New Haven, CT: Yale University Press.

Leibenstein, Harvey. 1957. *Economic Backwardness and Economic Growth*. New York: John Wiley.

Lewis, Arthur W. 1954. "Economic Development with Unlimited Supplies of Labour." *Manchester School* 22: 139–91.

Lucas, Robert E. 1988. "On the Mechanics of Economic Development." *Journal of Monetary Economics* 22: 3–42.

Maddison, Angus. 1991. *Dynamic Forces in Capitalist Development*. Oxford: Oxford University Press.

Malthus, T.R. 1959 [1798]. *Population: The First Essay*. Ann Arbor, MI: University of Michigan Press.

Mankiw, Gregory N., David Romer, and David N. Weil. 1992. "A Contribution to the Empirics of Economic Growth." *The Quarterly Journal of Economics* 107 (2): 407–37.

Marx, Karl, and Friedrich Engels. 1967 [1848]. *The Communist Manifesto*. Harmondsworth, Middlesex: Penguin Books.

Meade, J.E. 1961. *A Neo-Classical Theory of Economic Growth*. London: Allen and Unwin.

Mill, John Stuart. 1848. *Principles of Political Economy*. London: J.W. Parker.

North, Douglass C., and R. Thomas. 1973. *The Rise of the Western World: A New Economic History*. Cambridge, UK: Cambridge University Press.

Nurkse, Ragnar. 1953. *Problems of Capital Formation in Underdeveloped Countries*. Oxford: Basil Blackwell.

Pritchett, Lant. 1997. "Divergence, Big Time." *The Journal of Economic Perspectives* 11 (3): 3–17.

Ricardo, David. 1965 [1817]. *The Principles of Political Economy and Taxation*. London: Everyman's Library.

Rivera-Batiz, Luis A., and Paul M. Romer. 1991. "International Trade with Endogenous Technological Change." NBER Reprints 1691 (also Working Paper 3594). National Bureau of Economic Research, Cambridge, Massachusetts.

Rodriguez, Francisco, and Dani Rodrik. 1999. "Trade Policy and Economic Growth: A Skeptic's Guide to the Cross-National Evidence." NBER Working Paper 7081. National Bureau of Economic Research, Cambridge, Massachusetts.

Rodrik, Dani. 2000. "Development Strategies for the Next Century." Paper delivered at the Conference on Developing Economies in the 21st Century, Institute for Developing Economies, Japanese External Trade Organization, Chiba, Japan, January 26–27.

———. 2003. "Introduction: What Do We Learn From Country Narratives?" In *Search of Prosperity: Analytic Narratives on Economic Growth*, ed. Dani Rodrik, 1–22. Princeton, NJ: Princeton University Press.

Romer, Paul M. 1986. "Increasing Returns and Long Run Growth." *Journal of Political Economy* 94: 1002–37.

———. 1990. "Endogenous Technological Change." *Journal of Political Economy* 98, 71–102.

Rosenstein-Rodan, Paul N. 1943. "Problems of Industrialization of Eastern and Southeastern Europe." *Economic Journal 53* (2): 202–11.

Rostow, W.W. 1960. *Stages of Economic Growth: A Non-Communist Manifesto*. Cambridge, MA: Cambridge University Press.

Schumpeter, Joseph. 1939. *Business Cycles: A Theoretical, Historical and Statistical Analysis of the Capitalist Process*. London: McGraw Hill, Inc.

———. 1942. *Capitalism, Socialism and Democracy*. New York: Harper.

———. 1991. *The Theory of Economic Development: An Inquiry into Profits,*

Capital, Credit, Interest and the Business Cycle. Cambridge, MA: Harvard University Press.

Schultz, T.W. 1962. *Investment in Human Beings.* Chicago: University of Chicago Press.

Seers, Dudley. 1969. "The Meaning of Development." Reprint from the Agriculture Development Council, PC Box PLAN 310 (32): 1–11.

Smith, Adam. 1937 [1776]. *An Enquiry into the Nature and Causes of the Wealth of Nations.* New York: Random House, Modern Library Edition.

Solow, Robert. 1956. "A Contribution to the Theory of Economic Growth." *Quarterly Journal of Economics* 70 (1): 65–94.

Swan, Trevor. 1956. "Economic Growth and Capital Accumulation." *The Economic Record* 32: 334–61.

Wade, Robert. 1990. *Governing Markets: Economic Theory and the Role of Government Intervention in East Asian Economies.* Princeton, NJ: Princeton University Press.

Weber, Max. 1958 [1905]. *The Protestant Ethic and the Spirit of Capitalism.* New York: Charles Scribner's Sons.

Wei, Shang-Jin. 2000. "Natural Openness and Good Government." NBER Working Paper W7765. National Bureau of Economic Research, Cambridge, Massachusetts.

Yeager, Timothy J. 1999. *Institutions, Transition Economies, and Economic Development.* Boulder, CO: Westview.

Appendix

An Alternative Explanation of the Neoclassical Growth Model

The explanation of the neoclassical growth model given in the chapter is not the usual way in which this model is explained. The commonly used explanation of this model is thus presented below.

In the Harrod-Domar growth model, the production function was a fixed-coefficient relationship. Solow's production function can be written as in Equation (A1):

$$Y = F(K, L), \tag{A1}$$

where Y is output, K is capital, L is labor, and constant returns to scale are assumed. This means that if both K and L were increased in a certain proportion, Y would increase in the same proportion. Solow expressed his production function in per-labor units. If the production function is divided by L, we get production per worker that is solely dependent on capital per worker, given by Equation (A2):

$$y = f(k), \tag{A2}$$

where y is Y/L and k is K/L. This per-worker production function exhibits diminishing returns; that is, as capital per worker is increased, output per worker increases, but at a diminishing rate.

To understand the concept of equilibrium in this framework, the concept of investment has to be introduced. The economy reaches a steady-state equilibrium when capital per worker, k, does not change, or $\Delta k = 0$. Because all variables are expressed in per-labor units, an assumption about growth of labor has to be incorporated. According to Solow, labor grows exogenously at rate n. If there is no investment, then $k = K/L$ will automatically fall as population grows. Therefore, for k to be constant, there must be investment (capital must grow) at rate n. Thus, required investment can be written as in Equation (A3):

$$I^r = nK. \tag{A3}$$

In per-worker terms, this can be written as in Equation (A4):

$$I^r/L = nK/L; \tag{A4}$$

or as in Equation (A5):

$$i^r = nk, \tag{A5}$$

which is the required investment to maintain a steady k. The Solow model reaches equilibrium when required investment equals actual investment i. Just as the required investment i^r is a function of the capital-labor ratio, so is the actual investment per person. It is assumed, as in the Harrod-Domar framework, that investments are funded by savings. Thus, actual investment in the economy is given by Equation (A6):

$$I = sY, \tag{A6}$$

where s is the savings rate. Dividing both sides by L gives Equation (A7):

$$i = sy, \tag{A7}$$

or Equation (A8):

$$i = sf(k). \tag{A8}$$

Figure A1.1 **Steady-state Growth**

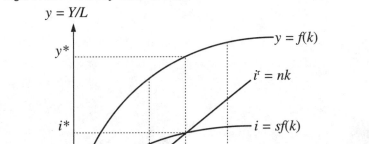

The steady state is achieved where actual investment equals required investment, or where $sy = nk$. The steady-state level of k is shown in Figure A1.1 as k^*. It is the equilibrium point since at k^* alone actual investment is equal to required investment, $i = i^r$.

When actual investment is more than required investment, k increases or capital deepening occurs. When this change is zero, when actual capital-stock K is growing as fast as population growth, capital widening occurs.

The two main conclusions from the neoclassical growth model were first, that an increase in savings rate or investment rate can only boost the economy in the short run by postponing the steady state from approaching. In order to achieve long-term growth, the production function itself will have to be shifted upward, and that can only be made possible through an improvement in technology. Thus, investment was not the key to growth in this model, it was technology. The second important conclusion that can be drawn from the Solow model was that, due to the operation of diminishing returns in production, countriés with lower-capital-per-worker ratios would grow much faster than more-developed countries, where capital per worker was already quite high. Thus, there will be a rapid convergence of wealth across countries. Simply put, convergence implies that countries' growth rates are correlated to initial levels of income.

Europe

2

European Emergence

The Industrial Revolution, which began in England, marked a dramatic change in the economic history of the world. Traditionally it has been thought that sometime during the late eighteenth century structural economic change began to occur in England. These changes involved the development of new technologies that were in turn applied to practical pursuits, namely economic and business activities. The result was thought to have been a dramatic increase in the overall rate of economic growth. Modern factories arose, involving large-scale production that required great supplies of relatively unskilled labor. Labor congregated in urban areas, with employment in the agricultural sector dramatically shrinking in size. Thus, growth seemed to be combined with dramatic structural change.

The economic development that set the stage for industrialization began long before the Industrial Revolution. As such, this development was evolutionary rather than revolutionary in nature. The estimated rates of growth achieved during the Industrial Revolution have been steadily revised downward, but a profound economic and structural transformation did occur, centered in northwestern Europe. England became the workshop of the world and the industrialization process began to diffuse to other parts of the world.

It is only natural to think that a study of this hitherto unique economic transformation might be useful in terms of analyzing the factors that play a key role in economic growth and development elsewhere. In other words, it seems natural to think that there might be useful lessons for today's developing countries in the experience of the Industrial Revolution (i.e., its evolution) in England and in Europe.

We will examine the economic emergence of northwestern Europe, in particular England. Of course, caution must be exercised when drawing lessons about the development process from the English experience. When this process began there were no other competitors in the world economy, and this lack of competition is quite different from the experience of developing nations today, which must try to industrialize within an environment dominated by competition from technologically sophisticated industrialized countries. This advanced competition may make it more difficult for developing nations today. However, the free flow of goods, knowledge, and investment that comes with the globalization of the world economy may make it somewhat easier for currently developing nations to promote rapid development.

Even with the above caveats in mind, it is indeed useful to examine the British experience. Patterns that emerged in England appear to have some rather important implications for the modern-day developmental process.

Growth During the Industrial Revolution

The English Industrial Revolution is conventionally dated as occurring between 1760 and 1830. During this period, there was a phenomenal expansion of cotton spinning, coke smelting, coal and iron production, as well as new commercial organizations (Ashton 1948). Some controversy remains over how rapidly England grew in this period, though, and as to the sources of this growth.

Estimates of growth rates are low by today's standards, ranging from less than 1 percent per annum to slightly above 3 percent. Furthermore, much of this growth may have been more the result of the accumulation of physical inputs (e.g., labor and capital) than as a result of overall increases in productivity. The advances, which did occur, were concentrated in certain sectors, such as cotton and iron manufacturing, and these sectors were initially too small to have a sizeable impact on the manufacturing sector as a whole. Therefore, there was no revolution in terms of speed of growth; it was more evolutionary in nature. What was revolutionary was the broad structural transformation, the reallocation of labor from agriculture to industry.

In these sorts of discussions it is perhaps helpful to make a distinction between extensive and intensive growth. Growth of output has occurred throughout much of human history. Much of this growth was extensive in nature (Jones 1993); that is, as the size of population grew, additional land was brought under cultivation. This allowed the larger population to be supported, but the level of per capita income was relatively unchanged.

The Malthusian perspective, of course, would argue that, in the long term, growing populations would eventually run up against the limited surplus of arable land, and the law of diminishing returns would eventually cause per capita food availability to decline. However, Boserup (1965) argues that as population bumps up against the environment social groups will, under certain conditions, innovate. The history of the world is punctuated by periodic innovations that have allowed larger populations to be supported on the land. However, extensive growth remained predominant for much of history.

Intensive growth occurs with a rise in per capita income that is sustained over long periods of time. It appears that the Industrial Revolution was a period in which intensive growth became established in England. It was not necessarily revolutionary, but a growth rate of 1 to 2 percent in per capita gross domestic product (GDP) can, over long periods of time, result in substantial changes in the standard of living. A simple formula, $Y_D = (70/\text{percent growth rate})$, gives the number of years required for something such as per capita income to double. If per capita GDP grows at 1 percent, income would double every seventy years. Incomes will double every thirty-five years for a 2 percent growth rate of per capita income.

England did indeed become the workshop for the world, to the extent that by the mid-to-late nineteenth century a huge gap had opened between it and all other countries. Specifically, in 1860 England accounted for 45 percent of the world's industrial production while comprising 2 percent of the world's population. In terms of international exchange, one-third of the world's commercial fleet was English, as was one-quarter of the world's exports and one-third of the world's imports. Within Europe itself, England produced 55 to 60 percent of the manufactures, 58 percent of the iron production, and accounted for 50 percent of European energy consumption.

Tremendous structural change occurred in England. By 1860, England displayed a sectoral composition that was achieved in other countries only many decades later. As early as 1846, only 22 percent of the economically active population was still employed in agriculture. England had indeed been transformed from an agricultural nation into the manufacturing workshop of the world (Senghaas 1985).

So, how might the economic processes occurring in England in the seventeenth and eighteenth century be described? These processes involved a dramatic restructuring of the economy with agriculture shrinking in importance relative to industry. This increasingly involved the migration of people to urban areas or the transformation of rural areas into towns and cities. This significant structural transformation resulted in a slow but persistent rise in the growth of income and, most importantly, in per capita income. One can call this economic evolution rather than revolution, but the result was an economic giant that dominated Europe and the world economy in the nineteenth century.

In order to understand how this restructuring of England's economy occurred, one must begin with an analysis of the system of feudalism. It was out of this system and its agricultural production that the new economy evolved.

Agricultural Growth

Several of the theories reviewed in Chapter 1 will be useful in explaining the process of industrial evolution outlined above. The dualistic models of Lewis (1954), Boeke (1953), and Ranis and Fei (1961) are particularly important. These models presume that a less-developed country is made up of two sectors: traditional and modern. The process of economic development unfolds as a result of the interaction of these sectors.

The traditional sector is assumed to be primarily agricultural in nature. The main inputs are labor and land—little capital is utilized. Population is relatively abundant, perhaps so abundant that surplus labor exists; that is, labor could be withdrawn without harming production. Techniques of production are highly labor intensive in nature. Economic units usually produce for subsistence rather than profit. Thus this sector is not commercialized and the primary motivation is survival. There is generally a land-owning elite or warlord class that owns or at least controls the usage of land. The landed elite extracts as much of the surplus agricultural production as possible.

The modern sector is usually presumed to be made up of manufacturing activities. The main inputs to the production process are capital and labor. This sector is commercialized, inputs and outputs are bought and sold in markets, and the main motivation of economic units is profit maximization.

The dualistic models described above usually are presumed to be closed; that is, they are not open to trade. Economic development is presumed to involve structural change, an expansion of the modern sector, and a contraction of the traditional sector—both in absolute and relative terms. However, it is immediately obvious that an expansion of the modern sector is constrained by a number of factors. First, for a modern sector to exist, the traditional sector must be able to produce enough food to feed the peasant farmers plus enough extra food (agricultural surplus) to feed the manufacturing workforce and entrepreneurs. Without this food surplus, there can be no urban, manufacturing sector. Moreover, the landed elite must refrain from consuming the food surplus and be willing to exchange it for the output of the modern sector. In addition, part of the labor (surplus labor) of the traditional sector must be available to provide the workers for the modern sector. If the modern sector is to expand it must draw more of the surplus food and labor from the traditional sector. If this becomes increasingly difficult (e.g., if food becomes increasingly scarce), then modern-sector expansion will cease.

Johnston and Mellor (1961) have argued that agriculture (i.e., the traditional sector) has a number of functions to perform. It must provide the food and labor for the expansion of the modern sector and the savings to finance the expansion of the latter. It is likely to also serve as the main market or main source of demand for the goods produced in the modern manufacturing sector.

While these dualistic models were not intended to describe development in Europe, they may nonetheless be helpful in examining the experience of fifteenth-, sixteenth-, and seventeenth-century England. In the early part of this time period, England was characterized by an economic, political, and social set of institutions commonly known as feudalism. This set of institutions arose out of the chaos stemming from the decline of centralized political authority. With this decline, political authority became concentrated in the hands of lesser and greater warlords, constantly in struggle against each other. Over time a particular warlord gained dominance over the others in a particular region. Peace was restored via a hierarchical relationship between or among greater and lesser lords. The predominant lord allowed the weaker to have access to sections of land in return for which the lesser lords pledged their loyalty. Each lord earned his "living" from organizing economic production within his particular fiefdom. Within the fiefdom, peasant farmers were given fields within which they would grow the food necessary for survival. They were protected from outside marauders by the lord's military might. In return, the peasants were required to provide labor services for the lord; for example, farm the lord's lands. Also, a share of various types of output produced by the peasant was often also made available to the landlord.

Agricultural production was done in a labor-intensive manner involving limited capital and technology. The agricultural surplus supported the feudal elite. Ideally, each feudal lord and his land and his peasants would form a self-sufficient production organization. In reality, however, this was never possible. Each lord and the peasants were dependent on the production of artisans for many nonagricultural products. The trade between the agrarian-based fiefdoms and the artisans was generally arranged by merchants. Towns were where the artisans and merchants generally resided.

In this context, international trade was generally limited. Given the poor state of transportation systems and security, only high-value, low-bulk items were traded over long distances. This long-distance trade was generally in luxury goods. Bulky commodities, like food grains, were rarely traded over long distances. Thus feudalism can be represented as a closed economic organization with a large traditional sector, feudalistic agriculture, and a relatively small modern sector made up of artisans and merchants engaged in the organization of small-scale manufacturing, usually based on artisanship rather than factory production.

The size of the modern sector was indeed limited by the amount of food surplus produced in the agricultural sector and the willingness of the landed elite to trade part of that surplus for simple manufactured goods. Also, peasant farmers were serfs, that is, they were tied to the land—they could not legally leave to earn a living in the town. Thus, the labor supply was restricted.

The implication of the above analysis is that a modern sector cannot expand unless there are increases in agricultural surplus traded for manufactured goods. The landed elite can seek to extract additional surplus by using force to further restrict peasant consumption. However, there are limits to this possibility. It seems indeed that a necessary condition for the expansion of the modern sector is a persistent increase in agricultural productivity, providing increased amounts of agricultural surplus.

The historical evidence seems to indicate that there was a significant growth in agricultural productivity from 1600 to 1800. Evidence for this growth can be seen by looking at the proportion of the population engaged in agriculture. While the total population of England rose by 210 percent from 1600 to 1800, the percentage of the population engaged in agriculture declined from 70 to around 36 percent (Wrigley 1985). By

1800, one-third of the population was able to provide the rest with food. As relatively little of this food was imported, this implies that output per person in agriculture expanded by three-quarters between 1700 and 1800. Robert Allen (1992) utilizes estate surveys and concludes that while the size of the agricultural labor force changed little between 1700 and 1800, agricultural output of both grain and livestock more than doubled.

There is significant controversy as to just how this agricultural revolution occurred. Some have argued that the enclosure of fields allowed cultivators to combine grain production with animal husbandry. In traditional feudalism, large fields were subdivided into small plots and families were allowed to farm a scattered number of the plots. Livestock was grazed on common pastures. Enclosure by landowners (allowing the consolidation of plots and the breaking up of common pastures) resulted in individual holdings, upon which animal husbandry and crop production were combined. The animals provided the power and the fertilizer, and this combined with new crop-rotation systems provided the foundation for rapid productivity growth. However, there is evidence that the productivity growth began much earlier and that agricultural productivity during the enclosure movement was rather sluggish (Allen 1998).

Robert Brenner (1982) offers a different view as to the cause of the agricultural growth. He believes that during the late fifteenth and sixteenth centuries the agrarian crisis caused by the Black Death (1348–49) resulted in a dramatic altering of the property-rights system in the countryside. The population decline allowed peasant farmers to succeed (through resistance and flight from the land) in disrupting the feudalistic system of the extraction of surplus by force that was the main tool of the feudal elite. Thus peasant labor increasingly became free of feudal restraint, though the landed feudal elite was able to maintain control over the land. This view has some traces of a Marxist theoretical perspective. Marx saw economic change as being driven by a dialectical process involving class conflict. In this context, the struggle between the feudal elite and the serfs (peasant farmers) resulted in a new distribution of rights. Peasants claimed rights to their labor while the landed elite retained control over the land. The landed elite could no longer maintain themselves by extracting rents via force. They would have to use other means to retain the services of labor. The peasant farmers controlled their labor, but if they were to maintain themselves they would have to gain access to land.

Thus market exchange on the input side began to occur, with the landed elite earning market rents and the laborers earning income via labor or managing tenant farms. According to Brenner (1982), market competition thus drove productivity growth through the evolution of a competitive landlord-tenant system of agriculture. Productivity growth in the short term enhanced the income of tenant farmers, and perhaps hired labor; in the long term, it added to the wealth of those controlling the land.

However one explains it, it is obvious that an "agricultural revolution" seems to have occurred in England from the 1600s to the 1800s. It was a slow, upward climb in agricultural productivity resulting in increases in the agricultural surplus.

Protoindustrialization and Trade

The agricultural growth discussed above set off a process of market expansion culminating in dramatic structural changes. That is, growing rural incomes led to the purchases of goods and services from the artisan sector, which in turn led to the expansion of merchant groups to handle the increased internal trade. These increased expenditures dramatically increased the market demand for nonagricultural goods. The expansion of production of nonagricultural goods has often been labeled *protoindustrialization*.

Protoindustrialization began as production by artisans and evolved into small-scale manufacturing, often based on a "putting-out system." Merchants would distribute raw materials to family producers and pay them to transform the raw material into finished products. Those processes became centered within evolving new urban areas. The expanding protoindustrial production in turn expanded the demand for agricultural raw materials. It then became possible for specialization to expand in both the rural and urban areas. This, of course, allowed the normal productivity increases that come with specialization.

Jan De Vries (1994) has likened this process to an "industrious revolution." The growth in employment in small-scale manufacturing provided employment opportunities not only for men, but also for women and children. Although wages for these new occupations were low, they raised total household income. This "industrious revolution was a process of household-based resource reallocation that increased both the supply of marketed commodities and labor and the demand for market supplied goods" (De Vries 1994, 249).

Thus, by the late eighteenth century, England had become a very different place. It was becoming increasingly urbanized, specialization in production was growing, and the commercialization of society was still under way. David Ricardo, who was living and writing at this time, certainly appreciated the dramatic changes that England had undergone, but he was skeptical that this process could continue. His conception of the law of diminishing returns indicated that this sort of expansion process would not last. After all, if land is fixed (or some important input is fixed or grows slowly relative to others), then ultimately the returns to applying variable inputs to this fixed input would decline, and this, if pushed far enough, would eventually lead to declines in output per person.

Ricardo was not rejecting the idea that the expansion of markets and the specialization that resulted could raise productivity. He was, however, skeptical that this sort of process could result in a persistent rise in productivity over extended periods of time. Wrigley (1985) has argued that one might characterize the English economy at this time as being organic in nature, or as being an organic economy. In this kind of economy, energy sources were largely limited to human and animal muscle, and these are, in turn, derived from land, a finite resource. In the Ricardian sense, it was this limitation that allowed for the operation of the law of diminishing returns. Thus, the organic, capitalist economy of the eighteenth and early nineteenth centuries would seem to have been established on a rather fragile base. The structural change that had occurred was reversible.

Ricardo argued that international trade might provide a reprieve, at least temporarily, from the law of diminishing returns. In order to understand his argument one must first understand a bit of England's agricultural history, especially as concerns the Corn Laws (which concerned grain of all kind). These laws were originally passed in the late seventeenth century and remained in force well into the nineteenth century. Under their terms, when the world price was higher than the domestic price, farmers were allowed to export their grain. When the world price was below the domestic price, imports were prevented. The Corn Laws were a high-price policy; they promoted a high price for domestically produced grains. They were a subsidy applied to agriculture. This stimulated an expansion of agricultural production as well as an expansion of investment into the agricultural sector. It would seem likely that the agricultural expansion of the late seventeenth and eighteenth centuries may very well have been stimulated by this agricultural subsidy.

From Ricardo's perspective, however, the Corn Laws posed a barrier to the expansion of manufacturing. If a nation, England, could via trade find alternative sources of food grains, which were relatively cheaper than what could be produced domestically, then they should be imported from other countries. This would lower the relative cost of food, and, at least temporarily, offset the law of diminishing returns and allow the market-specialization-driven process of economic expansion to continue.

How would food imports be financed? It was Ricardo's theoretical principle of comparative advantage that provides the answer. Let us presume that labor is the only input in the production process. Assume that in England it takes ten labor hours to produce a bushel of corn and five labor hours to produce a piece of manufactured cloth. In France, assume that it takes four labor hours to produce a bushel of corn and four labor hours to produce the same cloth. It is obvious that France is absolutely superior at producing both products. But does it make sense for France to produce both? Ricardo would answer "no!" France can produce corn with only 40 percent of the labor as England, but in producing cloth it uses only 20 percent less labor. Thus, relatively, France is best at corn and England's disadvantage is relatively the least in manufacturing cloth. Thus France can produce one more bushel of corn at the sacrifice of one unit of cloth. England can produce one more bushel of corn only by sacrificing two units of cloth. Therefore, France has a relative advantage in corn production, whereas England has a relative advantage in cloth production. Assume that England chooses to concentrate its resources in cloth production and trade with France for corn, and vice versa for France. If they agree to trade one corn for one and one-half cloths, it is obvious that both countries will gain. England, instead of sacrificing two cloths to produce one unit of corn, can now trade one and one-half cloths to France for one unit of corn. This is certainly to England's advantage. Alternatively, France, instead of sacrificing one unit of corn to produce one more unit of cloth, can now trade one unit of home-produced corn for one and one-half units of English cloth. Both nations benefit from the trade according to relative or comparative advantage.

Thus, free trade, based on the principle of comparative advantage, would allow England to offset the law of diminishing returns by drawing on food produced in the world. This would allow England to continue its economic expansion, at least temporarily. Temporarily might mean a century or more, especially given the untapped potential for food production worldwide and that, at the time, it appeared England would remain the only country producing manufactured goods, and would thus dominate the world.

Exploitation and Slavery

The principle of comparative advantage outlined in the previous section was used to illustrate the idea that the elimination of the Corn Laws may have allowed England, at least temporarily, to get around the law of diminishing returns. More importantly, it was shown that both England and France would both benefit from free trade.

There is a theoretical branch of economics, referred to in Chapter 1 as dependency theory, which argues that free trade was certainly a key to the rise of England. However, its interpretation of the role of free trade in England's growth is quite different. It was not through the exchange of goods that England benefited as much as via the extraction of profits. That is, the industrial expansion in England required significant amounts of investment, and the argument has been made that the profits from trade with North America, South America, Africa, and Asia provided the profits that financed the industrial expansion. In addition, the key inputs necessary for industrial expansion were extracted from colonies in Asia, Africa, and the Americas.

Dependency theorists divide the world into two regions: the center and the periphery. The center is made up of the economically advanced, industrialized countries, which generally produce and export manufactured goods to the periphery. The periphery is generally thought to be composed of the less-developed countries, which produce mainly primary commodities for export to the center. The theory of comparative advantage of Ricardo implies that both regions will benefit through specialization and trade based on comparative advantage. Dependency theory is not so optimistic; it tends to see the center benefiting at the expense of the periphery.

Dependency theorists emphasize the power differential that exists between center and periphery. Through the process of colonization, the elite establish themselves in the metropolitan areas of the periphery. According to Frank (1966), these metropolitan areas represent the organizational focus of a process by which surplus is extracted from the countryside, and then, via trade with the center, that surplus is transferred to the center. In the context of this chapter, England is seen as using its colonies to extract surplus from the primary production activities of its peripheral colonies, transferring that surplus (i.e., profit) to the center, and utilizing that surplus to finance its industrialization process.

How is the surplus extracted? There has been a variety of mechanisms put forward by a number of dependency theorists. Many of them involve a process by which the terms of trade are turned against the periphery and in favor of the center. The terms of trade for a region are the average price of its exports divided by the average price of its imports. The periphery generally exported primary commodities (e.g., copper, gold, sugar) while importing manufactured goods. Therefore, if the price of primary goods falls relative to manufactured goods, then, *ceteris paribus*, the profits accruing to the producers of manufactured goods will be increased.

How is the decline in the relative price of primary goods brought about? Most of the explanations have to do with the exertion of some sort of monopoly or monopsony power by the center countries. Monopoly power stems from being a single seller of a product, while monopsony power stems from being a single buyer. If the center has monopoly power, it can raise the price of what it sells to the periphery. In turn, the center can use its power as a single buyer to force down the price of what it buys from the periphery. The increased profits that result can then be saved and invested in the expansion of industry in the center. Thus, the argument is that England, and other countries in northwestern Europe that followed England and were able to industrialize, were able to use their superior power to extract profit from the periphery.

The expansion of the center was, argue the dependency theorists, at the expense of the periphery. That is, the expanding wealth at the center created poverty in the periphery. The increase in poverty is thought to be the result of several factors. First, if the profits of the periphery are siphoned out, then there will be less savings, and investment and growth will be slowed. Second, the penetration of the periphery by the center was highly disruptive. Indigenous civilizations and organizations were destroyed via warfare and/or disease. Previous institutional structures were eliminated and replaced with those imported from the center. The traditional manufacturing that often existed in these regions was quickly destroyed via imports of cheap manufactured goods.

There are a number of critical issues raised by the dependency theorists that are relevant to our discussion concerning the European emergence. First, how critical was the trade between the center (England) and the periphery (Asia, the Americas, Africa) in the center's industrialization process? Did the periphery provide the raw materials that were critical to the industrialization process? Did the periphery provide the profits that financed the Industrial Revolution in England and northwestern Europe? What was the impact of this relationship on the periphery? Were the developmental prospects of the periphery damaged?

First, how critical was the trade between northwest Europe and the periphery in terms of supplying key inputs for industrialization? Senghaas (1985) argues that the external economic links of Europe were mainly of an intra-European nature. That is, 70 percent of all European exports involved trade among European nations and 65 percent of all European imports involved trade among European nations. Beyond this, much of European trade with elites outside of Europe involved trade with North America, Australia, and other newly settled regions with substantial European settlement. Trade between Europe and what many have or continue to call the "third world" (though the term is nonsensical given the end of the cold war and the "second world" of the Soviet bloc) or developing countries amounted to only around 20 percent of European foreign trade. Senghaas goes on to argue that Europe was self-sufficient and not dependent on supplies of foodstuffs, agricultural raw materials, and minerals from the developing word of the nineteenth century.

The main imports from what would today be called the developing countries were cotton, sugar, tea, coffee, spices, tobacco, silk, china, rare timbers, and natural dyes. Most of these products were not consumed by the masses of Europe and were not critical industrial inputs. These goods would generally be labeled as luxury goods. In the twentieth century, the industrialized world's production of manufactured goods did become more dependent on materials and goods from the periphery. Thus, it seems that, in the nineteenth century, European expansion was not critically dependent on what would be today's less-developed countries for critical goods and inputs.

Trade does, however, provide benefits to the participating countries as a result of specialization and comparative advantage. In the European case, perhaps it was the large markets provided by the periphery that allowed significant gains in productivity to be made via specialization. However, one must remember that the size of available markets is determined not just by population sizes but also by the purchasing power (per capita income levels) available to those populations. In the nineteenth century, the purchasing power of countries outside Europe was quite limited. This is supported in the above discussion by the fact that only a small share of European trade involved that group of nations, which we would today call less developed.

Still, if the trading opportunities generated enough profit, and profit was the main source of investment, perhaps it was the profitability of trade with the periphery that provided the supply of funds for investment that drove the industrialization process. This thesis was first proposed by Williams (1944). However, quantitative evidence analyzed by Engerman (1972), Engerman and O'Brien (1991), O'Brien (1982), and Bairoch (1995) show that the volume of trade and profits generated appear to be too small to provide the main driving forces for industrialization. For example, O'Brien estimates that the contribution of profits from trade with the periphery to aggregate capital accumulation would be between 5.5 and 7.5 percent. Thus, only 5 to 7 percent of capital accumulation in the eighteenth and early nineteenth centuries could be explained by the profits of trade with the periphery.

Recently, an alternative view has been proposed by Inikori (2002). He argues that, although trade flows in general were intra-European in nature, and profits from trade with the periphery were small relative to total capital accumulation, this information is quite misleading. He points out that the Industrial Revolution in England was initially focused in particular regions, the counties in the northern part of England (Lancashire, the West Riding of Yorkshire, and the West Midlands). This is where the new industries (e.g., textiles and metals) were beginning to develop. "The successful industrializing northern countries sold the greater part of their manufactures overseas" (Inikori 2002, 476). The bulk of this trade involved trans-Atlantic commerce. "During the period the Atlantic basin became by far the most important center of international trade in the world" (ibid., 479). Most of this trade involved the Americas and Africa. "Between 1699/1701 and 1772/1774 increases in the sale of English manufactures in Western Africa and the Americas accounted for 71.5 percent of the increment in overseas sales of English manufactures" (ibid., 480).

Inikori thus believes the industrialization process in the northern English counties was export driven. The significant growth in external demand drove the new manufacturing industries there to innovate and expand production. This exporting would not have occurred without importing. Namely, for the Atlantic basin trade to function, the Americas would have to be able to export to Europe, that is, to England. Those exports produced in the Americas were produced utilizing plantation agriculture and labor-intensive mining and included such products as gold, sugar, cotton, coffee, rice, and tobacco. These were produced by African labor, which had been brought to the Americas via the slave trade.

Inikori believes it was African slave labor that was thus crucial to the Industrial Revolution in England. The abundance of land in the Americas meant that free labor migrating into the region sought to establish small, independent farms that were basically subsistence oriented. "Given this situation, legally free labor could not form the basis of large-scale commodity production in the Americas for Atlantic commerce" (ibid., 481). African slave labor was crucial for large-scale, commercial production. This labor was cheap not only because it was unfree (slave labor), but also such labor could produce much of its own subsistence (on small plots), thus dramatically lowering the cost of production. This provided the foundation for the Atlantic trade.

The Atlantic trade and slave labor seems crucial to the development of early manufacturing in England. Whether or not this is accurate, the impact of the industrialization of northwestern Europe did have a devastating impact on much of the periphery. The colonization of Central America, North America, South America, the Caribbean, and the Pacific region decimated the populations of the indigenous people. In South and Central America, existing civilizations were dismantled and replaced by imported institutions, the same for social and political structures. Political power, social status, and the control of land were held by a small foreign-born elite. In the Caribbean, native populations were replaced with African slaves and sugar production came to dominate the economics of this region. The distribution of wealth and political power were highly unequal. (These issues will be discussed in Chapter 6.)

The impact on Africa was equally devastating. The trade in slaves corrupted indigenous social and political organizations and structures. Infrastructure, roads, and communications were geared to extracting slaves or other products deemed of value. Ultimately, as a number of countries in Europe industrialized, the process of the colonization of Africa unfolded as the new industrial powers used their military power to divide up Africa. In this process, states were created within Africa that bore little relationship to preexisting social and political structures. These states often combined large numbers of different ethnic or tribal groups with different cultures and conflicting histories. This would pose a significant obstacle to future economic development in the region, as is discussed in Chapter 4.

The impact of colonization on East, Southeast, and South Asia was perhaps less extreme. Societies there appear to have been more resilient to the onslaught of the industrialized powers and their economies. In addition, since their indigenous economies were more commercialized and market development was more extensive, the colonial powers appear to have been less extractive in their policies. Extractive colonial practices did not introduce much protection for private property, nor did they provide checks and balances against government expropriation. In fact, the main purpose of the extraction process was to transfer as much resources as possible from the colony to the colonizer with the minimum amount of investment. This characterized much of Africa and Latin America, as outlined above. In parts of South, Southeast, and East Asia, colonial policy seems to have been less extractive.

Trade, as discussed above, may have played a direct role in the industrialization process, though this is still subject to significant debate. However, it seems that trade did have a clear, indirect impact on the industrialization process. Indirectly, the trade avenues that opened up through the Atlantic may have played a role through its impact on the evolution of political institutions. The role of such institutions will be discussed in the next section, and the indirect effect of trade on political institutions will be explained.

The Evolution and Role of Political Institutions

In examining the process of economic development, economists have traditionally ignored institutions, particularly political institutions, and the role of politics. Instead, concentration was focused on analyzing market malfunctions and designing policy solutions that it was implicitly assumed would be administered by a state whose main goal was the welfare of its citizens. In the last decade, this naïve perspective has been dropped and economists have turned their attention to the analysis of institutions, political as well as social. It is now recognized that successful economic development is very much dependent on the political, institutional environment. This new perspective is useful not only in examining the experience of today's developing countries, but also sheds some light on the European emergence discussed here.

A significant problem, which seems to limit commercial development and specialization, seems to be the inability of the state, whatever its form, to credibly commit to policies that uphold basic property rights. Weingast (1995) calls this the fundamental dilemma of an economic system. "A government strong enough to protect property rights and enforce contracts is also strong enough to confiscate the wealth of its citizens. Thriving markets require not only the appropriate system of property rights and a law of contracts, but also a secure political foundation that limits the ability of the state to confiscate wealth" (Weingast 1995, 1). Therefore, the question becomes or concerns how to solve this fundamental dilemma.

The upshot of the above discussion would seem to be that economic development and political development are intertwined. Political development can be seen as an evolutionary process by which the state attains the ability to independently set and carry out policy, but is constrained to do so in ways that enhance the overall productivity of society. This involves an interaction between the state and society, and the political institutional structure emerges out of this interaction. Moore (2001, 8) defines political underdevelopment as a regime that is both ineffective, "unable to rule many nominal citizens or to pursue any kind of collective interest in an authoritative fashion," and is arbitrary and unaccountable. Political development represents the opposite: a state that is constrained to pursue collective interests in an authoritative fashion.

The ruling elite of any society is presumed to make policy with the goal being to maximize their own welfare and their own wealth. Because they are a small minority of the population of any society, policies that maximize their welfare may not be the same sort of policies that raise the welfare of society in general. In other words, the ruling elite may very well view their society as prey from which wealth is to be extracted; thus the concept of the predatory state.

Political development is the evolutionary process by which the pursuit of wealth maximization by the elite comes to coincide with wealth maximization for society at large. In other words, political development is the process by which a ruling elite moves from killing the goose that lays the golden egg to nurturing the goose so that it lays many golden eggs. Political development is the process by which the state moves from being predatory to being developmental.

It would seem that the above process is most likely to occur if the survival probability of the ruling elite becomes increasingly dependent on the well-being of the bulk of its society. In other words, political development occurs when the ruling elite become dependent on society in general for their political survival. Moore (1998) provides a clear way to think about these issues by referring to a tradition in public policy called "fiscal sociology." He argues that one should make a distinction between earned and unearned state income. A state or ruling elite's income is dependent on or influenced by the extent to which it has put in effort working with its citizens in order to get its tax revenue.

The effort that Moore speaks of comes in two varieties. The first is organizational effort, the extent to which the state has to construct a bureaucratic apparatus for the collection of revenue, which increases the proportion of its citizens that it is able to reach. The second involves the extent of reciprocity between citizens and the state. Simply, it involves the extent to which the ruling elite provide services in return for revenue. Thus, more of the income for the elite is characterized as earned income when the proportion of the citizens that is provided services in return for that revenue increases.

Unearned income is the mirror image of the above. It derives from very few sources, requires little organizational or political effort to collect, and involves little interaction between the elite and the bulk of the society. An extreme example would be a ruling elite that is supported by revenue flow from outside the nation or region. In the twentieth and twenty-first centuries, unearned income would include mineral revenues, oil, and foreign aid. A broader view would include dependence on timber, diamonds, narcotics, and some kinds of primary product exports (coffee, cocoa, and others).

This concept of earned and unearned income can be broadened out a bit further. The organization of agricultural production comes in many forms. One can think of a bimodal organization in which the bulk of production occurs on large estates owned by a small proportion of the population while the bulk of the population is subsistence oriented. In this case, the rural elite and ruling elites are usually intertwined. The revenue provided to the state is likely to be earned in the sense that services are provided to the rural elite in return for tax revenues and, most importantly, political support. However, the limited extent of the interaction implies that policies are likely to favor the economic prospects of the small rural elite, not the population at large.

In contrast, consider an agricultural sector that is organized in a unimodal fashion. In this context, the operational size of farms is more uniform (although land ownership may be unequal). In this context, the revenue needs of the ruling elite will be dependent on providing services in return for revenue from the bulk of the rural population.

The distinctions made above are quite important. States that rely on income drawn from the population in general (i.e., unimodal) are more likely to become politically developed (i.e., regimes capable of pursuing collective interests). This is likely to happen because states relying on broadly based earned income have an incentive to recruit a capable and relatively honest public-service bureaucracy so that taxes can be assessed and revenue collected. In addition, the more prosperous the general population is, the potential revenue flows to the state increase, implying that the ruling elite and its citizens are likely to have significant areas of common interest. However, these common interests are not immediately obvious and a learning process is usually involved. This learning process is likely to take the form of periods of struggle between the ruling elite and society at large over rates of extraction and the allocation of revenues.

This struggle to develop common interests is likely to extend beyond the agricultural sector. A unimodal agriculture that is growing in productivity is likely to result in an expansion of the demand for simple manufactured goods, produced labor intensively. In the case of England, this resulted in rapid protoindustrialization. Much of this production was organized by rising merchant groups through the putting-out system discussed previously. Thus, new sources of revenue were emerging with the development of nonagricultural production and the rise of ambitious merchant groups.

England in the eighteenth and nineteenth centuries would seem to be a good example of a state that earned its tax revenue. The ruling elite resided within a society whose agricultural base was unimodal in nature. The growing agricultural sector, greater manufacturing, and rising merchant class represented a broad basis of potential revenue. The conditions were appropriate for a learning process to occur within which the ruling elite and the bulk of the citizens would slowly recognize their common interest in prosperity and the protection of property rights necessary for the prosperity.

By the sixteenth and seventeenth centuries, the English state had established a monopoly in violence and had created a foundation from which to rule. However, the significant problem that seemed to limit commercial development and specialization was the inability of the state to credibly commit to policies based on upholding property rights. For example, in the late 1500s and early 1600s the king was continuously in search of revenue in the form of taxes and loans. However, repayment of the loans was highly unpredictable, with the state often repudiating loans or arbitrarily altering the terms of payment (North and Weingast 1989).

As agricultural productivity began to grow and commercialization spread in the late seventeenth and eighteenth centuries, the behavior to the monarchy triggered recurrent clashes between the king and commercial interests in parliament. The latter was generally represented by commercial agriculture and merchants. However, the ruling elite was often able to maintain its position by exploiting differences in opposition groups, playing one against another. However, as time passed and the economy became increasingly commercialized, a consensus began to develop as to what was acceptable and unacceptable behavior on the part of the ruling elite.

It seems that, out of this struggle between the commercial interests and the ruling elite, a national economic interest or view was evolving in England, which represented a consensus as to individual rights in the pursuit of commercial interests and limitations on the state's ability to manipulate the terms of commercial exchange for its own benefit. The development of this consensus was reflected, at least partly, in what has come to be known as the Glorious Revolution of 1688. This began an era of parliamentary dominance that provided a strong check on abuses by the monarch. It also created a credible threat of punishment if rules were violated by the state. Finally, it provided parliament with a central role in financial matters. These changes provided a foundation for the continued economic integration of England.

The effect of the above developments was to dramatically increase the control of wealth holders and creators over the government. Representatives of wealth holders and creators could veto major changes that threatened their activities. Second, the routes by which the state could renege on its commitment to support wealth accumulation were gradually closed off. As a result, a variety of innovations occurred in both private and public credit markets that further supported specialization, productivity growth, and commercialization.

Recent research by Acemoglu, Johnson, and Robinson (2002) has added an interesting international dimension to the ideas presented above. They argue that the significant growth in the Atlantic trade after 1500 played a significant though indirect role in the European emergence. More specifically, those nations whose economies significantly diverged from the economies of the rest of Europe and the world were heavily involved in the Atlantic trade. The evidence that they examine implies that the rise of Europe between 1500 and 1850 was largely the rise of Atlantic Europe.

Acemoglu, Johnson, and Robinson argue that the Western European growth reflected the great opportunities offered by the Atlantic trade, but, most importantly, the emergence of economic institutions providing secure property rights to a large proportion of society. These institutions resulted from the evolution of political institutions constraining the powers of the ruling elite. These constraints were imposed by a rising commercial elite within England and a few parts of northwestern Europe.

The constraints discussed above arose because the Atlantic trade dramatically increased the wealth of the new commercial interests. This new wealth allowed these groups to exert increased political power, and this, in turn, allowed them to demand and obtain the institutional changes necessary for growth. Although, as argued in the previous section, profits from the Atlantic trade were small relative to GDP, they were still rather substantial. The recipients of these profits grew quite rich, by seventeenth- and eighteenth-century European standards, and socially quite powerful.

The process outlined above is the indirect way that trade may have stimulated the European emergence. It was not through the gains from specializing according to comparative advantage, and it was not through the use of profits from trade to finance the expansion of industrial investment; instead, the profits from the Atlantic trade strengthened the political power of the rising commercial interests and these interests were then able to use this power to constrain the ruling elite.

However, not all Atlantic traders reaped this benefit from the expansion of trade. For example, Spain was heavily involved in the Atlantic trade and yet this sort of process did not unfold. Institutional constraints did not evolve and the ruling elite of Spain was not able to credibly commit to property rights. Acemoglu, Johnson, and Robinson explain this by appealing to initial conditions. Spain, and for that matter, Portugal, had not gone through a long period of agricultural growth, with its attendant protoindustrial expansion. Instead, these economies were dominated by royal trading monopolies, and such were the main beneficiaries of early profits from the Atlantic trade. This increased the power of these monopolistic groups and enhanced their stranglehold over the Spanish and Portuguese economies. They utilized this power to restrain competition and commercial expansion. As a result, the treasure that flowed into Spain and Portugal had no impact on general domestic economic development.

While England represented the example of a ruling elite that was dependent on its own society for resources to survive, Spain in the sixteenth, seventeenth, and eighteenth centuries represented a ruling elite that relied on external sources of resources (treasure from the New World) to finance its rule and position. It is unlikely that an effective civil service would develop in states that were relatively autonomous from their populations in terms of revenues. There was no need to spend the time and resources necessary to construct such an institutional structure since the main source of revenue was elsewhere. Also, the ruling elite were likely to be little interested in the economic conditions of the bulk of its population, since the latter were not necessary for the survival of the elite. There was, therefore, little interaction likely to occur between the state and its citizens, with the latter incapable of articulating issues of concern. This description seems to be a fairly accurate portrayal of Spain, and also, perhaps, Portugal.

In summary, long-term economic development would seem to be dependent on the existence of states that can commit to policies and rules that enhance productivity. Ruling elites who are dependent on the bulk of their own population for the resources necessary to maintain their position are most likely to be able to solve the commitment problem. The solution emerges through a dialectical interaction and struggle between the elite and the commercial groups within its society. Through this interaction, constraints on state behavior arise or evolve through a learning process. In the English case, this process was aided by the impact of the Atlantic trade. The latter created a substantial stream of profit that went into the hands of growing commercial groups. These groups used this wealth to enhance their political power, and this power allowed them to temper the actions of the ruling elite. The foundation for a developmental state had been laid.

Culture and Nationalism

The analysis of the European emergence has been based on an implicit assumption that has yet to be clearly articulated. It has been argued that certain structural changes occurred within the English agricultural sector that allowed agricultural growth to become a persistent characteristic. That is, once incentives for investment into productivity enhancement come into existence, as a result of, say, institutional change, individuals respond by investing and innovating. The implicit assumption is that individuals are maximizers. Perhaps a less controversial way to put this assumption is to say that people, if given the opportunity, will seek to better themselves economically. Hence, given the opportunity, individuals will make choices to save, invest, accumulate capital, and innovate.

There is a vein in the social-science literature that would strongly dispute this implicit assumption. It would argue that the motivations to save, accumulate, and innovate are not found everywhere, that the development of such motivations was relatively unique and recent in economic history. Max Weber ([1905] 1976) was one such theorist, and the purpose of his work was to try to explain the shift in social attitudes taken toward valuing economic activity that is oriented toward growth. He did not dispute that human beings have been buying and selling for thousands of years; indeed, markets are not a recent historical phenomenon. What distinguishes the modern economy from what came before was the type and degree of rationalization and the institutionalization of the drive to acquire.

One might simply think of this feature of the modern economy in the following way. Before the European emergence, economic activities were a means to other ends, social and cultural. Accumulation would occur, but only up to a point, and only to fulfill certain cultural or social responsibilities. The economy was embedded with the culture, the latter constrained the former. Thus the motives to save, invest, and accumulate were subservient to other objectives. The motive for increasing accumulation did not exist.

According to Weber's view, the emergence of the modern economy could not have taken place without a new set of motivations and a set of ethics that could serve as justification for this new set of motives. The ethical system would serve as a support mechanism for the new set of motives. For Weber, this new ethical system arose out of the Reformation of the sixteenth century. The Reformation, he argued, provided the ethical foundation for a new set of motives.

Roman Catholicism represented an ethical system that denigrated the pursuit of profit and continuous and unending accumulation. The Protestant Reformation, specifically the rise of Calvinism, upended this ethical system. The doctrine of predestination indicates that God has already chosen "the elect"; they are predestined to reap the benefits and joys only available in the afterlife. How does one know who is and who is not among the elect? It is impossible to know for sure, but the "elect" will likely exhibit certain characteristics. They will live a sober life not given over to the pleasures of the body. Each individual has a gift given by God and is called to make diligent use of that gift through dedicated hard work. One must give to the poor, but in order to do so one must prosper, and as long as that prosperity does not come at the expense of the poor, profit is good. Thus, new motivations were created and condoned (i.e., rationalized).

Weber's analysis can be divided into two parts. First, the drive to continuous acquisition and accumulation is unique in history. Thus, the key to the European emergence must have been motivational in nature; that is, a new set of motivations came to the forefront of the human psyche though a process of rationalization. Second, empirically, much of the new, innovative economic activity characteristic of the European emergence seemed, according to Weber, to be concentrated in the areas that had been most strongly influenced by the Reformation and Protestantism. Hence, the Protestant Reformation and its new doctrines must have provided this rationalization (Greenfeld 1996).

Some modern scholars have accepted the first set of ideas while rejecting the second. Specifically, after closer examination, the correlation between new types of behavior and the Protestant Reformation have been increasingly found to be dubious. However, rejection of the Protestant Reformation as the rationalizing agent does not mean rejection of the idea that there must be a rationalizing agent. That is, the European emergence was the result of the dominance of new motivations that received the approval of a new set of system of ethics, but that new system of rationalization was not Protestantism (Greenfeld 1996).

If not the Protestant ethic, then what was the new system that provided the motivation that drove the evolution of modern capitalism? Greenfeld (1996, 434) argued, "I claim that behind this shift of societal attitudes toward the acquisitive drive stood a new, secular, form of collective consciousness (thus a new system of ethical standards)—nationalism." It is nationalism that represents the new spirit of capitalism. There are several factors why this hypothesis would seem reasonable. First, the chronology of nationalism lends itself as an explanation. It first appeared in England around 1600. Moreover, it was unique to England for about a century. England was thus the first to acquire this new spirit. Second, nationalism tends to promote a social structure that a modern economy needs to develop. According to Greenfeld, nationalism is inherently egalitarian in nature since one of its consequences is the creation of a system of social stratification that allows for social mobility. In other words, nationhood grants citizenship to all members of the nation and all citizens have certain rights and certain responsibilities.

Nations and their prestige are judged in terms of comparisons with others, that is, international competition. Nationalist societies commit themselves to a race with others, a race that never has a finish, or, as Greenfeld argues, has an ever-receding finish line. If the economy and its performance are included in the areas of performance on which competition is based, then the nation-state is committed to a perpetual quest for economic growth.

According to Tilly (1997), economic performance must become the core on which state performance is to be judged. According to him, the classic European experience involving state making had to do with how a particular lord made war so effectively as to become the dominant power over a particular territory. Thus, the establishment of a nation-state was not about the creation of a social contract, but about the establishment of a monopoly over violence in a particular area. The ability to effectively generate power, in particular military power, is therefore essential to the establishment of a state.

New states engage in a number of tasks. From Tilly's framework, one can classify these tasks in the following manner. War making is necessary to eliminate and neutralize rivals outside the controlled area. State making involves eliminating or neutralizing rivals within the territory and protecting the individuals within the controlled region from attacks from others. Finally, the state must extract from its clients (its citizens) the resources necessary to support the monopoly of violence established by the ruling elite. Thus, in this context, the ruling elite is in continuous competition with other forces seeking to usurp that monopoly.

The competition among nation-states will drive the ruling elite to experiment with various policies in an attempt to generate increased resources that can be used to enhance military power. Through this process of experimentation, states will begin to take on other functions, such as the provision of public goods, adjudication or justice (e.g., protection of property rights), roads, communication, and the provision of information. Ruling elites who take on these responsibilities will find that the flows of resources available for war making will be enhanced.

From this perspective, nationalism and the competition that it inspired often emerged from the nature of military conflict. Those societies that had productive economies could generally provide a larger material base for military power. Thus, economic performance became an important measuring rod in the international competition among nation-states. This provided the rationale for the motive of never-ending accumulation, which served as the foundation of modern capitalism.

So far, this section has argued that mechanisms or ideologies valuing persistent accumulation were essential for the industrialization process in Europe. In other words, ethical systems had to develop that placed high value on accumulation and rationalized it from society's perspective. In very simple terms, cultural changes prior to the industrialization experience were necessary. Without these particular cultural changes, there would be little possibility that modern capitalism could emerge in northwestern Europe.

Culture and Technology

A different sort of perspective on the role of culture in the European emergence comes out of the work of Goldstone (2002). Much of this chapter has implied that things happening in Europe from the late sixteenth to the nineteenth century were unique to Europe. For example, growth was intensive, not just extensive. The reader will remember that intensive growth results in rising per capita income, while extensive growth results in output growth that matches input growth (i.e., no change in per capita income). Extensive growth has occurred throughout much of human history, but intensive growth was unique to Europe.

Goldstone, however, argues that this interpretation is incorrect. He introduces a new term, *efflorescence,* which he argues is the opposite of crisis. Specifically, a crisis is a sharp unexpected downturn in economic and demographic indicators. An efflorescence, on the other hand, is a short, unexpected upturn in such indicators that is usually characterized by political expansion and the development of new institutions. From a pure economic perspective, an efflorescence involves both Smithian growth and Schumpeterian growth. Smithian growth is a productivity increase resulting from specialization and the expansion of the market, while Schumpeterian growth represents productivity growth stemming from innovation.

Throughout history there have been a number of societies that have experienced such efflorescence. Japan during the Tokugawa period (1600 to 1850) underwent a period of rapid commercialization. New agricultural techniques were developed and silk production increased rapidly. Song China (900 to 1200) developed extensive waterpower, iron works, and shipping. These societies went through extensive periods of productivity growth resulting from the expansion of markets, specialization and the application of innovations. Goldstone suggests there are at least two other examples of efflorescence. First, there was the "golden age" in the Netherlands. He dates this period from 1570 to 1680. During this period, real wages increased by 50 percent, as did the population. At the same time, agricultural productivity grew rapidly by historical standards. The second example would be from the Qing dynasty in China (seventeenth century), although there is significant debate as to how much economic progress occurred during this period.

Goldstone's main point is that the European (i.e., English) efflorescence of the eighteenth and early nineteenth centuries was not unique in the history of the world. From time to time a particular society would experience an economic efflorescence for a particular period, only for it to die out. Thus one gets the perception of efflorescence as flickering on and then slowly disappearing throughout history. They all eventually flickered out, except for that in England. How is this process to be explained?

The major problem with all preindustrial societies and their economies was not a limited amount of land or too rapid a rate of population growth. The real limitation was in terms of energy. "The amount of mechanical energy available to any preindustrial economy was limited to water flows, animals or people who could be fed, and wind that could be captured. In any geographically fixed area, this amount was strictly limited, as well as—for wind and water power—highly variable" (Goldstone 2002, 361). A second problem was it was extremely difficult to concentrate large amounts of energy or power at a single location. Concentrating wind- or waterpower sources, teams of animals, or large groups of people to provide the power factories needed were not feasible.

The solution to this energy problem came with the development of ways to harness energies in minerals. The crucial innovation in this process, according to Goldstone, was the steam engine. The key was a mechanism that could convert the relatively abundant fossil fuels into energy and, therefore, useful work.

As a result, the modern factory becomes possible. Large amounts of potential energy could be concentrated within factories, which could then apply that energy to do work on a large scale. It overcame not only the limited amounts of energy available from the water, wind, animals, and humans, but also allowed that energy to be effectively concentrated and focused within the confines of factory organization. "Circa 1700, the entire world's use of biomass energy for fuel amounted to perhaps 250 million tons of oil equivalent (Mtoe). By 1850, this had grown by perhaps 20 percent to 300 Mtoe. By contrast, energy produced from coal in 1700 totaled only about 5 Mtoe, but grew by 1,400 percent to 70 Mtoe in 1850; and what is even more striking is that over 70 percent (50 Mtoe) of the coal was extracted by Britain to power its engines" (Goldstone 2002, 363). Thus by 1850 the average citizen of England had "more than ten times the amount of moveable, deployable fuel energy per person used by the rest of the world's population" (ibid., 314).

However, the technological innovation was not the steam engine alone. It involved a whole series of innovations stemming from applying the modern principles of physics, mechanics, and chemistry to manufacturing, agriculture, and transportation. It was the widespread application of science to the production process that really distinguishes the European emergence (an efflorescence) from all others. This is what eventually truly revolutionized the production process. This was indeed unique to the English experience.

How does one explain this new development, the application of science to production? Goldstone believes this was the result of a cultural transformation that was peculiar to England. It is not a cultural change involving religious values or the development of the new motive of individualism; instead, one can think of this as the emergence of engine science or a scientific culture strongly associated with engines.

Engine science, or culture, was a particular strain within the broader context of European culture. This was a culture that lauded the practical application of science to solving problems. Practical science and engineering became dominant. A fascination with instruments had begun long before the European emergence, in a variety of different cultures and regions around the world. However, there is a difference between a fascination with instruments and a willingness to rely on them for generating knowledge. This way of thinking came to dominate England in the seventeenth and eighteenth centuries.

Mokyr (1999) argues that an intellectual bifurcation occurred in the seventeenth century. British science became more experimental and commercially oriented. Science on the continent became more abstract and formal. Newton's work, for example, was not widely studied on the continent for at least 100 years after the development of his ideas. Some of the continental churches found these ideas in conflict with their view of the world. "Only the Anglican Church initially embraced Newton and proclaimed from the pulpit the order of the universe as maintained by universal gravity and uniform mechanical laws, allowing a middle-class popular culture based on interest in mechanical demonstrations and physical laws to spread. While modern science thus had wide European roots, the branch of engine-based scientific inquiry spread freely into popular culture only in England from the mid-seventeenth to the mid-eighteenth century" (Goldstone 2002, 370).

One can think of scientific development as occurring throughout parts of Europe. However, this scientific development took a variety of forms, some more formal and abstract, while others were less formal and more pragmatic. It took a peculiar form in England. English craftsmen, artisans, and entrepreneurs became deeply involved in engine science. The result was that England became the center for what we would think of as modern engineering. Craftsmen who tinkered with machines in an attempt to practically apply the fundamental principles of natural philosophy were involved in the emergence of engineering. They, according to Goldstone, relied on precise measurement with scopes, graphs, and instruments. These were the people that developed the steam engine and a host of other practical engines.

Thus, the important change that differentiated the European efflorescence from others was the ability to tap new sources of energy (e.g., mineral) for the production process. This was made possible via the application of science to the production process. This resulted in the creation of machines that could transform fossil fuels into the energy to do enormous amounts of work. This broke the energy bottleneck that had strangled previous efflorescences and allowed for the possibility of the modern factory.

What We Have Learned

After examining the European emergence, what have we learned about the process of economic development? First, the Industrial Revolution was more like an industrial evolution. It was a slow series of changes that took place over a relatively long period of time. The key was that growth in income per person, while slow, was sustained. Growth persisted.

The European emergence was closely tied to growth in agricultural productivity and output. This growth in turn fostered a growth in spending, or, in other words, market size expanded. With this, Smithian growth, based on specialization in both agricultural and nonagricultural activities, became an integral part of the English experience. Protoindustrialization provided alternative employment opportunities for rural families, especially for women and children. The term industrious revolution might be called on to characterize this experience. That is, as specialization expanded and productivity grew, there were increased opportunities to increase the application of labor in productive ways.

In this process, international trade certainly played a role. According to Ricardo, free trade allowed for the importation of cheap wage goods and this allowed England to stave off the law of diminishing returns. Trade, according to comparative advantage, allowed England to reap the gains from a more efficient allocation of resources. The trading relationship between industrializing Europe and the periphery also allowed the former to reap substantial profit through both trade and investment, as well as through force and coercion. However, these profits do not seem to have been key to the European emergence. The processes by which much of it was extracted had extremely damaging effects on the periphery, effects that would be detrimental to long-term development for various regions in the world.

Trade seems to have had a much more important indirect effect on the experience of England. Specifically, the commitment problem plagues most ruling elite. That is, they can promise to promote situations conducive to investment by private individuals or groups, but once the investment is made, they have an incentive to extract all of the profit for themselves. Long-term growth and development is dependent on the resolution of this problem. Because the English ruling elite was primarily dependent on their own domestic economy for revenue, a struggle between the ruling elite and commercial groups ensued. This resulted in a process by which the ruling elite learned to be developmental rather than predatory. The profits offered by the Atlantic trade strengthened the commercial groups in this dialectical interaction and played an integral role in the solution to the political-commitment problem.

However, when all is said and done, the critical feature that allowed the European emergence to be more than just an efflorescence—one of many that have occurred in history—was breaking the energy barrier; that is, the creation of new ways to tap into the potential energy of fossil fuels via innovation. It was the practical application of science to industry that allowed this to occur. This was a peculiar cultural characteristic that developed in its most intense form in England.

This process can be briefly summarized as follows. A commercial revolution fostered by agricultural growth and the gains from Smithian productivity increases is necessary for industrialization, but it is not sufficient. Previous efflorescences appeared and died out. What is required for industrialization is the application of science to the practical problems of production. The peculiar machine culture that evolved in England seems to have been the key. Perhaps there is a simpler way to state this:

Without an agricultural revolution, Smithian growth, and commercialization, there would have been no long-term industrialization. Without the development of a machine culture, the application of science to production, there would have been no long-term industrialization. It was the fortuitous combination of both that led to the European emergence.

Key Terms

Industrial Revolution	Slavery
Extensive Growth	Political Development
Intensive Growth	Earned Income
Agricultural Surplus	Atlantic Trade
Protoindustrialization	Culture
Comparative Advantage	Nationalism
Dependency Theory	Efflorescence

References

Acemoglu, Daron, Simon Johnson, and James Robinson. 2002. "The Rise of Europe: Atlantic Trade, Institutional Change and Economic Growth." NBER Working Paper 9378. National Bureau of Economic Research, Cambridge, Massachusetts.

Allen, Robert. 1992. *Enclosure and the Yeoman.* Oxford: Oxford University Press.

———. 1998. "Tracking the Agricultural Revolution." Discussion Paper No. 98–18, Department of Economics, University of British Columbia.

Ashton, T.S. 1948. *The Industrial Revolution, 1760–1830.* Oxford: Oxford University Press.

Bairoch, Paul. 1995. *Economics and World History: Myths and Paradoxes.* Chicago: University of Chicago Press.

Boecke, J.H. 1953. *Economics and Economic Policy in Dual Societies.* New York: AMS Press.

Boserup, Esther. 1965. *The Conditions of Agricultural Growth: The Economics of Agarian Change Under Population Pressure.* Chicago: Aldine.

Brenner, Robert. 1982. "Agrarian Class Structure and Economic Development in Pre-industrial Europe." *Past and Present* 97 (November): 16–113.

De Vries, Jan. 1994. "The Industrial Revolution and the Industrious Revolution." *Journal of Economic History* 54: 249–70.

Engerman, Stanley. 1972. "The Slave Trade and British Capital Formation in the Eighteenth Century: A Comment on the Williams Thesis." *Business History Review* 46: 440–43.

Engerman, Stanley, and Patrick O'Brien. 1991. "Export and the Growth of the British Economy from the Glorious Revolution to the Peace of Amiens." In *Slavery and the Rise of the Atlantic System*, ed. Barbara Solow. Cambridge: Cambridge University Press.

Frank, Andre Gunder. 1966. "The Development of Underdevelopment." *Monthly Review* 18 (September): 17–31.

Goldstone, Jack A. 2002. "Efflorescences and Economic Growth: Rethinking the 'Rise of the West' and the Industrial Revolution." *Journal of World History* 13: 323–89.

Greenfeld, Liah. 1996. "The Birth of Economic Competitiveness: Rejoinder to Breckman and Trägardh." *Critical Review* 10 (summer): 409–70.

Inikori, Joseph. 2002. *Africans and the Industrial Revolution in England: A Study of International Trade and Economic Development.* Cambridge, MA: Cambridge University Press.

Johnston, Bruce F., and John Mellor. 1961. "The Role of Agriculture in Economic Development." *American Economic Review* 51: 566–93.

Jones, E.L. 1993. *Growth Recurring: Economic Change in World History.* Oxford: Oxford University Press.

Lewis, W. Arthur. 1954. "Economic Development with Unlimited Supplies of Labour." *Manchester School* 22: 139–91.

Mokyr, Joel. 1999. *The British Industrial Revolution.* Boulder, Colorado: Westview Press.

Moore, Mick. 1998. "Death Without Taxes: Democracy, State Capacity, and Aid Dependence in the Fourth World." In *The Democratic Developmental State: Politics and Institutional Design*, eds. Mark Robinson, and Gordon White, 84–121. Oxford: Oxford University Press.

———. 2001. "Political Underdevelopment: What Causes 'Bad Governance.'" *Institute of Development Studies.* March. 1–40.

North, Douglas, and Barry Weingast. 1989. "Constitutions and Credible Commitments: The Evolution of the Institutions of Public Choice in 17th-Century England." *Journal of Economic History* 49: 803–32.

O'Brien, Patrick. 1982. "European Economic Development: The Contribution of the Periphery." *Economic History Review* 35: 1–18.

Ranis, G., and J. Fei. 1961. "A Theory of Economic Development." *American Economic Review* 51: 533–65.

Senghaas, Dieter. 1985. *The European Experience: A Historical Critique of Development Theory.* Dover, NH: Berg Publishers.

Tilly, Charles. 1997. *Roads From Past to Future.* Lanham, Marsland: Rowman and Littlefield.

Weber, Max. 1976 [1905]. *The Protestant Ethic and the Spirit of Capitalism.* New York: Scribner's.

Weingast, Barry. 1995. "The Economic Role of Political Institutions: Market Pre-serving Federalism and Economic Development." *Journal of Law, Economics, and Organization* 11: 1–32.

Williams, Eric E. 1944. *Capitalism and Slavery.* Chapel Hill, NC: University of North Carolina Press.

Wrigley, E. Anthony. 1985. "Urban Growth and Agricultural Change: England and the Continent in the Early Modern Period." *Journal of Interdisciplinary History* 15: 683–728.

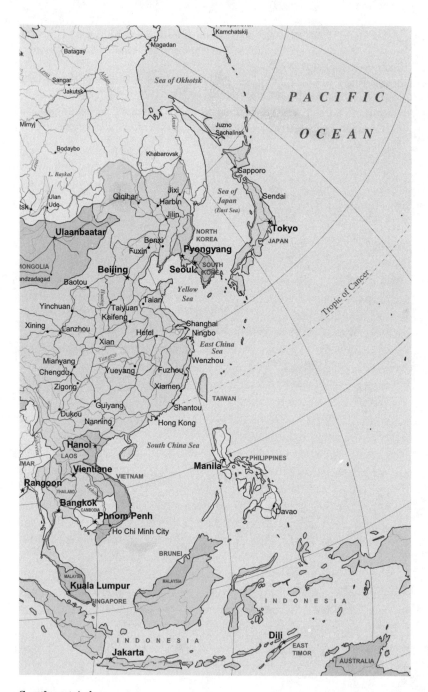

Southeast Asia

3

East Asian Experience

In the previous chapter, the economic emergence of Europe was studied in some detail. It represented the first example of a process of economic development that significantly diverged from that of the world in general. East Asia would also enter a development trajectory that was different from the rest of the world, although this would be somewhat later than that of Europe's. However, economic growth and development were no strangers to East Asia. China went through several periods of economic efflorescence before 1900, and Japan went through such a period from the 1600s to 1868. However, neither country managed to make the transition to industrialization based on the application of science to the production process. Both came into contact with the West, and this contact, in one way and another, set off a process that ultimately led to the unfolding of an industrialization process (based on applying science to production), first in Japan, and then, more recently, in China.

As Japan industrialized, in the late nineteenth and early twentieth centuries, it also engaged in a process of colonization (specifically involving Taiwan and Korea, both North and South). Through this process of colonization, a foundation was inadvertently laid for the industrialization of these regions in the post–World War II period. Of course, foundations mean nothing unless they are properly built on and the postwar experiences of South Korea and Taiwan were the result of many other factors in addition to its common colonization experience.

In this chapter, East Asia is defined to include China, Japan, South Korea, and Taiwan. The experiences of these countries represent successful examples of catching up; that is, this region was exposed to the Western industrial powers (England, France, Germany, and, most importantly, the

United States) at a time when it was behind in terms of the industrialization experience. As a response, it attempted in various ways to initiate a rapid catching up. The theme of this chapter is on catching up; that is, the learning process of East Asia.

We first examine the early experiences of Japan and China. In the case of Japan, it will be shown that, during the period 1600 to 1868, a vigorous Smithian growth process was well underway. It was driven by rapid agricultural growth, which, in turn, stimulated protoindustrial development. China, on the other hand, actually experienced several phases of intense Smithian growth. They too were powered by a pick up in agricultural growth, which fueled protoindustrial development. Neither country was able to make the transition to industrial growth via an evolutionary process. Both were confronted by strong industrial powers from the West. This confrontation set off frantic efforts to catch up.

In the third section of this chapter, we will discuss, from a theoretical perspective, the key differences between the early (i.e., English) and late (i.e., Japanese and Chinese) industrialization process. In the latter, a key role is played by the learning process. Neoclassical economists argue that open and free trade and open and free flows of capital between countries will allow for fast learning to occur in those countries which are trying to rapidly industrialize. An alternative perspective is based on the infant-industry argument and its many derivatives, and this is explored in the fourth section. The argument here is that the state may have to play an important role in the learning process, that free trade, in and of itself, may actually hinder the learning process. The difference between this perspective and the neoclassical view revolves around different views of the state; that is, how it functions and its role vis-à-vis the economy. Three views of the state will be discussed: the rent-seeking state, the developmental state, and the relational state.

In the fifth and sixth sections, we utilize the theory discussed previously to examine the postwar experiences of China and Japan. With respect to Japan, the relational-state perspective will be used to analyze both the rapid economic development of Japan, as well as the stagnation that afflicted the country in the 1990s. With respect to postwar development in China, this chapter will stop prior to the economic reforms of the 1970s. The analysis of China's reforms and growth after the 1970s will be examined in Chapter 8.

The experiences of Japan and China are then used as a backdrop for the analysis of the economic experiences of South Korea and Taiwan.

The colonial experiences of these two states will be reviewed. The story will emphasize their roles as suppliers of rice and sugar for mainland Japan. During this time, the foundation for rapid agricultural growth was constructed. The postwar period was characterized by both dramatic land reform and further rapid agricultural growth. Both economies proved adept at making the transition to the production and export of manufactured goods. It will be argued that a combination of internal and external circumstances allowed both states to overcome the political-commitment problem discussed in Chapter 2. Ultimately, these two countries have become democracies, though this seems to have been the result of the economic process rather than a cause thereof.

The chapter will close, as the previous chapter did, with a discussion of what has been learned. This includes the notion that catching up is a different process from that which occurred in the initial industrializing country, England. This type of industrialization is nested within a market expansion or commercialization process. International trade is important, but not necessarily free trade. Solving the political-commitment problem is, however, essential. Finally, cultural flexibility seems to be an overarching need, with consistency required between institutional structures and culture.

Early Experiences of Japan and China

This section will be concerned with the early economic experiences of Japan and China. With respect to Japan, two historical periods will be discussed: the Tokugawa (1600 to 1868) and the pre–World War II (1869 to 1939) period. The latter encompasses what is typically called the Meiji period.

It is interesting the number of similarities that exist between the English and Japanese experience. They were both island nations off the coast of large continental landmasses. They were both relatively isolated. More importantly, Japan too experienced a period of decentralized feudalism, during the Tokugawa period.

In late sixteenth-century Japan, warriors were scattered across the land in villages, where they essentially behaved as overlords. Peasants were permanently attached to the land and were allowed to farm it in exchange for paying a tax, usually in-kind, to the ruling warrior. In addition to levying taxes, the warrior also administered justice and kept the peace. To defend their land, the warriors banded together into regional military organizations, which were composed of a lord and his vassals. As Smith (1988, 137) puts it, "the normal state among such groups was war or the preparation for war." (Much of what follows on Tokugawa Japan is drawn from Smith.) During this period, much of the agricultural surplus was extracted and utilized for war making.

At the turn of the seventeenth century, Tokugawa Ieyasu succeeded in conquering most of the important areas of mainland Japan. This was the beginning of a period of almost 200 years of internal peace and stability. Tokugawa Ieyasu did not destroy the feudal structure, but instead exerted his control over it (Smith 1988). As a result, many changes occurred. One of the most important was a change in the relationship of the warriors to the land. The warriors were removed from the land to reside in the towns that grew up around their lord's castle. Thus, land and the seigniorial rights associated with it became consolidated in the hands of a few hundred noble families. The warriors became townspeople who depended on a rice stipend paid by the feudal lord.

The central government, represented by the Tokugawa shogunate (military rule), took over the power of taxation and, in turn, used much of the revenue generated to pay the warriors their stipends. The latter thus became dependent on the feudal government. In order to prevent the feudal lords from becoming too powerful, the Tokugawa shogunate instituted an elaborate hostage system, which required local feudal lords to spend alternate years in residence at Edo (modern-day Tokyo), the shogun's castle town. Further, feudal lords were often rotated from region to region. All of these changes provided the foundation for 200 years of internal peace.

The new Tokugawa shogunate was faced with significant financial burdens, mainly composed of the warrior stipends. In the past the warrior class had collected the tax, but this was no longer possible since they had been removed from the land. Therefore, a new tax structure had to be created. Taxes levied on farmers were to be based on the estimated productivity of the land, and this tax was levied not on individuals but on whole villages. Thus, collecting the tax became a responsibility for the entire village (ibid., 50–70).

Here it appears there is another significant similarity with England. The central governments in both countries were dependent on earned revenue to support the activities of the ruling elite. By earned revenue it is meant that the ruling elite must put significant effort into the construction of a bureaucratic apparatus for the collection of revenue, and this apparatus reaches a large proportion of the population. In addition, this effort required by the ruling elite also involves reciprocity; that is, the elite must provide services in return for the revenue.

Income earned by the ruling elite from the bulk of the population involves the elite in a dialectical interaction with its citizens. As discussed in Chapter 2, this dialectical interaction involves a process of learning whereby common interests are constructed and constraints on the behavior of the ruling elite are likely to evolve. This ruling elite is likely to become less predatory and more developmental. The political-commitment problem is thus resolved.

This process seems to have unfolded within the context of Tokugawa Japan. Tax data for several villages have been examined by Smith for the period 1680 to 1850. It seems that there is no indication that there was a long-term increase in the tax rate. Thus the ruling elite seems to have been unable to extract the maximum amount of revenue from agriculture. This inability would seem to have been related to the strength of village peasant groups in resisting increased extraction. Vlastos (1986) indicates that during this period there were some 3,000 uprisings by peasants against feudal authority and another 3,000 intravillage disputes. The average number of peasant protests per decade was 113, and the protests occurred in every province. The most common purpose of such uprisings was to oppose higher taxes and interference by the ruling elite with rural commerce and production.

The willingness of peasants to engage in collective action was significantly influenced by the mechanism by which tax was administered. The lord announced annually to each village what its land-tax liability would be and the village would allocate the tax burden among families. There was an internal structure within each village to carry out this process. However, an organization created to administer these taxes could also serve as a focus for resistance. Thus the peasants had a mechanism by which dialectical interaction between the ruling elite and peasant farmers could occur. In this way, peasant farmers were able to restrain the extractive impulses of the ruling elite; hence, the problem of political commitment to growth-enhancing policies was solved by restraints placed on the ruling elite.

Because of these changes, peasant farmers now had an incentive to invest in activities that would increase overall productivity. As long as tax rates remained unchanged, a share of any increase in output could be retained by the farmers. The revenue of the ruling elite would also rise as overall productivity increased. Indeed, this happened, and productivity slowly grew throughout the Tokugawa period. The resulting increases in income fueled the demand for simple, labor-intensive manufactured goods. Protoindustrial or protomanufacturing activity expanded, providing increased off-farm opportunities for employment. Because of these activities, a commercial transformation occurred in much of the Japanese economy. Specialization in the production process expanded dramatically and internal trade grew rapidly.

The growing demand for rice resulting from growth stimulated merchants to serve as intermediaries between suppliers in rural areas and buyers in urban areas. This in turn led to the creation of networks of buyers and sellers throughout the rural areas. The rice market tended to center on Osaka, and the city also began to develop as a center for trading with other communities, and merchant specialization began to occur.

Thus, by 1868 Japan had been economically transformed; it was experiencing an economic efflorescence in which per capita income was rising and extensive market networks were forming. However, industrialization had yet to occur. The utilization of fossil fuels and the application of large amounts of energy (i.e., nonbiological in nature) to the production process had yet to take place on a large scale. The economy was therefore still faced with the constraint imposed by available traditional energy sources (wind, water, animal, human).

It was at this time, however, that the Americans appeared off the shore of Japan with their gunboats and gunboat diplomacy. The shock posed to the Japanese system undermined the rule of the Tokugawa shogunate. It was immediately evident that the Japanese would not be able to militarily resist the might of the United States and the other Western military powers that quickly followed the Americans. As a result, the Tokugawa shogunate collapsed and was replaced by an oligarchy of the ruling elite from the outlying regions. A nation-state was established and the Meiji era would begin. The main goal of the new regime would be to catch up with the West in terms of industrialization. It was felt by the new ruling oligarchy that catching up was necessary if Japan was to be able to create a military that was capable of resisting intrusions by the West.

The early experiences of China were, in some ways, similar to those of Japan. However, it seems that China had experienced several periods of growth efflorescence. Jones (1993) has vigorously argued that the Sung dynasty, from the tenth to the thirteenth century, was one such efflorescence. Jones points to the performance of the iron industry in support of his contention. Their technique for iron production was well developed. Coal was used in the smelting process, which was not achieved in Europe until the eighteenth century. Some historical estimates seem to indicate that China's iron output in 1078 would not be achieved by Europe until 1700. This resulted in a significant decline in the relative price of iron, which, in turn, induced increased iron usage. Specifically, it was used for weapons, farm implements, and other types of tools.

There was also a significant change in the land system. Like the Tokugawa period in Japan, the Sung dynasty began with the reunification of a fractured political system. A national civil-service commission was established and neoconfucianism was established as a national philosophy. The government ceased reallocating land and converted taxes to cash payments. This led to the development of a commercial land market (Jones 1993). Agricultural productivity appears to have grown as a result; the population of China grew rapidly in the early part of this period, which could not have occurred unless agricultural production had risen significantly. Part of this rising prosperity resulted from the introduction of early ripening rice, which increased annual rice yields.

Because of these processes, specialization and market integration increased dramatically. The state, in turn, seems to have heavily invested in public goods such as communication and transportation. Peasants in areas most favorable for rice growing tended to concentrate on rice production, while other regions specialized in tea and sugar production, orchards, fish rearing, and market gardens. In addition, significant amounts of protoindustrial activity also occurred. Many peasants became part-time producers, while a smaller proportion became full-time producers of simple manufactured goods (Jones 1993).

According to Jones, this efflorescence was a response to the relaxing of political controls and demands, a switch to taxation in money (as opposed to in-kind), and to the improvement in transportation and communication. Merchant groups and small manufacturers played an increasingly important role in the economy.

However, this was not the only instance of growth efflorescence in Chinese history. In 1644, the Ming emperor was facing rebellion and upheaval. He invited the Manchu (a powerful nomadic group in the northeast) to help suppress the internal rebellion. The Manchu were successful, so successful that they seized power for themselves and established the Qing dynasty. This ushered in significant change within important parts of China.

During the Ming dynasty, the vast agricultural sector had become dominated by huge bondservant and subservient tenant-farmed estates. These were eliminated and a largely free and independent peasantry was established. In addition, markets for grain were freed. According to Goldstone (2002, 348–49), it was "the combination of a large-scale shift to a free peasantry, combined with a shift from direct to more market-oriented control of the peasantry" that was an essential component of productivity growth and the specialization that ensued. In addition, the territorial expansion by the Qing created an entity several times larger than that controlled by the Ming, and this new entity included a large number of different peoples and cultures. Thus, market exchange within this entity expanded dramatically.

The economic growth that took place in China during this time was astonishing. In 1700, the population of China was approximately 160 million. By 1800, it had more than doubled, to approximately 350 million. However, living standards seem to have been higher in the eighteenth century than in the previous century.

Agricultural productivity and output seem to have dramatically increased. Food availability and health improved, and a variety of raw (unprocessed) goods was consumed, even by the peasant farmers. This increase in agricultural productivity was accompanied by a rapid growth in protoindustrial activity. Yet this expansion process (like that of the Sung) did not last. After 1750 there was a slowdown in economic expansion, and rapid population growth seems to have eroded much of the previous gain.

China seems to represent a socioeconomic system that underwent periodic efflorescences. Deng (2003) characterizes China as being a symbiotic economic system. This system is made up of three interlocking types or sectors: the rural, private, customary, mercantile sector; the urban, private, mercantile-customary sector; and the state-run, command, mercantile sector. Customary and mercantile here perhaps need further explanation. Customary production by households in either the rural or urban sectors was generally for the household's own use or consumption. Mercantile activities involved production and exchange, which are market oriented. The three sectors were linked together by two kinds of domestic markets: producer and consumer goods and services, and land and property.

This system waxed and waned throughout Chinese history. During periods of prosperity, commercialization increased, mercantile activity expanded, urbanization increased, and the overall size of the economy expanded. During periods of decline, the economy deurbanized, decommericalized, and the absolute size of the economy contracted.

The center of economic gravity was undoubtedly the rural sector and its customary component, peasant household farmers. They were involved in both traditional production for subsistence purposes and market production via specialization. The balance between the two was constantly altering as conditions altered. The core of Chinese family farms arose, probably through a trial-and-error process, by the seventh century BC. Through time, the family link to land holding became established by law. Household, peasant farming on a relatively small scale became the dominant structural form. The advantage of this form lay in the reward it offered to farmers to produce more and innovate. After paying taxes and rent, the residual was left to the peasant farmer.

The state, in turn, was greatly dependent on the rural sector for the revenue necessary to support the ruling elite. In other words, the state and ruling elite were dependent on earned income. Taxes levied on producing households provided a stream of revenue for the state, which was enhanced by productivity growth within agriculture. As long as the state did not extract all of the productivity gains from the farmers, both the rural elite and peasant farmer could benefit. The former would find its income stream enhanced, and the latter would have provided an incentive to expand productivity. The farmers would also gain from the public goods provided by the elite: irrigation, roads, and security. "The ruler of such a state had an agenda: to build up and maintain his economic and military might. This was met without too much trouble by the rural sector once private land holding created jointly by the peasants (who claimed it) and the state (which endorsed it) had been institutionalized" (Deng 2001).

The key question here is how the political-commitment problem was resolved. Remember, the ruling elite has every incentive to promise not to extract all productivity gains (thus providing an incentive for peasant farmers to expand productivity). However, after the farmer has invested and productivity has grown, the ruling elite has every incentive to break their promise and extract as much as possible. However, in China, as well as Japan, the elite's dependence on the peasant farmers for earned income set off a dialectical interaction from which common interests were forged between the elite and farmers. The key to such successful dialectical interaction, which results in constraints on the ruling elite, is the extent to which the peasants are capable of resisting.

In China's case, it seems that peasant farmers were able to resist deviant state activities. Peasants rather frequently arose to oppose unpopular regimes. Deng (2001) believes that the Chinese peasantry qualifies as one of the most rebellious among all farming classes in world history. From 210 BC to 1900 AD, there were 2,106 major peasant rebellions, each lasting an average of seven years, with an average of 226,000 participants. Rebels were responsible for establishing at least forty-eight regimes. The political regimes of the peasant rebellions always included land issues and an emphasis on private ownership. Most importantly, it was the better-off regions that most often rebelled.

The impact of these rebellions was both obvious and important. They served as an important deterrent to policies that attempted to extract too much from the agricultural sector. "Indeed, the correlation between a heavy tax burden on the rural sector and armed rebellions was so obvious that increasing taxes became a taboo" (Deng 2001, 26).

One can view the Chinese system as a carefully balanced system of incentives on which the economic and political structure was built. As long as the balance between the ruling elite and the peasant farmers was maintained, productivity growth in agriculture would occur. The rising incomes would stimulate specialization in both the rural and nonrural sectors. Protoindustrial development would occur. Standards of living and population size would grow. However, shocks from the inside and outside would very often disrupt this balance. Then the commercialization process would be thrown into reverse, specialization would decline, productivity would fall, and, in the face of rising populations, living standards would collapse. Such is the dynamic rise and fall that is characteristic of Chinese history.

However, throughout these periods of expansion and contraction, industrialization failed to occur. The efflorescences in economic activity (i.e., the prosperity booms) did not set off industrialization, just as in Japan. The application of fossil-fuel energy to the production process did not occur on a large-enough scale. There was no widespread shift from biological to mineral-energy sources. More simply, there was no widespread application of science to the production process.

Thus, at the end of the nineteenth and beginning of the twentieth centuries, neither Japan nor China had been able to construct a heavy industrial base, although both had constructed highly commercialized societies that, from time to time, appeared to be on the verge of the industrialization process. However, the arrival of the Western powers to this region of the world created upheavals in both China and Japan that would lead to the demise of old political orders and the rise of nationalistic attempts at catching up. The Japanese were, in the short run, more successful at achieving this than the Chinese. Civil war, which engulfed China in the twentieth century and resulted in the establishment of a highly centralized communist state there, certainly slowed the process of catching up in China. However, this story began to change quickly in the 1970s.

Before exploring these two stories of learning and catching up, the next section will first examine the theoretical perspectives on this process. This will give an analytical structure that can then be used to analyze the experiences of China and Japan.

Catching Up: A Neoclassical View

One can visualize the problem for the countries that were left behind by the industrial expansion of northwestern Europe. In Figure 3.1, a production-possibilities curve is drawn for two types of goods, agriculture and manufacturing. Point B illustrates the position of an industrialized country, while point A represents the position of a society left behind. The latter operates closer to the agricultural axis, specializing in agricultural production, relative to the former. In addition, the society left behind operates inside the production-possibilities curve. Thus, it lags behind—it is not attaining the highest possible standard of living (given the existing technology). The existing technology (the position of the production-possibility curve) is determined by the industrialized nation.

In order to catch up, the society left behind must engineer a movement to the production frontier; that is, it must learn how to utilize the newer technologies to attain higher productivities. This will involve a process of learning. The situation is complicated in that the industrialized nation is continuously engineering new ideas that push the production frontier further outward. Thus, the lagging society must learn how to close the gap in a situation in which the gap has a tendency to increase.

How does this learning take place? Neoclassical economics has a particular story to tell about this process. The Solow (neoclassical) theory of economic growth had important implications for the process of convergence, the tendency for less-developed nations with lower per capita gross domestic product (GDP) to grow faster than already

Figure 3.1 **Catching Up**

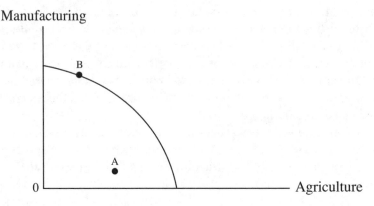

industrialized or developed countries (the explanation of convergence provided here is different from what is usually provided—a more detailed explanation is provided in the Appendix). They will grow more rapidly because they have lower capital-output ratios for the same underlying technology. Remember that the stationary state equilibrium for a country is when $s/v = n$. Thus if two countries, R (rich) and P (poor), have identical values of s, v, and n, then one would expect that the poor country would grow more rapidly. Its capital-output ratio would increase until it reached the same value as in the rich country. In this case, they would converge to the same standard of living if the underlying fundamentals were the same.

Divergence in per capita income levels will occur if $s_R > s_P$; that is, if the savings rate is higher in country R relative to country P. In the case of $s_R/v_R > n_R$, per capita income will rise in R relative to P, the law of diminishing returns will set in, and v will rise until a new stationary state is achieved. In this stationary state, per capita income will be higher in the rich country relative to the poor country because the savings rate is higher. Alternatively, if $n_R < n_P$, per capita income will grow in R relative to P until, once again, the law of diminishing returns sets in and a new stationary state is achieved, with per capita income higher in the rich country relative to the poor, as a result of population growth being lower in the former relative to the latter. Finally, if R uses a more productive technology relative to P ($v_R < v_P$), then once again the result will be a higher income in R relative to P. Thus, absolute convergence between rich and poor countries will not occur if the underlying fundamentals are different (although both rich and poor countries always converge to their own stationary state; i.e., conditional convergence).

The lack of absolute convergence outlined above is the result of presuming that differences in underlying fundamentals persist through time. However, if one allows for the free flow of capital among nations, the story changes. If $s_R > s_P$, then $v_R > v_P$ in the stationary state; that is, the productivity capital is lower in rich relative to poor countries. If the return to capital is related to the productivity of capital, then investors will perceive there to be a higher rate of return on investment in P, the poor country. Thus, savings would flow from R to P until $s_R = s_P$, and per capita incomes would converge. In the same manner, if $n_P > n_R$, then one would expect that, *ceteris paribus*, the return to labor is less in P relative to R, and that labor would migrate from P to R until per capita incomes were identical in both rich and poor countries. Finally, if knowledge were free to flow between countries, one would expect $v_R = v_P$, and thus absolute convergence in per capita income would tend to occur.

Therefore, if a poor country is to catch up with the rich, it should encourage foreign investment and encourage the free flow of new knowledge into its economy. At the same time, it should allow its workers to migrate to regions where the return to labor is higher. However, there is significant resistance to allowing the free flow of labor between countries. Sometimes barriers to capital also exist. In these cases, trade may serve as a substitute (a complete substitute under certain stringent conditions) for the free flow of the factors of production.

In a situation where capital and labor are immobile, rich countries are generally relatively abundant in capital, whereas poor countries are relatively abundant in labor. The Hecksher-Ohlin theory of trade argues that countries will have comparative advantages in those goods that use those factors of production that are relatively abundant. Rich, capital-abundant nations will have a comparative advantage in the production and export of capital-intensive goods, while poor, labor-abundant countries will have a comparative advantage in the production and export of labor-intensive goods. The rich countries will get the labor-intensive goods they need and the poor countries the capital-intensive goods they require. Through this process, the standard of living (i.e., per capita income) in the two types of countries will tend to converge through trade.

The above process would likely be enhanced by another factor. Bear in mind that the divergence between rich and poor countries discussed in the previous two paragraphs revolved around barriers to the mobility of capital and labor. Free trade will allow the poor country to expand the production of labor-intensive goods, increasing the demand for labor, thus driving up the relative wage. In addition, if foreign investment flows into the poor country it will enhance the productivity of labor and labor's income. At this point, the demographic theory of transition becomes relevant.

Demographic transition theory evolved out of Malthus's work. As you will recall from Chapter 1, he argued that the availability of education (in his day in the form of apprenticeships) would lead to a fall in population growth (due to the postponement of marriage). Transition theory (Thompson 1929, Notestein 1949) adds to this by arguing that social norms and mores determine fertility, and that these eventually adjust to society's needs. Initially, cultural inducements to high fertility were necessary to offset high mortality. As economic growth occurs, mortality rates will decline, resulting in a spurt of population growth. However, fertility eventually falls, as religious doctrines, moral codes, laws, education, customs, and marriage habits gradually respond to reduced mortality.

The implication of this discussion is that the flows of capital and knowledge, as well as free trade (according to the Hecksher-Ohlin perspective), will cause income to rise in poor relative to rich countries, reducing mortality rates in the former, which eventually also reduces fertility rates. Thus $n_p = n_R$ and absolute convergence in income levels will occur.

As can be seen, a common theme runs through neoclassical analysis. Countries that have fallen behind the industrial leader will tend to follow a process that allows them to naturally catch up. As long as capital and labor can flow freely among nations, or as long as free trade in goods occurs between countries and as long as knowledge is allowed to flow freely among nations, then absolute convergence will tend to occur. Capital, new knowledge, and capital-intensive goods will tend to flow into the poor countries, while labor and labor-intensive goods will flow into the rich ones; both will get what they need. Thus, living standards will tend to converge, and the poor will catch-up relative to the rich.

Now, this whole story breaks down if there are obstacles to the free flow of goods, inputs, and knowledge among countries. If states (ruling elites) put up barriers to the free flow of goods, inputs, and knowledge, then the convergence process will be short-circuited. Thus, bad government policy and interference with competitive-market economics will prevent the poor from catching up. Why would the ruling elite of poor countries knowingly engage in bad policy? The answer to that lies in the realm of neoclassical political economy.

Neoclassical political economy is based on the notion of rent seeking. That is, restrictions on the free flow of goods, inputs, and knowledge among countries creates rents (i.e., extraordinary profits) for a select group within a particular nation. From the poor-nations' perspective, the supply of capital is scarce and the returns to that capital are high. If capital or capital-intensive goods are allowed to flow into a poor country, it will drive down the return to native capitalists (the owners of the capital). The latter would favor restricting the inflow of foreign capital and foreign-produced, capital-intensive goods as a mechanism to generate extraordinary profits for themselves. A ruling elite that provides such policies could certainly rely on the political support of the capitalist group and thus maintain its position of political power.

The free flow of knowledge into a less-developed country may also likely undermine the dominant position of domestic capitalists and landlords. Thus, a ruling elite that supported policies that interfered with the free flow of knowledge would once again enhance the profitability (i.e., rents) of certain groups of domestic capitalists and landlords. This would increase the likelihood that they would support the political elite that makes such policies.

The policies outlined above all have a common element; they short-circuit the operation of free markets and allow subgroups within the poor country to earn extraordinary returns (i.e., rents) in return for supporting (politically) the ruling elite. The cost of these policies is that all of them reduce growth rates and the overall productivity of society in general in order to enrich a minority. Society's interests are sacrificed for the interests of the politically powerful minority. One might ask why the bulk of society, the majority, allows themselves to be impoverished in order to enhance the wealth of a few?

The answer comes in several parts. First, most countries left behind in the industrialization process are not democracies. As such, the bulk of the population often has no direct political voice in influencing policies. One would think that the bulk of the population could still influence policy indirectly via protest or perhaps the threat of revolution. However, Olson (1971) has provided a fundamental explanation as to why the bulk of population often has no political influence, direct or indirect. He argues that a group's goals resemble a collective good. If such a good is provided, everyone within the group will get access to it whether or not they contributed to the cost of achieving it. Therefore, if the goal of a group is to bring about the construction of a new road, everyone along the road is likely to benefit whether or not they contributed resources to the construction (it is too costly to exclude those who do not contribute). This creates a "free rider" problem for the group. If I stand to benefit from the achievement of the group's goal regardless of whether I contribute to the cost of achievement, I will be tempted not to contribute (to free ride on the effort of others). If everyone feels that way, however, then no one will contribute and the goal will not be achieved.

The free-riding problem will be less acute for small groups since free riders are easier to detect and pressure can be brought to bear. Thus, small groups are likely to be able to organize to achieve their goals. However, with larger groups, free riding will be more difficult to detect or more difficult to prevent. As a result, large groups—representing society at large—are less likely to be able to organize and become politically powerful. Alternatively, small groups are more likely to be able to organize and achieve political power. These groups are likely to pursue rent-seeking policies, policies that restrict the flow of labor, capital, goods, and knowledge among countries. This will likely enhance their well-being at the expense of society at large, but society at large has no political power (i.e., it is not sufficiently organized).

In summary, the neoclassical perspective argues that the free flow of goods, labor, capital, and knowledge among nations is likely to lead to absolute convergence, and that poor countries initially left behind will be able to catch up with the industrialized nations. Difficulties arise when ruling elites seek to maintain their hold on power by restricting the free flow of these things. These restrictions will enhance the returns to small subgroups within society (create rents for them), and these small groups are likely to be politically powerful. Thus, the ruling elite uses its power to create rents to satisfy a politically powerful minority in order to ensure their continued hold on power. This comes at the expense of lower productivity, lower growth, and a lack of absolute convergence. Thus, for much of the world, convergence can occur only with political reform—reform aimed at reducing the influence of the state (i.e., the ruling elite), and economic reform (e.g., a greater reliance on free markets).

Catching Up: A Role for the State

There is a second theoretical perspective on the catching-up process. It argues that in many situations catching up will not automatically occur, that absolute convergence will not occur. More specifically, even if the elite do not engage in restrictive policies to benefit a few at the expense of the many, it is still unlikely that the countries left behind will be able to catch up with the initial industrializers. The ruling elite and the state may be a problem in less-developed countries, but they are not the fundamental problem. This perspective is based on the theoretical notion of multiple equilibria.

The neoclassical argument discussed in the previous section presumed that the free flow of goods, land, labor, and knowledge guaranteed the existence of one high-income equilibrium toward which all countries will, in the long term, converge. More importantly, if a country (for whatever reason) is moved away from the equilibrium, then there are convergence forces that will move the country back to the equilibrium. However, there is another group of theorists whose models involve multiple equilibria (at least two). The first equilibrium is a low-income one in which GDP per capita, and the capital-to-labor ratio, are at a low level. In the neighborhood of this equilibrium, all economies are drawn to it. Attempts to move from the equilibrium are likely to be thwarted by counteracting forces, which will drive the economy back to the low level. There is a second equilibrium where GDP per capita and the capital-to-labor ratio are quite high. There are forces at work that tend to keep an economy in the second equilibrium once it has been able to attain this equilibrium.

For accidental, historical reasons, some countries are caught in the low-level equilibrium and are trapped there. Others, for the same historical, accidental reasons, find themselves in the high-level equilibrium. In this kind of model there is no tendency to absolute convergence, the poor or the left behind are locked into their poverty (i.e., a low-level equilibrium).

These multiple-equilibria models come in a wide variety of types. Perhaps the earliest articulation of this idea is to be found in the work of Rosenstein-Rodan (1943), in what has come to be known as the parable of the shoe factory. Imagine there is a country or region where there is significant potential for investment in a number of areas. Further, presume that all of the production that occurs in the region must be sold there. In other words, there is no possibility to export (or import) products, and thus no international trade. In this situation, presume that a giant shoe factory is set up that produces $1 million worth of shoes and also $1 million worth of wages, interest, rent, and profit (all forms of income). If all of this income was in turn spent on shoes, a market for all the shoes would exist and the factory would prosper.

However, it is not likely that all $1 million worth of the income generated would be spent completely on shoes. It is more likely that it would be spent on a variety of things. The shoe factory will not be able to survive, as there will not be enough demand. However, if, simultaneously, several different enterprises were set up, consistent with the ratios with which people spend their money on different commodities, then jointly all of these enterprises would be successful in a way that the single shoe factory was not. For example, presume that people spend 50 percent of their income on food, 30 percent on clothing, and 20 percent on shoes. If three enterprises are set up such that 50 percent of income generated comes from food, 30 percent from clothing production, and 20 percent from shoe production, then income would be spent in such a way that all three prosper.

This situation illustrates how coordination becomes important. If any single producer (shoes, food, clothing) invests while the others do not, then he will fail. Thus, it is unlikely that any single investor will step forward to invest. Given that all firms face the same situation, this is an example of a low-level equilibrium. However, if each investor could be assured that the others, too, would invest, then all would succeed; such is high-level equilibrium. In order to attain that, the expectations of all the investors must be coordinated. Who would play the role of the coordinator? The most likely answer is the state.

There is a problem, however, with the previous example of multiple equilibria. The constraint giving rise to the problem comes from the demand side. If we drop the restriction on exporting and importing (allowing free trade), then the multiple-equilibria situation would tend to disappear. If the shoe factory were constructed in isolation, it might very well be able to survive by exporting a share of its output (i.e., selling outside of the region). The lack of demand would thus pose no problem and multiple equilibria would not exist.

However, an alternative multiple-equilibria model is not subject to such criticism. Let us presume that there are two types of final goods: simple and complex. The simple good is produced using very few intermediate goods (specialized machinery, specialized services, etc.) and lots of labor and land. Alternatively, presume that the complex good uses many intermediate goods relative to land and labor. Further, presume that the greater the variety of intermediate goods utilized, the higher is the overall productivity in the complex good industry (increasing returns). Finally, assume that the intermediate goods, which can come in almost a limitless variety, are produced under conditions of increasing returns. Now there is the possibility for multiple equilibria (Rodrik 1996).

One can think of it as follows. If an economy finds itself producing the simple good, it utilizes very few intermediate goods. Because the latter are produced under conditions of increasing returns, this implies that their cost per unit, and, therefore, their price, will be quite high. Thus, any individual investor who is contemplating investing in the production of the complex good will face very high costs for intermediate goods, and thus will find it unprofitable to produce them. The economy is locked into a low-level equilibrium. However, if all investors decided to simultaneously invest in complex goods, there would be a high demand for intermediate goods, and, because of increasing returns, the costs of such goods would decline, their price would be low, and the production of complex goods (in high-level equilibrium) would be profitable. Once again, the coordination of investment plans is necessary if movement from the low- to high-level equilibrium is to be achieved.

If the above country is allowed to engage in free trade, will the multiple equilibria disappear, and the need for coordination cease? It depends on how tradable are the intermediate goods. If they are completely tradable, then all that investors would have to do when they invest in complex goods is to import them from places that already produce them at low cost (and which are thus low priced). The more they are nontradeable, the more they must be produced domestically (within the country), and the more likely it is that multiple equilibria will exist.

Many economists argue that intermediate goods are largely nontradeable. Intermediate services, such as insurance, finance, and marketing, are not easily tradable either, especially in the rural areas of less-developed countries. Construction activities are also less tradable in nature. Even though specialized equipment can be imported (i.e., they are tradable), it often must be modified to fit local circumstances and it must be serviced locally (nontradeable elements). If it is accepted that intermediate goods are nontradeable, than coordination will be important in the process of moving from a low- to high-level equilibrium.

This perspective generally views the state as playing a key role in this coordination process. The state is seen as serving a developmental role therein. The neoclassical perspective tends to view the state as being predatory; that is, it often engages in policies that harm society in general in order to benefit a politically powerful few. Of course, in the real world, developmental and predatory are at opposite ends of the scale.

Real-world states governed by real-world political elites are likely to be varying mixtures of both. Therefore, the real question certainly revolves around what variables influence the degree of mixture toward the developmental end or toward the predatory end.

That question is difficult to answer. There are, however, several interesting hypotheses. First, it would seem that the distribution of wealth is critical, and since much of the wealth in countries that have fallen behind is in the form of land, the distribution of land ownership would seem to be important. In those countries where land is held in the hands of a few, the landed elite are likely to be powerful influences on policy making by the political elite. The landed elite are likely to oppose any policies that seek to undermine their economic position since this would, in turn, undermine their political influence, and vice versa.

A second factor that is likely to be important in determining how developmental or predatory the ruling elite are has already been discussed in some detail here and in Chapter 2. Specifically, a ruling elite will tend to be more developmentally oriented if it relies on tax revenue that has to be earned from the bulk of the population. A ruling elite, which must earn its income, must interact with the bulk of its citizens, providing services in return for revenue. If the bulk of the population prospers, then the ruling elite will have a larger flow of revenue from which it can seek to maintain its political power. Through a dialectical-interaction process, the ruling elite is constrained from engaging in predatory policies and they learn how to enhance their own resource flows by enhancing overall productivity. Ruling elite that are dependent for the bulk of their revenue on sources external to society, or on a small subset of the domestic society, are likely to readily engage in policies that benefit the few at the expense of the many. Predatory policies are likely to dominate.

A third factor that influences the mix of predatory versus development policies has to do with the existence, or lack thereof, of multiple equilibria. That is, if multiple equilibria do not exist, then attempts to coordinate a movement from a low- to a high-level equilibrium are bound to fail. Thus, there is no incentive for the ruling elite to try to pursue developmental policies; rather, there is every incentive to be predatory, to engage in policies benefiting the few at the expense of the many. What factors are likely to influence whether or not multiple equilibria exist? Rodrik (1996) argues that one important factor might very well be the level of human capital—the extent to which the members of society have been able to improve their skills via formal or informal forms of education. The higher the level of human capital, the more productive intermediate goods are likely to be, and intermediate goods are the key to a high-productivity equilibrium. With low levels of human capital, the productivity of the intermediate-goods sector is likely to be very low, and thus the high-level equilibrium is not likely to exist.

In addition to the level of human capital, the existence of multiple equilibria is also likely to be dependent on the overall productivity of the agricultural sector. The logic for this argument is as follows. As agriculture becomes more productive, it will need more intermediate inputs to carry out production. In addition, the growth in income will stimulate the demand for manufactured goods, which in turn will require more intermediate goods. The intermediate-goods sector will thus expand in size and, because of increasing returns, become more productive. The more productive the intermediate-goods sector, the more likely multiple equilibria will exist, and the more likely the high-level equilibrium will exist. If it does, then it is more likely that the ruling elite will be more development oriented, less predatory.

A fourth factor influencing the mix of predation and development followed by the ruling elite relates to centralization versus decentralization of political power. That is, within a region there must be some centralization of power in order to provide the resources necessary to defend against external marauders, to provide for internal peace, and to maintain a single integrated market. By the latter, it is meant that goods should be free to flow within the region (no tolls, tariffs, etc.). Of course, if power is centralized too much it gives incentive to the ruling elite to disregard the interests of others and to seek to extract as much surplus output as possible. This will tend to strangle the economy (i.e., economic predation). Alternatively, there must be some decentralization of power since this will allow the bulk of the population to somewhat constrain the ruling elite so that the latter are developmental in terms of policy. However, too much decentralization leads to the disintegration of the internal market within a region. When this occurs, subregions create barriers to the free flow of goods and services, and overall productivity suffers. Thus, there must be a delicate balance between these two, between centralization and decentralization (MacFarlane 1994).

A final factor has to do with external threats. External threats to the continued control by the existing ruling elite will, if not too extreme, lead to the latter focusing on more developmental policies. Simply, an external threat is likely to induce the elite to enhance the wealth of its citizens, for two reasons: a wealthier population is unlikely to join an outside aggressor; in addition, the enhanced wealth will likely result in increased tax flows to the ruling elite, enabling them to strengthen themselves militarily against any outside aggressor.

However, the analysis is not as simple as it sounds. If the external threat is extreme—by extreme it is meant that the probability of the ruling elite surviving is very low or zero—then the ruling elite may actually find predatory behavior a better choice: capture the spoils before they are captured by the external aggressor. Furthermore, the reaction to the external threat may drain resources away from investing in the economy and toward maintaining an expensive military.

One can envision the impact of an external threat in the following way. Initially, an external threat at low levels of threat is likely to lead the ruling elite to seek to enhance overall wealth. As the threat rises, this tendency among the ruling elite will likely increase. At some point, however, the threat will become so great that the elite will turn predatory.

The five factors discussed above would certainly interact in various ways, thus influencing, in perhaps contradictory ways, the mixture of predation versus development in the policies of a ruling elite. However, they give some structure to the thinking concerning how states that have been left behind economically react to this situation; that is, it sheds light on whether they will be able to organize, under the auspices of a ruling elite, so as to catch up and close the economic gap with those states that have prospered, or whether they will succumb to predatory policies fostered by a ruling elite that seeks to benefit the few at the expense of the many. In the next section, the theoretical work discussed here will be applied to the experience of Japan and China.

Catching Up: Japanese Success

The intrusion of the West on Japan occurred, as discussed previously, in the late nineteenth century (much of the following discussion is drawn from Francks 1992). The Japanese were forced to open their ports to American (and later other nationalities') ships, and this was followed by a series of treaties with various Western powers that gave foreign traders virtually unrestricted access to the Japanese market. These treaties were similar to those earlier imposed on China. The rights of the Japanese government to restrict imports or levy tariffs were limited.

The sudden inclusion of Japan into the international economic system had significant effects. The local governors (feudal lords) became increasingly hostile to the shogunate, demanding that it do something to protect the country. Leaders in the southwest banded together and, in 1867, toppled the shogunate. The small oligarchy of new leaders were not united in their views, and this resulted in a struggle that eventually culminated in the late 1870s in those favoring economic modernization gaining the upper hand.

The new government sought to establish a modern nation-state through which economic modernization could be organized. A bureaucratic system of government organization was established and the feudal system of governance was abolished. The land tax was reformed, titles to land ownership were clarified, and the tax was converted from in-kind to cash. This became the main early source of revenue for the Meiji government (named after the restored emperor).

Initially, a large share of government revenue was utilized to pay off feudal officials and samurai, and to construct a modern military. The rest was used for roads, the construction of railroads, the establishment of a modern postal system, and the creation of a modern educational system. In terms of the industrial sector, the government went about establishing model factories in a variety of different areas. However, the state quickly found itself unable to efficiently run these firms and thus they were sold. In terms of agriculture, the state moved to construct a research and extension system that would develop and disseminate new technology.

During this period prior to World War II, modern Japanese industry came to be dominated by the *zaibatsu*, large-scale conglomerate industrial groups or combines. The common feature of these groups was that they were composed of a number of legally distinct companies, which were linked to other members of the group through personal, historical, economic, or financial interrelationships. These groups tended to have interests in a wide range of industries. These entities acted as conduits via which skilled labor and capital found its way into modern production.

It should be pointed out that although large-scale industry came to be dominated by the zaibatsu, small-scale manufacturing remained important in the early industrialization process. Specifically, up until World War II the majority of manufacturing sector workers were employed in relatively small-scale manufacturing enterprises. Thus, one can think of the manufacturing sector in Japan as being composed of two parts: large-scale, capital-intensive industry, and small-scale, labor-intensive manufacturing. The two were, to some extent, interlinked through subcontracting arrangements. One should not suppose that the large-scale sector was dynamic and the small-scale static; in fact, both were dynamic.

By historical standards, the Japanese economy grew rapidly during this period. It is estimated that gross national product (GNP) grew at an average annual rate of 3.25 percent from the late 1880s through the end of World War I. Investment was around 13 percent of GNP (18 percent in military investment included). The value of exports and imports grew steadily, from 6 to 7 percent of GNP in the late 1880s to 20 percent by 1910. Initially, exports of primary products dominated. However, by the 1920s, manufactured goods, in particular textiles, dominated exports. Thus, prior to World War II, Japan was undergoing structural change, as it increasingly became a producer of manufactured goods. Although the rate at which this occurred was rapid, compared with the same transformation that occurred in postwar South Korea and Taiwan, the process was slow.

The industrial capacity of the rising Japanese economy translated itself into increased military power. Eventually, Japan came into conflict with the West, chiefly the United States, in World War II. Japan's defeat and subsequent occupation resulted in a number of reforms. First, a democratic political structure was constructed. Second, a major land reform was carried out that virtually eliminated the landowning elite. Finally, the *zaibatsu* were broken up. Within this context, Japanese reconstruction took place.

Of these three reforms, perhaps the most successful was the land reform. This was basically a land-to-the-tiller program of reform. Landlords were paid compensation for their lost land. The result of the reform was that most farmland under tenancy came into the hands of the actual cultivators. The proportion of owner operators increased from 31 percent in 1941 to 70 percent in 1955. As a result, landlords as a group or class basically disappeared (Kawagoe 2001).

After creating an owner-dominated agricultural sector, the Japanese state took the next crucial step. They continued to invest heavily in the development and dissemination of new agricultural technologies and the provision of crucial inputs (e.g., fertilizer). As a result, postwar agriculture in Japan remained dynamic and vibrant. From 1945 to 1965, total agricultural production grew at an average annual rate of 3.3 percent. Overall productivity grew at a little less than 2 percent (Yamada and Hayami 1979).

The breaking up of the *zaibatsu* proved to be an ineffective reform, however. They were broken up, but large conglomerates (*keiretsu*), each with a bank at the center, grew up in their place. Thus, heavy industry was dominated by these large complexes. However, small manufacturing firms continued to form a dynamic part of the Japanese economy. Thus, dualism persisted within the manufacturing sector, with the large conglomerates and small manufacturers again linked through the process of subcontracting (Friedman 1988).

The term "developmental state" has often been applied to postwar Japan (Johnson 1982). The idea is that the state selected certain industries to promote, and then used its control of the banking system to direct credit to these industries. Tax incentives and programs also were used to direct subsidies to such. In addition, tariffs and quotas were used to protect these industries from foreign competition.

In simple terms, the Japanese model of postwar economic development was to subsidize the expansion of particular industries. However, the targets for the subsidies were ever changing. That is, as time passed the type of industries subsidized altered. Initially, these subsidies were directed at labor-intensive, technologically simple manufactured goods. Through time, the subsidies were redirected at more complex, capital-intensive products. This strategy did not eliminate markets—the reliance of Japan on markets has always been great—rather, it relied on the regulation of markets.

In an idealized version of the Japanese model, markets are regulated (i.e., subsidies are provided to firms), but not on a permanent basis. The subsidies are conditional on economic performance, and the latter was often measured by the ability, after a period of time, to export the product and compete internationally; that is, subsidies were given with the understanding that the recipients would become productive enough to compete internationally.

Others have preferred to describe the Japanese model as one in which the state sought to enhance the market. Most markets in developing nations are limited or imperfect in their operation. For example, credit markets rarely operate in an effective and efficient way. The state in Japan sought to correct these imperfections and limitations by fostering intermediary organizations, such as business associations and banks, and to operate through these intermediary organizations rather than take direct action. From this perspective, it is the interaction between the government and the state that is critical. For example, the government monitored and directed the banking system, which in turn monitored and gave direction to firms (Aoki, Kim, and Okuno-Fujiwara 1997).

This sort of situation has been labeled by Li (2000) as "relation-based governance." In perfectly organized markets, the relationships guiding buyers and sellers are in the form of rules that are enforced by a third party (generally, state agencies). However, in many poor and developing nations, rule-based governance is just not possible since states often lack the ability to adequately enforce contracts and rules. In relation-based government, most transactions are based on long-term relationships and rely on personal and implicit agreements. Thus, in the Japanese context, a long-term triangular relationship occurred between the main banks, business organizations, and the state. It was through this process that knowledge and capital were focused on certain industries in Japan.

The results of the catching-up process in Japan were most impressive. From 1950 to 1973, GDP growth per year averaged about 10 percent, which allowed output to double every seven years. This was basically the result of rapid capital accumulation, along with rapid learning by doing in manufacturing. This period of extremely rapid growth was followed by a period, (1973–91) of moderately high growth, at an average annual rate of 4 percent. However, the 1990s saw slow growth on the order of around 1 percent per annum. Overall, though, despite the "lost" 1990s, the Japanese economy caught up with the Western industrialized economics in the postwar period.

There are some analysts who would quarrel with such an explanation of the rapid catching up. Basically, it has been argued that the state used selective industrial policy to spur the Japanese economy up the technological ladder. Some argue that the state made many mistakes and did not act as the catalyst for rapid growth. They argue that it was Japan's outward orientation (its export-driven growth) that principally fed the growth. It was through trade that Japan gained the knowledge with which to upgrade its industrial production. However, even these critics recognize that the state in Japan was not inordinately predatory; it did not derail the rapid growth process, and probably enhanced it through investments in transportation, communication, education, and other public infrastructure. Whatever your perspective, the state did play a critical role in the catch-up process.

How would one explain the highly productive response of the ruling elite to the problem of catching up? The explanation is at least partially given by the theoretical factors discussed in the previous section. The first factor concerns that, prior to intrusion of the West, prior to the Meiji Restoration (reestablishment of the nation-state), the Japanese economy was already a highly developed commercial society with extensive market development. Intermediate goods production had already undergone significant development. This created a situation in which multiple equilibria were likely to exist.

The new nation-state was highly dependent on its domestic agricultural sector for the bulk of its revenue. The ruling elite was thus locked into dialectical relationships with the bulk of the producers. From these dialectical relationships, constraints were established over state behavior, and the state came to credibly commit itself to policies that enhanced overall productivity. The state and the ruling elite had to earn the revenue they needed to survive. This held true in both the Meiji period and the immediate postwar period.

In both the periods, Japan was faced with external threats. In the Meiji, it was the threat of being colonized by the industrial West that motivated the ruling elite to pursue policies that promoted growth. Postwar, it was the threat posed by the cold war conflict between the United States on one side and China and the Soviet Union on the other. These threats were enough to focus the attention of the ruling elite, but not so extreme as to cause the ruling elite to ravage the economy before external powers did.

In addition, the landed elite and their power were on the wane prior to World War II. Smethurst (1986) has shown that as Japanese farmers became wealthier they were increasingly able to disrupt the countryside to reduce their rental rates and restrictions on the use of the land Thus, the balance of power had already begun to swing against landlords. In the postwar period, land reform eliminated any remaining influence that the landed elite had.

Catching Up: Early Chinese Failure

In China, the process of catch-up was significantly delayed. Specifically, it was not until the 1970s that China began to grow rapidly and close the gap with the Western industrial nations, although the gap remains large to this day. In the previous discussion, it was argued that China had gone through a number of periods of economic efflorescences followed by decline. However, unlike Japan, the intrusion of the West unleashed a process of decentralization of authority (much of what follows is drawn from www.chaos.und.edu/history/modern2.html).

In the early part of the eighteenth century, most of the trade between China and the West was carried out under the guise of tribute. That is, foreigners were forced to follow age-old rituals that had been imposed on envoys from China's tributary states. After 1760, all foreign trade was restricted to Guangzhou and it was handled by a dozen or so officially licensed Chinese merchant firms.

Trade evolved into a three-party or triangular structure. The British sold goods to India and Southeast Asia for raw materials and semiprocessed goods that were then sold to China. By the early 1800s, imported cotton and opium became major British imports into China. The Qing government attempted to stop the flow of opium into China, thus setting off the Opium War (1839–42). The Chinese were defeated, and, under the Treaty of Nanjing, China ceded Hong Kong to the British, abolished the Chinese system of trade, opened five ports to British residence and trade, limited Chinese tariffs to no more than 5 percent *ad valorem*, granted British citizens extraterritoriality, and paid a huge indemnity. This set the stage for other nations, as they too pressed China for similar rights and privileges.

While Japan faced the same sort of intrusion, it was less invasive. One can think of China as being the main attraction for Western, industrial nations, while Japan was only a sideshow. The pressures of foreign intrusion were much stronger in the case of China.

The intrusion by the West set off unrest within China, which expressed itself in a number of rebellions and movements aimed at strengthening China against the threat of the West. These movements largely failed partly a result of efforts by the Western imperialists to keep the weak Qing administration in power. At the same time, foreign powers took over the peripheral states that had previously acknowledged Chinese suzerainty. France colonized Cochin China and established a protectorate over Cambodia. Britain gained control over Burma, while Russia penetrated Turkistan. Japan also took part in this process, eventually wrestling away Chinese control of Taiwan and Korea.

This intense external pressure eventually led to revolution and the overthrow of the Qing regime in the early part of the twentieth century. Sun Yat-sen set up headquarters in Nanjing as the provisional president of the new Republic of China. However, power in Beijing had already passed into the hands of the commander in chief of the imperial army, Yuan Shikai. Yuan, who had control of the army, eventually seized control of the state, eventually establishing a dictatorship.

Widespread rebellion occurred throughout much of China, with numerous provinces declaring independence. The nation was breaking up into warlord factions, which only intensified with Yuan's death in 1916. From this point on, shifting alliances of warlords fought for the control of the Beijing government. In 1917, Sun Yat-sen became commander and chief of a rival military group centered in Guangzhou, in alliance with certain southern warlords. He also reestablished the Kuomintang (or Nationalist) Party. With Sun Yat-sen's death in 1925 the Kuomintang came under the control of Chiang Kai-shek. A split occurred in the Kuomintang Party, with the left wing moving the seat of the Nationalist government from Guangzhou to Wuhan, while the right wing of the party, led by Chiang, resided in Nanking, and a warlord government remained in control of Beijing. Thus, there were now three capitals in China. However, by 1928 most of China was under Chiang's control.

The new regime was immediately faced with two significant threats. Mao Zedong was leading a group of communist supporters who sought to gain control of power. In addition, the Japanese posed a significant external threat. Conflict with Japan began in the 1930s and continued until the end of World War II. It was this threat that led to an uneasy alliance between the Kuomintang and the Communist Party against Japan. However, the alliance was a very uneasy one, with frequent clashes.

With the end of World War II, civil war once again broke out, pitting the Kuomintang against the Communists. The Kuomintang forces were defeated and Chiang Kai-shek and a few hundred thousand supporters retreated to the island province of Taiwan and declared Taipei the new capital of the Republic of China, while Mao established the People's Republic of China in Beijing. The mainland was then dramatically transformed into a socialist state. Industry was nationalized and directed by the state. In the countryside, a major land reform was undertaken to destroy the landlord class. Eventually, the state moved to eliminate private ownership of land and to establish large collective farms.

The simplest way to describe the economic policies followed by the Communist government is that they represented a turning away from the market system. That is, central planning was substituted for markets that were, for the most part, eradicated or suppressed. Nationally, China strived to be self-sufficient, to rely as little as possible on international trade. Several attempts were made, in the following three decades of Communist rule to mobilize the Chinese population to make dramatic economic breakthroughs by appeal to revolutionary zeal and self-sacrifice. Most of these plans failed, however. By the 1970s, China still remained an impoverished nation.

How is one to explain the contrasting experiences of China and Japan? Japan was able to rapidly catch up through the activities of a developmental state. If you were a neoclassical economist you would argue that this state kept barriers to the free flow of goods, services, and ideas to a minimum and made significant investments in public infrastructure (education, transportation, and others). A more interventionist point of view argues that Japan selectively chose particular industries and nurtured them via subsidy and international trade in order to climb the technological ladder. Both views are based on the idea that the Japanese state was not extremely predatory—it nurtured long-run growth and the catching-up process.

However, this did not occur in China. By the early 1970s, successful catching up had yet to occur. There are several factors that can explain this phenomenon. First, recall that China underwent several economic efflorescences. The Qing efflorescence, however, had begun to decay by 1750. Recall that efflorescences occur when agricultural productivity grows, thus leading to market expansion, increased specialization, and protoindustrial development. By 1750, the population growth stimulated by the Qing economic efflorescence was beginning to overburden the complex agro-manufacturing system. This is a normal course of events as long as the base of the economy remains biological in nature. However, this decline implied that the commercial environment was deteriorating at the time when the foreign intrusions began in earnest.

The situation in China after 1750 is important relative to the theoretical arguments concerning multiple equilibria discussed earlier. As you will recall, a country may be stuck at a low-level equilibrium because the cost of intermediate goods is too high to make it profitable for any investor to switch to the use of modern technology. However, if enough investors would shift to using modern technologies, the demand for intermediate goods would be large enough and their resulting costs low enough to make a shift to a high-level equilibrium possible. However, in the Chinese case after 1750 the economy was in decline, the intermediate-goods sector was shrinking, thus a high-level equilibrium was becoming increasingly difficult to attain. In this context, states are more likely to behave in a predatory way in order to maintain the existing ruling elite, since developmental policies are less likely to succeed.

A second factor that made successful catching up difficult for China concerned the external threat. It was argued previously that an external threat could focus the attentions of the ruling elite on pursuing wealth-enhancing policies as a mechanism to increase military power. This is indeed what happened in Japan. However, the relationship between an external threat and wealth enhancing policies by the ruling elite is non-linear in nature. That is, initially, as external threats rise, it drives the ruling elite to enhance wealth as a mechanism to ensure its survival. But as the threat level reaches certain critical values, the likelihood of the ruling elites' survival drops dramatically, no matter what kind of economic policy is pursued. The ruling elite will become predatory, grabbing what wealth it can no matter what the economic consequences.

In terms of Western imperialism, China was the main attraction, Japan a sideshow. Thus, although both China and Japan were threatened by foreign intrusions, the pressure was greatest on the Chinese ruling elite. The result was a predatory elite and a situation in which political authority began to fragment. The delicate balance between the centralization and decentralization of power was upset, and resulted in the significant decentralization or fragmentation of power (in this case, a many-sided civil war).

Eventually, the Communist Party, led by Mao, gained dominance in China. The subsequent turning away from markets, specialization, and the flow of knowledge doomed China to the low-level equilibrium. The rapid catching up that Japan achieved was not going to happen in China, at least not until the 1970s. The story of this catching-up process in China will be discussed in Chapter 8.

Taiwan and Korea

In the discussion above, we alluded to the imperialist activity of the Japanese; that is, as Japan industrialized before World War II, its industrial success allowed it to become a military power within the region. As a result, it was able to establish itself as a colonial power, and two of these colonies were Taiwan and Korea. The catching-up experiences of these two countries are the subject of this section.

In 1683, China gained control over Taiwan and, over time, established a three-tier system for land control that placed the emperor at the top. For much of this time, China did little to develop Taiwan. Indeed, the main value of Taiwan to China was as a source of tax revenue (Ho 1978). For its part, Korea, before colonization, followed an exclusionary policy aimed at keeping foreigners out. The land was controlled by a king who controlled access to the land. In return, taxes had to be paid to the royal family. Landlords were largely absent, and they, along with the ruling elite, extracted much of the agricultural surplus (Choy 1971).

With Japanese colonization, much would change in the two regions. The Japanese sought to use their colonies as a source of agricultural commodities, especially rice in Korea and sugar and rice in Taiwan. Japan acquired Taiwan in 1895 and initially collected a land tax in the traditional way. In 1897 it began to undertake an exclusive land survey that would serve as the basis for collecting taxes. In doing this, the survey uncovered 40,000 households basically operating as absentee landlords. The Japanese colonial administration, believing that rapid productivity increases could not occur within this environment, forced these households to give up their property.

The land tax itself tended to promote the commercialization of agriculture since farmers had to sell a portion of their output in order to pay the tax. In addition, the colonial government allocated funds to operate research and experiment stations. The major achievements of these research and experiment stations were the successful adaptation to Taiwan of high-yielding seed varieties that were responsive to fertilizer and water. In order to disseminate this technology, the colonial government created farmer's associations, small agricultural units, and agricultural cooperatives. The cooperatives worked to supply credit to farmers while the associations served as coordinators and suppliers of information and inputs. The small agricultural units sought to deal specifically with smaller farmers and their problems (Myers and Ching 1964).

The result was that agricultural productivity grew relatively rapidly for the period before World War II. Of course, much of this output was exported to the Japanese mainland since Taiwan basically served as a supplier of primary commodities. As a result, the Japanese mainland certainly benefited, but it also seems that Taiwanese farmers gained as well. Ho (1978) argues quite persuasively that the Taiwanese also gained. Specifically, it seems that per capita availability of food and other commodities rose steadily until the late 1930s. In addition, real wages rose throughout much of the period.

Korea became a colony of Japan in 1910. Compared with Taiwan, its economy was much less developed in terms of both the degree of commercialization and in investment in infrastructure. Just as in Taiwan, the Japanese began by undertaking a land survey that identified uncultivated land, land owned by the Korean nobility, and land owned by the royal house. Much of the royal land was brought under the control of the Japanese, while much of the nobility was given formal title to the land. A land tax was imposed on agriculture, which forced farmers to farm more intensively and also spurred commercialization (Myers and Saburō 1984).

In addition, the Japanese also invested in infrastructure, such as roads, railroads, and harbors. Also, a number of experimental stations were set up in the countryside to promote the development and dissemination of new seed varieties. In addition, agricultural technology bureaus were created in every province to plan the development of agricultural production.

These efforts, aimed at raising agricultural productivity in Korea, were not as successful as those in Taiwan. Agricultural growth for the period 1912 to 1937 was a little over 2 percent per year on average. This difference in performance was attributed to the lower level of initial overall development in Korea (Ho 1984). This slow growth, combined with tremendous increases in the amount of rice exported to Japan, placed a great strain on the Korean countryside. In fact, Kuznets argues that there was a decline in average per capita consumption of rice and food grains.

The colonial period was certainly not one of benign policy by the Japanese. They sought to utilize their colonies for the benefit of the homeland. They used them to provide cheap sources of food. However, as an unintended consequence the Japanese also created the infrastructure to support productivity increases in the agricultural sector. In other words, the foundation for a highly productive agricultural sector had been laid in both Korea and Taiwan. A significant degree of commercialization had already occurred and the intermediate-goods sector in both countries had become, compared with other nations in the region, relatively well developed.

After World War II, the new states of Taiwan (which enjoys *de facto* but not legal sovereignty) and South Korea (Korea divided into two political entities, the other being North Korea) continued to invest in the agricultural sector and in the development and application of new technologies to agricultural production. In Taiwan, agricultural growth was 4.7 and 4.2 percent for the periods 1950 to 1959 and 1959 to 1969. For South Korea, the growth rates were 4.1 percent and 3.8 percent for the same periods (Hayami, Ruttan, and Southworth 1979). Both regions also underwent fundamental land reforms, largely at the urging of the United States. The reforms began in 1949 in South Korea and 1952 in Taiwan. They had two important implications: first, landlords as a class were eliminated in both areas; second, the rapid agricultural growth was spread relatively equitably among the rural populations in the two countries. Importantly, the departure of the Japanese meant that commercial activities dominated by the colonial power now were carried out by Taiwanese and South Koreans.

Initially, both countries faced significant external threats. South Korea faced invasion by North Korea, which came in 1950, and Taiwan, where the Kuomintang government seated itself in 1949, faced invasion from the Communist Chinese mainland. Both being regarded by the United States as frontline states in the incipient cold war, they received large inflows of foreign aid and, in the case of South Korea, military defense. However, these aid flows were dramatically reduced in the late 1960s, although the political and military commitments of the United States to this region persisted. Thus, while foreign aid may have initially kept these economies afloat, they were very quickly forced to find their own way.

Although the above has emphasized the similarities between South Korea and Taiwan, their initial level of economic development was quite different. In 1961, the per capita GNP of South Korea was only 55 percent of that of Taiwan's. The level of savings in South Korea continued to be significantly lower than in Taiwan. Thus, the level of market development and commercialization was lower in South Korea relative to Taiwan (Hattori and Satō 1997).

Initially both nations followed what has been labeled an inward-oriented strategy; that is, tariffs were used to keep out foreign goods and domestic production expanded to replace imports. Industrialization was based on servicing the domestic market. This sort of policy generally tends to act as an implicit tax on the export sector since it raises the relative cost of inputs used in that sector. Initially, both countries overvalued their exchange rates since this cheapened the price of foreign currency (especially the U.S. dollar) and allowed foreign aid to go a lot further in terms of the purchase of foreign-produced inputs. However, the overvalued exchange rates made exports appear expensive, once again acting as a tax on them. As long as the aid continued, these policies could continue. However, with the decline of foreign aid both countries were forced to deal with the balance-of-trade (exports/imports) problem.

Both countries reoriented their policies in the mid-to-late 1960s. Exchange rates depreciated, making exports cheaper and imports more expensive. Imported inputs that were utilized for the production of exports were allowed in duty free. The ruling elite, through the apparatus of the state, allocated credit to particular industries. Subsidies of one sort or another were allocated so as to promote learning in terms of simple, labor-intensive manufactured goods, with exporting as a measure of the achievements of the particular industry. In other words, subsidies came with conditions. These conditions were based on performance, often measured by the ability to export. The idea was that as capability was achieved at the low end of the technology spectrum, then exports, subsidies, and the learning scheme would be applied to more technologically complex industries.

This represented the common elements in the catch-up strategies followed by South Korea and Taiwan. However, one must not lose sight of the significant differences in the process by which catching up was carried out. Biggs and Levy (1991) have talked of two strategies for catching up or learning. The first, which characterized South Korea, is government-directed learning. Government-directed learning is hierarchical in nature and refers to direct and specific efforts on the part of the government to improve the capabilities of individual firms by driving them along their learning curves. The first task of the state is to pick specific firms that are likely to be winners (i.e., to become highly productive) and are subject to significant potential economies of scale. That is, the larger the firm, the more productive it is, the lower the unit costs. Then the government takes vigorous control over the allocation of resources, making them readily available to specific firms.

The best example of this strategy in South Korea can be seen with respect to the allocation of credit. The banking system was initially nationalized in South Korea, allowing the state to have 100 percent control over the allocation of this critical ingredient in the growth process. Credit tended to be allocated to larger industries and firms. Direct tax breaks also were allocated to large firms and industries.

As a result of the above, a large network of interrelationships began to develop between the government and the *chaebol*. The latter were large conglomerate groups, which in some way resembled the Japanese *zaibatsu* (in prewar Japan). These business confederations encompassed a diversified group of large-sized firms. There were a small number of *chaebol*, and this became the main mechanism by which the South Korean state fed credit and resources to the industrial sector.

It should be reiterated that South Korea did not neglect the agricultural sector—investments continued to be made, and productivity grew—but the aim was to provide cheap food and savings for the rapid expansion of industry. Also, South Korea invested heavily in collective goods, especially education. Taiwan also continued investing in agriculture, and it too heavily invested in education. However, its catch-up strategy was different.

Taiwan has followed what Biggs and Levy (1991) have called an unbalanced growth strategy. Positive externalities or spillovers are the heart of this approach. Positive spillovers can take several forms. As workers in one firm become better educated, the benefits often will spillover to other firms as workers move from one to another. Another sort of externality has to do with the expansion of one industry's demand for the goods of another, causing the latter to expand and become more productive by expansion. So growth in one set of firms spills over and spurs productivity growth in another set of firms. The main avenue by which these externalities spread is through the operation of the market. In this situation, the government is less of a direct and driving force; instead, it plays a subtler role. It seeks to engage in activities that induce responses from private entrepreneurs in other parts of the economy.

The above ideas are very similar to Hirschman's (1958) theory of induced innovation. He argued that every production activity has backward and forward linkages. The expansion of firm A creates demands for inputs that induce expansion in industry B, C, D, and so on. These are backward linkages. The expansion of A also stimulates the expansion of industries X, Y, and Z that use A as an input in the production process. These are forward linkages. Thus the expansion of industry A stimulates or induces expansion in other parts of the economy. Hirschman argued that the government's role is to initiate projects that unbalance the economy, which create incentives and pressures for further action. Then private entrepreneurs will respond by carrying out new production activities and innovating.

From this perspective, the government's role is indeed more subtle and nuanced. There is a much bigger role here for the private sector. Biggs and Levy (1991) argue that this strategy was followed by Taiwan. The state played a significant role in inducing change. The general strategy was the same: to allocate subsidies among groups of firms under the condition that the firms use the subsidies productively. The criteria used to judge productivity improvement was export success. Taiwan also invested heavily in agriculture (there was no agrarian neglect) and education.

In carrying out this strategy, the ruling elite did not attempt to form large confederations of business enterprises, like the *chaebol* in South Korea. The ruling elite, largely from mainland China, was resented by the native Taiwanese. The mainland elite was not interested in stimulating large concentrations of economic power since business and commercial activities were dominated by the native Taiwanese. Also, because markets were well developed in Taiwan, the expansion of the rural sector, via agricultural productivity growth, stimulated the expansion of small- and middle-sized manufacturing firms. As a result, the structure of industry that evolved in Taiwan was much different from and less concentrated than in South Korea.

Taiwan also engaged in policies that selectively allocated credit to particular firms and industries. However, the banking system was not nationalized and the volume of these loans and the preference margins on interest rates were not as extreme as what was found in South Korea. In South Korea, the fiscal incentives provided to various firms were quite varied, from tax holidays to accelerated depreciation allowances. However, the allocation of these incentives was highly selective.

Thus, the Taiwanese economy evolved in a very different way from that in South Korea. While the latter developed a highly concentrated industrial structure, dominated by large firms and large business conglomerates, the former developed a highly flexible, niche pattern of production characterized by much smaller firms. Flexible production concentrates on short product cycles, quick delivery, short production runs, and mixes of products aimed at particular niches.

Although following different catch-up paths, both South Korea and Taiwan were economic success stories. Between 1965 and 1983, GNP per capita rose at an average annual rate of 6.5 percent in Taiwan and 6.7 percent in South Korea. This growth process was not only rapid, but the fruits of this growth were relatively equitably spread among the population, probably the result of two factors. First, the land reform saw that the predominant asset of the early development process was relatively equitably distributed. Second, the early stages of development were characterized by the rapid expansion of labor-intensive industries, thus providing rapid growth in employment opportunities.

Both South Korea and Taiwan were dominated by autocratic governments during the process of catching up. In the case of South Korea, it was a seizure of power by the military that was the prelude to rapid economic growth. In Taiwan, the mainland ruling elite governed the country in an autocratic style, with the in-exile mainlanders dominating political decision making. Still, both countries became functioning democracies in the 1990s. It seems that, in this case, democracy was an outcome of their enrichment.

In summary, the experiences of South Korea and Taiwan are similar in some important respects. Neither country turned away from the market, domestic or international. Neither engaged in free trade, however, but instead managed trade with the purpose of trying to move up the technological ladder via use of subsidies, taxes, tariffs, and so on. Both invested heavily in education and neither neglected its agricultural sector. Both had a common colonial experience, which created productive agricultural sectors that would provide the foundation for future industrialization. Both faced external threats, but were protected by the military of the United States. Initially, both received large amounts of foreign aid, but both had to fend with dramatic reductions in that aid.

Taiwan was, however, much more developed in the prewar period than was South Korea, and more commercialized. The development strategies followed after World War II were significantly different in some ways. South Korea chose to foster the development of large business combines and industries that were subject to significant economies of scale. Thus, the industrial structure of the economy became heavily concentrated. Taiwan, alternatively, sought to promote small- and medium-sized industries, and therefore its industrial structure was much less concentrated.

Both nations succeeded dramatically in terms of raising their standard of living. Both have managed to dramatically reduce the distance between them and advanced industrialized countries. How can one explain their successful catch-up experience? They did not turn away from the market. In addition, agricultural productivity grew rapidly in both the pre- and postwar periods. There was significant development of the intermediate-goods sector, especially in Taiwan. This created conditions under which multiple equilibria would exist and government coordination could succeed. Ruling elites in both regions were fundamentally dependent on the revenue that they could raise from their domestic populations. Thus, they interacted with their domestic producers and faced constraints that evolved to limit predatory behavior. Land reform eliminated the landlord class and provided an equitable basis for future growth.

What We Have Learned

What have we learned from the study of the East Asian experience? It would seem that one of the common elements in this region was that those countries that succeeded in catching up had productive and dynamic agricultural sectors. Reliance on markets appears to be essential, although free trade according to the principle of comparative advantage may not be a key. Instead, engaging with the international market within a context in which the ruling elite finds it in their interest to promote rapid growth, via regulated trade, seems to have been important. Governments that were committed to economic catch-up also seem to have been critical. The state did not overly engage in predatory policies, but seemed to be developmental. Part of this commitment by the ruling elite to economic development seems to have been the result of responding to an external threat. Another part of this commitment seems to have risen out of the fact that the ruling elite had to earn the revenue necessary to maintain their position.

In the case of China, a number of factors seem to have inhibited the catching-up process. The external threats to international sovereignty seem to have been much greater. So much so that the pressure fractured political power and created government by warlords, which presented a significant barrier to the development of an effective state. At the time that China was being vigorously confronted by Western industrial powers and Japan, the rural-based economy was in decline. Economic efflorescences occurred often in China, representing Smithian growth. These would involve periods in which specialization and productivity would rise dramatically and then decline or wane. When China was confronted by the West, it was in a period of decline. Finally, when political power was finally concentrated, it was in the hands of a regime that was motivated by an antimarket ideology. Markets were eliminated. This most certainly doomed catching up.

Key Terms

Feudalism	*Zaibatsu*
Tokugawa	Land Reform
Meiji	Developmental State
Symbiotic Economic System	Credible Commitment
Peasant Rebellions	Warlord
Catching Up	Communism
Rent Seeking	Colonization
Multiple Equilibria	Chaebol
Coordination	Linkages

References

Aoki, Masahiko, Hyung-ki Kim, and Masahiro Okuno-Fujiwara. 1997. *The Role of Government in East Asian Economic Development: A Comparative Institutional Analysis.* Oxford: Clarendon Press.

Biggs, Tyler, and Brian Levy. 1991. "Strategic Interventions and the Political Economy of Industrial Policy in Developing Countries." In *Reforming Economic Systems in Developing Countries*, ed. Tyler Biggs, and Brian Levy. Cambridge, MA: Harvard Institute for International Development.

Choy, B.Y. 1971. *Korea: A History.* Rutland, VT: Charles E. Tuttle.

Deng, Kent. 2003. "Development and Its Deadlock in Imperial China." *Economic Development and Cultural Change* 51: 479–522.

Deng, Kent. 2001. "Development and Its Deadlock in Imperial China." Department of History Working Paper no. 47. University of Manchester.

Francks, Penelope. 1992. *Japanese Economic Development: Theory and Practice.* London: Routledge.

Friedman, David. 1988. *The Misunderstood Miracle: Industrial Development and Political Change in Japan.* Ithaca, NY: Cornell University Press.

Goldstone, Jack. 2002. "Efflorescences and Economic Growth in World History: Rethinking the 'Rise of the West' and the Industrial Revolution." *Journal of World History* 13: 323–89.

Haltori, Tamio, and Yukihito Satō. 1997. "A Comparative Study of Development Mechanisms in Korea and Taiwan: Introductory Analysis." *The Developing Economies* 35 (December): 341–57.

Hayami, Yujiro, Vernon Ruttan, and Herman Southworth. 1979. *Agricultural Growth in Japan, Taiwan, Korea, and the Philippines.* Honolulu, HI: University Press of Hawaii.

Hirschman, Albert. 1958. *The Strategy of Economic Development.* New Haven, CT: Yale University Press.

Ho, S.P. 1984. "Colonialism and Development: Korea, Taiwan, and Kwantung." In *The Japanese Colonial Empire, 1895–1945*, eds. Ramon H. Myers and Mark R. Peattie, 347–98. Princeton, NJ: Princeton University Press.

Ho, S.P. 1978. *Economic Development of Taiwan, 1860–1970.* New Haven, CT: Yale University Press.

Johnson, Chalmers. 1982. *MITI and the Japanese Miracle: The Growth of Japanese Industrial Policy, 1925–1975.* Stanford, CA: Stanford University Press.

Jones, E.L. 1993. *Growth Recurring: Economic Change in World History.* Oxford, UK: Oxford University Press.

Kawagoe, Toshihiko. 1999. "Agricultural Land Reform in Postwar Japan: Experiences and Issues." World Bank Working Paper No. WPS 2111.

Kuznets, P.W. 1977. *Economic Growth and Structure in the Republic of Korea.* New Haven, CT: Yale University Press.

Li, John Shuhe. 2000. "The Benefits and Costs of Relation-Based Governance: An Explanation of the East Asian Miracle and Crisis." Working Paper, Department of Economics and Finance, City University of Hong Kong.

Macfarlane, Alan. 1994. "The Origins of Capitalism in Japan, China, and the West: The World of Norman Jacobs." *Cambridge Anthropology* 17: 43–66.

Malthus, Thomas R. 1959. *Population: The First Essay*. Ann Arbor, MI: University of Michigan Press.

Myers, R., and A. Ching. 1964. "Agricultural Development in Taiwan Under Japanese Colonial Rule." *Journal of Asian Studies* 23: 555–70.

Myers, R., and Y. Saburō. 1984. "Agricultural Development in the Empire." In *Japanese Colonial Empire, 1895–1945*, ed. R.H. Meyers, and M.R. Peattie. Princeton, NJ: Princeton University Press.

Notestein, Frank. 1949. "Population–The Long View." In *Food for the World*, ed. Theodore Schultz, 36–57. Chicago: University of Chicago Press.

Olson, Mancur. 1971. *The Logic of Collective Action: Public Goods and the Theory of Groups*. Cambridge, MA: Harvard University Press.

Rodrik, Dani. 1996. "Coordination Failures and Government Policy: A Model with Applications to East Asia and Eastern Europe." *Journal of International Economics* 40 (February): 1–22.

Rosenstein-Rodan, P. 1943. "Problems of Industrialization of Eastern and Southeastern Europe." *Economic Journal* 53: 202–11.

Smethurst, Richard. 1986. *Agricultural Development and Tenancy Disputes in Japan, 1870 to 1940*. Princeton, NJ: Princeton University Press.

Smith, Thomas C. 1988. *Native Sources of Japanese Industrialization, 1750–1920*. Berkeley, CA: University of California Press.

Thompson, Warren S. 1929. "Population." *American Journal of Sociology* (May): 959–75.

Vlastos, Stephen. 1986. *Peasant Protests and Uprisings in Tokugawa Japan*. Berkeley, CA: University of California Press.

Yamada, Saburo, and Yujiro Hayami. 1979. "Agricultural Growth in Japan, 1880–1970." In *Agricultural Growth in Japan, Taiwan, Korea, and the Philippines*, eds. Yujiro Hayami, Vernon Ruttan, and Herman Southworth. Honolulu, HI: University Press of Hawaii.

Appendix

In Figure A3.1, output per capita (y) is measured along the vertical axis, while the capital-to-labor ratio (k) is measured along the horizontal axis. The technology is represented by $y = f(k)$, which is subject to the law of diminishing returns. The curve $sf(k)$ represents new capital accumulated per person, while nk represents the amount of new capital accumulation required to keep the capital-to-labor ratio constant (s is the propensity to save and n is the rate of population growth). The equilibrium k is given by k^* and the equilibrium y is given by y^*.

Poor countries—those left behind—might have a capital-to-labor ratio of k_1 and an output per person of y_1. Because capital is so much more productive in the poor country (the slope of $sf(k)$ is greater at y_1 relative to y^*), the poor country will grow faster than the developed country and the poor country's k and y will approach k^* and y^*. Convergence in this

Figure A3.1 **Absolute Convergence**

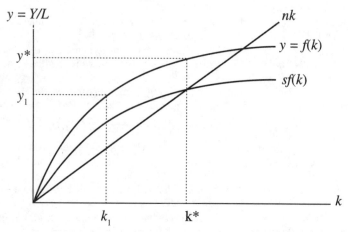

sort of model occurs naturally, whereas unnatural events may prevent convergence. If the state or ruling elite were to extract too much profit or surplus in the form of taxation of one sort or another, then the process of convergence would be prevented. In addition, if property rights do not exist, or if they exist but cannot be enforced, then convergence would not occur. If physical infrastructure (roads, communication, etc.) is not provided, then convergence may not occur, and catching up may fail.

Of course, convergence as presented above is much too simplistic since it is couched in terms of absolute convergence. A more realistic perspective is provided by thinking in terms of conditional convergence. That is, different countries may have different propensities to save, different technologies, and different rates of population growth, and this would mean that each different country would have a different equilibrium toward which it was converging. For example, suppose country 1 has a savings rate that is less than that of country 2 ($s_1 < s_2$). This is illustrated in Figure A3.2.

As can be seen, country 1 will converge to k_1, y_1, while country 2 will converge to y_2, k_2. Convergence occurs, but it is conditioned on the different savings rates. Because country 2 has a higher saving rate, it will converge to a higher per capita income level relative to country 1.

However, neoclassical economists would tend to make the additional argument that the return to capital will be higher in country 1 relative to country 2 since it is relatively scarcer. As a result, if capital is free to move from country to country, then one would expect capital to flow out of country 2 and into country 1 until the k and y in the two countries are

Figure A3.2   **Conditional Convergence**

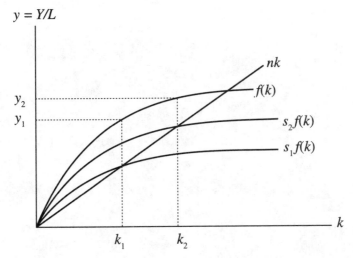

identical, until absolute convergence. Thus, as long as governments do not interfere with the free flow of capital among countries, poor countries should catch up with rich countries.

One can make similar arguments about differences in technology. If country 2 utilizes a superior technology relative to country 1 (assume ($sf_2 >$ sf_1), then country 2 will converge to a higher level of per capita output (y_2) and capital-to-labor ratio (k_2) than country 1 (y_1, k_1). However, country 1 will certainly have every incentive to try to learn and utilize this superior technology. Thus, as long as knowledge is free to move from country to country, one would expect country 1 to learn the superior technology and then incomes would converge in an absolute sense once again. If governments interfere with the free flow of knowledge, absolute convergence will not occur.

Population growth rates may also diverge: country 1 may have a higher population growth rate than country 2 ($n_1 > n_2$). As a result, per capita output and the capital labor ratio in country 1 will converge to equilibrium levels less than that for country 2. However, if populations are free to move across borders, then the following logic would apply. If labor is growing faster in country 1, then, *ceteris paribus*, the relative return to labor would be lower. The excess labor in country 1 would then seek to migrate to country 2, where, *ceteris paribus*, relative wage rates are likely to be higher (since the availability of capital is greater). Thus, once again the free movement of an input, in this case labor, would allow for absolute convergence in living standards to occur.

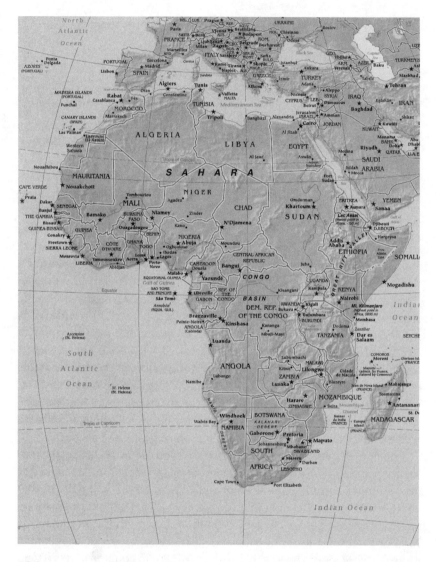

Africa

4

Sub-Saharan Africa

Sub-Saharan Africa has lagged far behind the rest of the world in terms of economic development. While there are a few bright spots, such as Botswana and South Africa, these seem to be overshadowed by the negative experiences of the rest of the region. Per capita gross domestic product (GDP) has actually declined, on average, during the past several decades. In contrast, the next poorest region, South Asia, has seen a 2.3 percent increase in real per capita GDP in the same period. This poor economic experience has been accompanied by severe political instability, civil war, and violence on an appalling scale. The misery that affects parts of Africa seems never ending and beyond comprehension.

This chapter will attempt to analyze the experience of the region in light of the theories discussed in Chapter 1, as well as the experience of other regions discussed in previous chapters. Featured are some fundamental similarities with those regions, but there are some significant elements unique to this region.

The section immediately below will briefly examine the precolonial period within the context of the notion of economic efflorescences utilized in previous chapters. This will be followed by an examination of the impact that European colonialism had on the institutional, physical, and social infrastructure in the region. This experience had a significant impact on the political development of the region resulting in the predominance of illegitimate state and institutional structures. This in turn has led to the development of a patron-client form of state structure, which is also discussed. The inward-oriented trade and exchange policies, implemented by the patron-client-based political structure, are discussed in the section on urban-based policy. The role of migration in this process is also analyzed. Within this context, the limited extent of rural development, and thus the limited development of linkages throughout the rural sector, is also explored. This is integrated with a discussion of the demographic experience. In the penultimate section of the chapter, the success story of Botswana is examined. A summary of the chapter is then presented, which emphasizes what has been learned.

Precolonial Period

Africa is thought to be the cradle of humanity. About 50,000 to 100,000 years ago, small bands of human beings began migrating out of Africa into the Middle East. These became the ancestors of the human population of the world. (The following historical synopsis is drawn from Compson 2001.)

Between 2,500 and 5,000 years ago, the Bantu people of the western part of Africa expanded and eventually became the dominant people of much of Sub-Saharan Africa. It is thought that the use of iron in the region began around 500 BC. The Bantu were skilled in smelting iron and making the iron tools necessary for the expansion of agricultural productivity. As Europeans began to explore the coast of Africa (after 450 AD), farmers there were found to be growing a wide variety of crops. Many regions were heavily dependent on raising cattle.

It is estimated that by 1500 AD there were approximately 47 million Africans living in farming communities scattered throughout the continent. Large towns and cities had not yet developed. This precolonial society was characterized by broadly similar languages spoken over wide areas. African loyalties were linked to extended families, clans, and patron-client relationships. Some regions saw the emergence of powerful individuals who exerted influence over wide areas by controlling valuable trade routes and manipulating extended family and marriage ties.

A number of African kingdoms developed, expanded, and then collapsed. For example, it is generally agreed that the ancient state of Ghana emerged sometime in the seventh century AD. Its expansion into an empire was fueled by economic vitality, spurred by agricultural growth, trade, and increased division of labor. Its economy was made up of extensive agriculture, iron smelting, stonemasonry, carpentry, pottery, goldsmithing, and cloth manufacturing.

In the western part of Africa the great Kingdom of Mali evolved, which after 750 AD became the center of culturally and politically dynamic cities and kingdoms. It was under one leader, Marsa Musa, that Timbuktu became one of the major cultural centers of Africa.

Near central Africa arose another great empire, around 1200 AD, called Korem. At the height of this empire, the controlled territory ran from Libya to Lake Chad to Hausa. Korem was based on sedentary agriculture and the trade that flowed through the region.

Thus, it appears that the concept of economic efflorescences is equally applicable to the African continent. Wherever property rights and rules allowed for the development of sedentary agriculture capable of producing an agricultural surplus, the foundation for trade, commercialization, and economic and political expansion was established. As in East Asia and Europe, these intensifications of economic activity allowed for the centralization of political authority and the creation of power. Exogenous shocks, as well as limits to the environment, almost always brought an end to these efflorescences. However, the tools, knowledge, and institutional structures connected with these efflorescences did not completely disappear. The rise of these kingdoms involved increasingly complex economic, political, and social constructions.

The processes that unfolded in precolonial Africa were similar to those that unfolded within Europe and East Asia. However, there were significant differences. First, the population densities in Africa appear to have been lower than those found in Europe and Asia at similar periods of development. This implies that the intensification of agricultural production and division of labor was more limited. More importantly, the slave trade served as a destabilizing factor that served to disrupt this cyclical process of Smithian growth based on biological sources of energy. Thus, the question of the application of science to the production process and why it did or did not occur becomes, in this context, irrelevant.

The Atlantic slave trade is thought to have started in the middle of the fifteenth century. It lasted approximately 400 years, and it is estimated that between 10 and 13 million people were taken and removed, with most being sent to Brazil, the Caribbean, with smaller numbers going to North America. The peak of the trade was in the eighteenth century, and it was driven by the rapid expansion of plantation agriculture in the New World. It should be noted that, at the same time, there was a thriving slave trade centered in East Africa, the Indian Ocean slave trade, dominated by Arab traders. However, this trade was quantitatively much smaller compared with the Atlantic trade. Slavery was abolished throughout the Americas in the 1850s and 1860s.

The Atlantic trade was conducted mainly by European traders based on the West African coast. They traded guns, cloth, and other manufactured goods. Slavery was not new to Africa, it had been long practiced by victors against the vanquished in wars. However, the scale of the Atlantic trade was immense.

There is much debate as to the impact of the slave trade on African politics as well as its economics. The general consensus seems to be that this was an extremely destabilizing influence. The guns that flowed into Africa fueled this instability, and the need for these arms provided a strong incentive to expand the slave trade. Economically, the trade disrupted the process by which economic efflorescences occurred. However, it did not halt the process. According to a number of scholars, it seemed that as the late nineteenth century progressed indigenous political entities would centralize authority and develop nation-states. In western Africa, the Kingdom of Ashanti had acquired a central government, an advanced system of roads, and a national language (Davidson 1992). Buganda, in East Africa, had become the chief naval power on Lake Victoria and was characterized by rapid growth in trade (Oliver and Atmore 1994). A number of other empires that relied on imported European technology were also emerging. Many of these were based on a Muslim social model and their expansion promoted the spread of Islam in the region.

The colonization of the African continent disrupted this political development and restructured the economic organization of the continent as well. The next section will analyze the impact of colonization on the long-term economic development of the region.

The Colonial Era

The colonization process and its impact varied dramatically from region to region. In the earlier chapter on East Asia, the argument was made that Japanese colonization of Taiwan and Korea, however distasteful and painful for the indigenous populations, provided a strong foundation for future economic development. The same seems to hold for the colonization of North America and Australia. However, this appears not to be the case for much of Sub-Saharan Africa. How is this difference to be explained?

According to Acemoglu, Johnson, and Robinson (2000a), there are two types of states that colonizing powers can construct or set up in their colonies. Extractive states are those whose major purpose is to extract surplus or wealth from the colony as quickly as possible. The only investments that are made are for the rapid transport of resources and a level of security high enough to protect this process. As a result, the institutions constructed do not provide for the protection of private property since the objective is to extract resources. In addition, institutions are not constructed to check and balance state power as mechanisms to limit predatory state behavior. In fact, the whole purpose of such a colonization process is to create a set of rules that maximize the predatory activities of the state. The best example of such is provided by the Belgian colonization of the Congo of the nineteenth century.

At the other end of the scale, some colonizers sought to construct institutional structures that were more developmental in nature. Specifically, they acted to create incentives for saving, investment, and innovation. That is, institutions were constructed that protected property rights and provided checks and balances to offset predatory tendencies of the state. European colonizers in these colonies tried to replicate European institutions. Primary examples of this include Australia, New Zealand, Canada, and the United States. The Japanese transferred Japanese institutions to Taiwan and Korea.

What determines which type of environment is to be created, predatory or developmental? Acemoglu, Johnson, and Robinson argue that this was greatly dependent on the mortality rates expected by the first settlers in the respective colonies or regions. Their argument is straightforward. In those regions where settler mortality rates were low, extensive settlement was quite likely. In turn, these sorts of settlements would push for the development of an institutional structure similar to that found in the mother country. This would generally result in the construction of institutions to protect property rights and restrain predatory state behavior.

Alternatively, in those regions where settler mortality rates were quite high, a quite different result emerged. Because few settlers from the mother country migrated to the colony, there was little push for the development of appropriate governmental restraints and property rights. Instead, the state apparatus was extractive in nature. This environment was also a fertile one for the development of ethnic animosities. Ethnicity is not a natural characteristic with which one is born. It is a social construction, a product of the construction of the social structure of the society. Colonial, extractive states often sought to minimize opposition to their regime through a "divide-and-conquer strategy." That is, if the indigenous population could be divided into opposing groups, this would pose a significant barrier to the formation of a united opposition. Thus, colonial powers sought to promote differences based on language, kinship relationships, and ethnicity as a mechanism of control. Ethnic rivalry became an important tool for this sort of strategy.

Thus, where European settler colonies were established the institutional structures were much more developmental in nature. In cases where these institutions did not arise naturally, the settlers themselves were often ready to fight for them against the wishes of the mother country. This struggle occurred in Australia, New Zealand, and, to some extent, the United States (i.e., the thirteen colonies).

The same sort of argument can be made with respect to Japanese colonization. Settler colonies Korea and Taiwan were developmental in nature. In fact, in both regions there were indigenous forces that pushed for the transfer of Japanese institutional forms, especially in the agricultural sector.

This is in sharp contrast with much of the experience of Latin America, parts of Asia, and most importantly, Africa. The main objective of Spanish and Portuguese colonization was to obtain gold and silver from the New World. "For example, soon after the conquest the Spanish crown granted rights of encomienda to a favored few and set up a complex mercantile system of monopolies and trade regulations to extract resources from the colonies" (ibid. 8).

Much of the African experience is quite similar, and probably King Leopold of Belgium in the Congo provides the most extreme case of extraction. Leopold's philosophy was that "colonies should be exploited, not by the operation of a market economy, but by state intervention and compulsory cultivation of cash crops to be sold to and distributed by the state at controlled prices" (ibid. 9).

There was significant investment in physical infrastructure in much of Africa. However, much of this was meant to serve as a mechanism for transporting resources and crops extracted from African colonies to world markets. Much of the production involved in extracting these crops and other resources had few linkages with the rest of the indigenous economy. One can view many regions in Africa during this period as being characterized as enclave economies. That is, there were small subsectors of the economy that were commercialized and, to some extent, modernized, but these were isolated from the rest of the indigenous society.

Educational systems were also expanded during the colonial period. However, this expansion occurred for three somewhat contradictory reasons. First, they were meant to provide education for European immigrants. Second, they sought to provide minimal training for selected native workers and civil servants. Third, education was meant to spread Christianity and other Western values. As a result, literacy levels were low during the colonial period. The availability of education was largely limited to favored persons and often based on ethnicity.

The tax system was designed to provide the necessary labor to produce exports. Taxes were levied in cash, but access to the resources necessary to produce cash crops was limited. Only settlers and selected ethnic groups were allowed to hold land suitable for growing cash crops. The bulk of the population was involved in subsistence farming. The need for cash pushed this labor to seek employment in the commercialized resource or crop sector. This resulted in temporary migration to seek employment in the modern sector, the enclave.

As a result, colonization in Africa was accompanied by an extreme degree of inequality. Access to land, resources, and credit was strictly limited. Property rights for the indigenous population were not well developed and were regularly violated. There were few checks and balances placed on the behavior of colonial states. Predatory, extracting institutional structures dominated Sub-Saharan Africa.

The important aspect of this analysis is that the institutional structure created during the colonial period has persisted into the present. In other words, an institutional persistence characterizes recent African history. Much of the region is still dominated by predatory, illegitimate states and institutional structures. There are a number of mechanisms that might explain this institutional persistence. Setting up functioning institutions is generally thought to involve large set-up or fixed costs. New ruling elites at independence may find it too costly to change these institutional structures, thus they persist. North (1990) has referred to this situation as the lock-in effect.

The gains to an extractive strategy would seem to be partly dependent on the size of the ruling elite or ruling coalition. A small ruling elite implies that each member of the group would receive a large share of the revenues extracted from a resource-based economy. Such an elite would thus have a much greater incentive to be predatory or extractive. European colonizers in Africa often delegated the everyday sort of activities of running the bureaucracy to a small, indigenous elite. The latter very often played a pivotal role in the aftermath of independence. This environment provided incentives to maintain the existing situation of extractive institutions. The only change would be who receives the revenues from extraction.

An example of the above sort of arguments is related to the use of marketing boards in Africa. During the colonial period, these boards were used to extract revenue from the countryside. They profited from the difference between the international price of a commodity and the price paid to farmers. The elite who came to power in many African states had little to gain from abolishing these boards. Instead, they merely stepped in and used them as a major revenue source.

The extractive institutions created by the colonial powers persisted into the post–World War II period of independence. The newly independent countries were constructed on extractive institutions, not developmental ones. This, combined with the arbitrary way national borders for the new African states were drawn, practically guaranteed that these states would be viewed as lacking legitimacy in the eyes of the bulk of the indigenous population.

Patron-Client Political Structure

Legitimate states are those whose rules and regulations and mechanisms for succession are accepted by the bulk of the population as being appropriate and acceptable. In other words, the rules are obeyed not just because of the fear of punishment if a violation occurs, but because they are viewed as reputable and right. In an illegitimate state, people readily circumvent the formal rules since their obedience rests solely on the fear of punishment.

Legitimacy is not something that is conferred on a state. Instead, it is the outcome of a struggle between the ruling elite and the rest of society. This is strongly related to the concept of political development discussed earlier. Political development is a process by which the difficult commitment problem for a state and the ruling elite is overcome. As discussed, states have difficulty credibly committing themselves to policies that promote overall development. For example, a state can offer to allow investors to retain the profits stemming from high fixed-cost investments. However, once the investment is made, the state has every incentive to break the commitment and extract the profits for itself. This predatory action will not happen if investors—society in general—have mechanisms to punish the ruling elite for such behavior.

The process by which a state and its ruling elite achieve legitimacy is not completely understood. However, it would seem to be related to our earlier discussions involving the notion of political development. Political development—the ability to resolve commitment problems similar to those outlined above—is the result of interaction, dialectical conflict, and resolution between the ruling elite and the bulk of the population. If the reader will recall, Moore (2001) has argued that the ruling elite in societies that are dependent on external sources of revenue has little incentive to nurture the development of the indigenous economy; instead, it has every incentive to behave in a predatory fashion. More generally, if the ruling elite is dependent on a small part of indigenous society for the bulk of its revenues, the likelihood is high that the state's policies will seek to extract revenue rather than nurture the development of the economy at large. As a result, property rights are likely to be enforced for only a small segment of the population, with the vast majority subject to some probability of confiscation.

Legitimacy for a ruling elite and its state apparatus would seem to arise in a different sort of situation. If a ruling elite is dependent on the bulk of its domestic population for the revenue necessary to remain in power, then the ruling elite will construct tax and revenue structures that deeply penetrate the society. This dependency creates a process of interaction whereby the producers in society respond to the policies carried out by the ruling elite. There is, of course, significant conflict between the state and society. Out of this conflict the ruling elite face constitutional constraints that limit the extent to which they can engage in arbitrary actions and behavior. In other words, these institutional constraints are the mechanism that allows the state to commit itself to policies aimed at enhancing long-term economic growth. With the solution of the commitment problem, the state develops legitimacy.

In the African case, the colonial legacy created an environment in which most of the newly independent indigenous elite was dependent on enclave economies for the bulk of their revenue. This environment, combined with the institutional structures inherited from the colonial period, implied that in the post–World War II period most of these newly independent states were not viewed as being legitimate or were teetering on the edge of illegitimacy.

In this sort of an environment, a form of politics based on illegitimacy came to dominate many of these nations. Scholars have labeled it "patron-client politics." According to Kurer (1996), political clientelism is based on an exchange of political support for a patron in return for material benefits provided to a client (by the patron). In other words, the ruling elite provides certain benefits to their clients; the latter in return provide political support, which can come in a variety of forms. Governance is hierarchical in nature with a pyramiding of patron-client ties via networks of relationships. This network is based on face-to-face relationships between patrons and clients rather than on formal rules.

The income needed for the patron-client system of political organizations to work originates from the control over government institutions exercised by the ruling elite. Thus, the governing elite is the ultimate patron. They favor policies that short-circuit the operation of markets, creating shortages of key variables: foreign exchange, finance, and food. These strategies allow the ruling elite, through the apparatus of the state, to allocate these scarce resources only to political supporters and to deny access to political foes. In addition, the elite in this environment are likely to favor private over collective goods and to try, as best as possible, to privatize the benefits of public goods. This allows the patron elite to allocate such goods and benefits on the basis of political rather than economic criteria.

Corruption is likely to run rampant in such regimes. Patrons (i.e., the elite) will override bureaucratic procedures and allocate resources based on political support rather than abstract rules and regulations. Officials in this situation will cease to be bureaucrats and will instead be dispensers of favors. Such regimes will certainly lack legitimacy for two reasons. First, support for the regime is based on the receipt of benefits rather than myths and traditions, and this kind of support is likely to be both weak and fickle. Second, the regime disregards official or standard morality through its means of allocating favors.

In summary, these regimes are likely to under allocate resources to public goods and under-distribute those public goods that are provided. In addition, there will be a relentless pressure to increase the amount of resources available for payoffs. Thus, the ruling elite will continually seek to distort the existing market system to siphon off ever more resources for their own use.

The under-provision of public goods, such as infrastructure, has a strong negative effect on private production. Specifically, transportation infrastructure is crucial for development and is in short supply in Africa. For example, Sub-Saharan Africa has less than 10 percent of the roads per square mile as India and about 40 percent of the diesel trains as Asia. The lack of roads means that it is difficult for small firms, which sell their product within a country, to grow. This makes it easy to understand why there is so little trade within the region itself. Hence, there has been little possibility for the development of the traditional sector, in particular agricultural production. The type of increased specialization through production for the market envisioned by Adam Smith and other classical economists simply could not and has not occurred.

Another type of public infrastructure and public good involves investment in human capital. Included here are public health, health-delivery systems, and the educational system. In general, these public goods are not widely available to the bulk of the population. The availability of these services is often related to the particular ethnic group that one is a member of, with those favored groups receiving the bulk of the services.

An additional inefficiency in the provision of public services concerns the misallocation of variable inputs. One type of inefficiency that may occur happens when labor expenditures are too high and expenditures on other variable inputs, such as antibiotics and medicines in hospitals, are too low. It may be that the nonlabor, variable inputs are largely imported. Import restrictions and foreign-exchange shortages, brought about by the ruling elite, may make these inputs very difficult to obtain.

In addition to the above, policies carried out by the elite patrons are likely to be characterized by urban bias (Lipton 1977). That is, resources tend to be more readily available to urban residents, and at relatively lower prices, than for rural residents. Thus health, education, and other social services are not only made more readily available to political supporters of the ruling elite, but these supporters are most likely to be urban residents and groups. In addition, the relative price of commodities consumed by urban residents is generally lower than the social-opportunity costs. Thus, urban groups and residents tend to be favored relative to rural interests in much of Africa. For example, consider the experience with marketing boards. These boards' stated goal is to help groups of small farmers market their crops. However, as has sometimes been the case, the price offered to farmers is kept low to allow the board to generate significant revenue by selling the crops at international prices. Thus, marketing boards have been used to extract revenue from the rural sector by reducing the relative price received by farmers. The revenue is then used to provide benefits for the urban elite.

Because the bulk of the population in Africa still resides in rural areas, one must wonder how and why it is that patron-based politics has resulted in policy bias in favor of urban dwellers in Africa. Part of the answer to this can be found in the work of Mancur Olson (1971). His work was referred to in Chapter 3. He argued that small groups are more likely to successfully organize to achieve their goals than large groups. This is because the goal of any particular group can be thought of as a collective good, and thus any person in the group will benefit if the goal is achieved, whether or not they contributed resources to the achievement of the goal. Thus, individual members are subject to the temptation to free ride, and if everyone becomes a free rider, then no one will contribute resources and the goal will not be achieved.

It was Olson's contribution to point out that smaller groups are more likely to be able to overcome this problem. This is due to the fact that in smaller groups there is a great deal of interdependency. That is, if someone does not contribute, others will notice and retaliate. Within large groups, the failure of a single individual to contribute is not generally noticeable, free riding will dominate, and the group will fail. These small groups find it easier to organize. Thus, they will find it easier to influence policy making and they will achieve political power. Within a patron-client political system, the ruling elite is likely to seek the support of small, cohesive, politically influential groups. Urban groups representing employers and employees, the urban-based military, and others are likely to find it easier to organize and wield political influence relative to farmers in the countryside. The latter are likely to find it difficult to create organizational mechanisms to wield influence. Thus, the ruling elite is likely to seek to form ruling coalitions based on urban groups.

Bates and Rogerson (1980) add a more sophisticated theoretical argument that serves to also explain urban bias. According to these authors, policy is not made by a single group, but instead by a coalition of groups. They argue that agrarian-interest groups are unlikely to ever be members of such ruling coalitions. They explain this by assuming that people specialize in production but generalize in consumption. "That is, they earn their incomes from the production of a particular good and they spend their incomes broadly, allocating only a portion to their consumption of the good that they themselves produce and the remainder of the purchase of a wide variety of other goods" (Bates and Rogerson 1980, 215).

Thus, their real income depends on the price of what they produce relative to the prices of the things they consume. Hence, any elite that seeks to construct a ruling coalition will seek to attract groups by offering to raise the price of what they produce (relative to all other prices).

Given the above analysis, it is now relatively easy to see why farming-interest groups make unattractive members of a ruling coalition. In most less-developed countries, individuals devote a large share of their budgets to the purchase of food. If farming interests become a member of a ruling coalition, and the relative price of farm products increase, other members of the coalition could suffer significantly. Alternatively, for coalitions made up of urban, manufacturing interests, this is less likely to be a problem. No group belonging to such a coalition is likely to spend a large share of its budget on a good produced by another coalition member.

Thus, for the reasons outlined above, patron-client political regimes are likely to be characterized by the ruling elite, whose ruling coalition is likely to be made up of urban manufacturing interests. Rural interests are not likely to be courted by the ruling elite. Policy will be oriented to reward the urban coalition at the expense of the rural areas. It is likely to be characterized by a distinct urban bias and rural neglect. This has had a significant influence on international trade and migration as well as rural development. The next section will examine the impact on trade, with the following section examining migration.

Urban-biased Policy

Urban biased policy, as outlined above, seeks to protect the politically powerful clientele in urban areas. They form the base of the coalition for the ruling elite. Most countries in Africa did not, at or since independence, possess comparative advantages in urban-based manufactured goods. Instead, most of these countries had comparative advantages in minerals or other natural resources or primary agricultural products.

A set of policies aimed at promoting the interests of urban-based manufacturing would then likely involve some sort of protection for such economic activity. Protection from international competition would involve both tariff and nontariff forms of protection. Tariffs, of course, represent taxes on foreign-produced goods. Nontariff barriers would represent rules and regulations imposed by the state that increase the cost of importing foreign-produced manufactured goods.

Urban-biased ruling elites often combine such protection of manufacturing with policies aimed at promoting the overvaluation of exchange rates. This overvaluation creates a shortage of foreign exchange, which is then allocated by the ruling elite. This foreign exchange is often allocated to urban groups to allow them to import the capital equipment they need at artificially low prices. At the same time, overvaluation of exchange rates makes primary agricultural products and mineral-resource exports more expensive on international markets. This, in other words, acts as a tax on the export sector.

The net result of this sort of policy is to allocate domestic resources to import substitution and nontradeable goods and away from exports. This resource misallocation is certainly inefficient and reduces the level of economic activity (level of GDP per capita). However, its effects on economic growth are unclear. This is because growth seems to be driven by factors that are not directly, at least, influenced by the extent of trade.

The experience of Africa with respect to trade policy would indeed seem to reflect the logic outlined above. Two facts stand out. First, government-imposed trade barriers have generally been higher in Africa than in East Asia, although the differences are not huge. Second, until the 1990s, trade barriers in Sub-Saharan Africa have been comparable to those that exist in Latin America (Rodrik 1998).

Sub-Saharan Africa's trade has grown at relatively low rates since the 1950s. The result is that today the region's share in world trade stands at around 1 percent, down from 3 percent in the 1950s. Much of this poor trade performance is, of course, due to lagging output growth. The main conclusion drawn by Rodrik (1998) is that trade policies have indeed mattered in Africa in terms of both determining the volume and growth of trade. In addition, the variation in the trade-GDP ratios among countries in the region can be explained by income per capita, geography, and trade policy. Variations in the growth of trade are also significantly influenced by trade policy.

Thus, the urban-biased policies dominating much of the African region have reduced the role of international trade in these countries, and this in turn has certainly lowered the standard of living. The impact on long-run growth is less clear. However, several successful countries (such as Botswana and Mauritius) have engaged in more open trade policies, although they have combined these policies in unorthodox ways. The key conclusion is that urban-biased trade policies have indeed negatively affected trading opportunities in the region. These policies have also significantly affected migration within the region, and the next section explores this issue.

Urban Bias and Migration

Perhaps the best-known models of Africa have to do with the impact of this urban bias on migration. One of the best-known models of migration was developed by Harris and Todaro (1970) and was explicitly based on the African experience. The Harris-Todaro model has influenced how economists view migration, employment policies, and international trade.

To understand the Harris-Todaro model, we need to first understand the factor-flow model of migration on which it is based. In the factor-flow model, labor moves to regions with high wage rates from regions with low wage rages. Capital moves, through investment, to regions with high profit rates. This notion is quite natural and easy to understand. Suppose there are only two regions, A and B, and that region A is wealthy because it has lots of capital per worker. Region B is much poorer because it has little capital per worker. Standard economic theory says wage rates will be higher in A than in B, but profit rates will be higher in B than in A. It seems reasonable to suppose that workers would like to move from region B to A to seek higher wages and capital will tend to move in the opposite direction to seek higher profits.

Because we are mostly interested in migration, we will discuss labor movements and not capital movements. Of course, there could be restrictions on the movement of capital or of labor. However, if at least one of these factors of production is able to move for economic gain, then the results will be the same. Wage rates will fall in region A as the supply of workers in that region increases and will rise in region B as workers become dearer. Similarly, profit rates will rise in region A and fall in B. Migration will continue until wage rates are the same in both regions and profit rates are the same in both regions. In other words, migration is the mechanism whereby equilibrium occurs in both the labor and the capital market.

Suppose rural Africa is poor but that urban Africa is much better off in terms of real income due to the effects of urban bias. This relative situation does appear to be the case. Workers, according to this theory, would like to move to the urban area to gain higher wages and income. They will move if they can finance the move and if there are no barriers or prohibitions on their moving. Competition for jobs in the high-wage region will reduce the wage rates in that region. Similarly, wages in the low-wage region will rise. After some time, the wage rates in the two regions will be the same.

A major question concerning the factor-flow view of migration is whether there is any evidence that wage rates are becoming equitable through migration. This narrowing of wage rates does not appear to have occurred. There are many possible explanations as to why some depressed regions continue to be depressed. One is that there are other important differences between the regions, such as cultural ties. People may choose lower wages because they like a particular location. Harris-Todaro provides an explanation based on the urban bias in African policy.

Consider Equation (4.1), which describes the factor-flow model:

$$M_{BA} = \beta \, (W_A - W_B), \tag{4.1}$$

where M_{BA} is migration from B to A, W_A is the wage rate in region A, W_B is the wage rate in region B, and β is a positive constant determining the speed of adjustment. Migration will occur as long as $W_A > W_B$. Hence, in equilibrium, the wage rates are equal.

Harris-Todaro contends that the wage rates are not narrowing because we are already in equilibrium. Wage rates are not the same, however, because urban wage rates are kept high through the actions of the government. Let A be the urban area and B the rural. The government's urban constituency, through its ability to exercise significant political power, achieves a wage rate in the urban area that is above the market-clearing wage rate. The result is unemployment. For simplicity, this wage rate is assumed to be fixed. At the same time, because land is abundant, no unemployment in the rural sector is assumed, and the rural wage rate is assumed to be fixed. Consequently, rural workers must consider both the probability that they will be unemployed and the wage rate in making a decision to migrate. The migration becomes Equation (4.2):

$$M_{BA} = \beta(\lambda W_A - W_B), \tag{4.2}$$

where λ is the probability the migrant will be employed. Hence, as long as $\lambda W_A > W_B$, rural to urban migration will occur. Migration will reduce λ, the probability of employment in the model, but will not affect the wage rates. The probability of employment will fall until it reaches the equilibrium level, where expected income is the same in both regions and migration is zero.

The Harris-Todaro model emphasizes that rural development might be preferable to urban development. This case can most strongly be made in terms of what has been called the "Todaro paradox." The Todaro paradox is that the creation of jobs to combat urban unemployment causes more unemployment. In the discussion of the paradox, it is assumed that the economy is in equilibrium. The creation of high-paying jobs in the urban

Table 4.1

Urbanization

Country/Region	Urban growth rate, 1940–95 (in percent)	Percent urban		
		1975	1995	2025
Country				
Botswana	7.0	12	28	56
Burkina-Faso	11.2	6	27	66
Burundi	6.6	3	8	21
Ghana	4.3	30	36	58
Kenya	6.8	13	28	51
Lesotho	6.2	11	23	47
Malawi	6.2	8	14	32
Mozambique	7.4	9	34	61
Nigeria	5.2	23	39	62
Tanzania	6.1	10	24	48
Uganda	5.8	8	13	29
Zimbabwe	5.0	20	32	55
Region				
Africa	4.4	5	34	55
South America	2.5	64	78	88
Asia	3.3	25	35	55
Europe	0.6	67	74	83

Source: The World Resources Institute (1996).

area will increase λ, the probability of employment in the urban area. This rise in λ will temporarily cause rural to urban migration until λ falls to its equilibrium level. Hence, the number of unemployed workers would rise and the unemployment rate in the economy as a whole would rise if the urban unemployment rate were higher than the rural unemployment rate.

Job creation in the rural area has two advantages over urban job creation. First, it actually reduces unemployment and problems associated with unemployment. Jobs are created in the rural area where potential workers do not have to sacrifice employment to search for a new job. Second, the costs associated with both migration and urban congestion would be reduced.

Examining the data on Africa, urban bias in policy making does indeed seem to be correlated with high urban growth rates. Looking at Table 4.1, it is obvious that the rate of urbanization has been high. In fact, projections indicate that more than 50 percent of Africa's population will reside in urban areas by 2025.

The model presumes that as people migrate to urban areas unemployment rates in those areas are likely to remain high. In reality, most of these new migrants cannot afford to remain unemployed. For the most part, those migrants who fail to find jobs within the modern sector with formally registered firms are often absorbed into the urban informal sector. These firms are usually small in scale, labor intensive, and unregistered (for tax purposes). They are engaged in a remarkable array of activities, ranging from hawking, street vending, letter writing, knife sharpening, carpentry, and so on. Studies reveal that the share of urban labor engaged in such informal sector activities ranges from 20 to 70 percent.

Along with the rapid urbanization and urban bias in policy has come the prolific growth of huge slums and shantytowns. In Africa during the 1980s, 92 of every 100 households established in urban areas were located in slum areas. Most of the settlements lack clean water, sewage systems, and electricity. Thirty percent of the population of Abidjan, Côte d'Ivoire, lives without piped water and 70 percent without sewers. Similar conditions can be found in Nairobi, Lusaka, Kinshasa, Dakar, and Lagos.

This seems to be the result of an urban bias in policy structure that has played a role in augmenting migration to cities. Ultimately, this is the result of a type of politics, patron-client politics, practiced in much of Africa, which in turn is the outcome of a lack of legitimate state authority. What has been the impact of this sort of politics on rural development? The bulk of the population is still located in rural areas. Is there any role for rural development in terms of successfully reducing poverty? These questions are examined in the next section.

Risk Management and Lineage Groups

In order to understand the process of rural development in Africa it is necessary to understand something about property rights. The notion of private property is new and does not have complete legitimacy in Africa. The traditional economy in Africa is a combination of lineage groups as the source of social security and "use ownership" property rights. Each of these features of the traditional economy will be defined in order. Then their implications for African growth will be discussed.

What has come to be known as private property is the type of property relationship most widely used today in the West. A more correct term is "fee simple." Fee simple means that the property is yours in two senses. You have the right to use the property in any manner as prescribed by law. For example, if you have a fee-simple right to land that has been used to grow wheat, you have the right to grow some other crop, grow nothing, or turn it into a parking lot as long as those uses are legal. In addition, you can permanently transfer those rights to another person. In other words, you can sell the land. With use ownership, custom and social pressures limit how you can use a piece of land. In addition, you cannot sell that land. Use ownership can be transferred to others in the person's lineage group, however, such as children.

A lineage group is an extended family. Extended families differ from the nuclear family to the extent and the strength of obligations to aid relatives. Extended families consist of related persons living in different households who accept strong mutual obligations to help each other. For example, cousins, uncles, and other relatives might help finance a move for a job search, provide assistance when a crop fails, or pay for some of the costs of an education. In other words, the lineage group provides many of the social and risk-protection services that are provided by the state or by private financial markets in advanced industrialized economies.

There are two basic ways a lineage group can protect itself against risk. The first way is to reduce risk through diversification. Diversification of earnings sources plays a dominant role in financial economics as a way of trading off risk and income. Choosing uncorrelated income streams reduces risk. The less the correlation, the more risk is reduced. In financial economics, this diversification occurs through purchasing financial assets whose returns are thought to be uncorrelated or not highly correlated. A second way of dealing with risk is to even out the consumption stream. A family can save during good years and use these savings to consume more in bad years than they could otherwise have consumed.

Both of these ways of dealing with risk involve sophisticated financial markets. Such deep financial markets may not be available in the rural sector of many developing countries. In Sub-Saharan Africa, lineage groups have stepped in and developed ways of dealing with risk that do not involve largely nonexistent financial markets. Diversifying productive activities, crops, or both can reduce risk. Furthermore, lineage groups help individual families to cope with risk by providing aid in times of difficulty.

A difficulty that lineage groups face in reducing risk is that, typically, members of a kinship group live and work in the same geographic area, where they face similar risks such as crop failure due to inadequate rainfall. Nevertheless, risk can still be reduced by engaging in a variety of occupations in addition to farming, such as raising some animals (including cattle, which are mobile) and raising several crops, some of which are less susceptible to drought and others that have higher yields in good years.

There are both static and dynamic costs to risk reduction through diversification. Static costs occur because families will engage in low-return activities if the return is not correlated with the returns to other activities. Dynamic costs occur because they limit learning by doing. Learning by doing occurs as workers become proficient in a task by repetition in performing that task. While both these costs are important, the static costs will be emphasized because they help to explain the organization of rural production and the impact of attempts at agricultural reform on the rural economy.

One implication of diversification is that small plots of land are devoted to a crop. These small plots of land, in a land-abundant region, may appear to be inefficient. However, they are part of the costs of reducing risks. Small plots reduce transportation costs. In addition, they become necessary in a subsistence economy, given the limited time a farmer has to engage in a number of activities, both agricultural and nonagricultural. Attempts to increase plot size have been unsuccessful because it would require farmers to face more risk. The best way to increase plot size would be to provide the social infrastructure that would allow farmers to reduce risk without diversifying.

Because lower productivity and perhaps stagnation are a response to risk, the introduction of marketable property rights (i.e., fee simple) could be effective. Marketable property rights have not, however, been able to override traditional rights in many cases. A key determinant of reliance on lineage groups is the extent of risk in an area. Lineage groups are strongest in the dryer north, where rainfall is less reliable. Private property has emerged in areas where crops and rainfall are more reliable. Furthermore, diversification is most common in areas with unreliable rainfall.

Another way of dealing with risk is consumption smoothing. Farmers save and accumulate assets during good times and consume those assets during bad times. A difficulty with this consumption-smoothing activity is the lack of a safe asset to accumulate. Food is perishable and costly to store. Cattle do a little better, but must be slaughtered and consumed before drought becomes too severe. The lack of reliable financial assets and the ability to accumulate them makes consumption smoothing a costly endeavor. Protection of nonfinancial assets can also be difficult unless one is a member of a strong lineage group.

Thus, the institutional organization of African agriculture has been strongly shaped by the lack of a variety of different markets. Specifically, the lack of insurance possibilities—formal mechanisms for reducing risk—have resulted in a system within which the extended family plays that important role, and the extent of commercialization is limited. That is, families are less engaged in the market and therefore are less capable of specialization and reaping the productivity increases that come from specialization and division of labor.

Within this context, the urban-policy bias has been a disaster for the agricultural sector. Relative prices have been turned against this sector and this, combined with overvaluation of exchange rates and taxation, has crippled commercial agriculture. These effects are revealed in Table 4.2. It shows the trend via a net per capita production index for agriculture for the Sub-Sahara region from 1961 to 2000. As can be seen, the dismal picture persists with net per capita food production lower in 2000 than it was in 1961.

Recently (i.e., the 1990s), steps have been taken to deal with some of the issues discussed in the sections above (see World Bank 2000). Exchange-rate overvaluations have been moderated and trade policies have been somewhat liberalized. The result is that the antiexport, antirural sector bias has been eased. In all of this, emphasis has been placed on moving domestic prices to border parity levels. As part of this process, marketing boards have been reduced in their importance or eliminated.

Between 1990 and 1991, real domestic producer prices for agricultural exports increased in fifteen of nineteen African countries. This trend is the result of favorable world price trends as well as better policies. This has resulted in some improvement in agricultural growth, as illustrated at the bottom of Table 4.2. In the period 1990 to 1997, twenty-five countries had recent agricultural growth rates in excess of 2 percent, which is a substantial improvement over the 1980s. The export shares for five of the nine main crops in the region rose in the 1990s.

However, significant problems remain and these relate to a lack of investment in rural infrastructure (irrigation, roads, power, telecommunications), agricultural research and extension, and farmer education and health. Without this investment the response to price liberalization will be significantly muted and fragile. The response will be fragile in the sense that if world commodity prices continue to drift downward, much

Table 4.2

Net Agricultural Production and Net Food Production (per capita), 1961–2000

Year	Net agricultural production	Net food production
1961	115.7	115.6
1962	116.7	116.2
1963	117.4	117.0
1964	117.9	116.6
1965	116.4	115.4
1966	115.3	113.5
1967	118.1	117.2
1968	116.1	115.0
1969	120.2	118.2
1970	121.4	119.6
1971	118.9	117.5
1972	113.6	111.6
1973	111.5	109.6
1974	115.7	114.4
1975	112.7	111.6
1976	109.8	109.5
1977	107.3	106.8
1978	105.8	105.7
1979	102.2	102.3
1980	101.1	101.2
1981	101.8	102.1
1982	99.6	99.8
1983	97.6	97.7
1984	94.4	94.2
1985	98.2	98.0
1986	99.7	99.5
1987	96.0	95.7
1988	100.3	100.5
1989	99.9	99.9
1990	98.2	98.2
1991	101.8	101.9
1992	98.9	99.3
1993	98.4	99.2
1994	98.4	99.3
1995	99.4	99.8
1996	102.9	102.9
1997	100.5	100.2
1998	102.2	102.2
1999	102.7	103.2
2000	101.4	102.1

Source: Food and Agriculture Organization of the United Nations, www.faostat.fao.org

of the recent gain in growth and productivity will likely disappear. Thus, there is too little investment and much of it is inefficient. Urban bias in terms of investment still exists, and this poses a significant obstacle to long-run economic development.

The agricultural sector has been greatly harmed by the political structure that has come to dominate much of Africa. The structure of the rural sector and development process within the rural sector has also greatly influenced population growth in Sub-Saharan Africa. The next section will examine population growth in Africa.

Lineage Groups, Fertility, and the Demographic Transition

A population can grow three basic ways. It can grow through migration, births, or reduced mortality. All three sources of demographic change have played important roles in Africa's economic development. Sub-Saharan Africa has particularly higher birth rates. The total fertility rate is the highest for any region of the world. It has 5.8 births per woman, versus 4.1 in Arab states (the next highest) and 3.6 in South Asia (the third highest). The fertility rate tells us, on average, how many children a woman will give birth to if births continue at their current pattern, ignoring mortality. A fertility rate of 5.8 births per woman is extremely high. However, these birth rates may be set back by the epidemic of HIV/AIDS in many parts of Africa.

It is not clear that high fertility retards economic growth, although except for a few population economists in the United States, the common belief is that high fertility has made it more difficult for most less-developed countries to grow. Children are both producers and consumers of goods. Each child will initially consume more than that child produces. Eventually, however, as they age children will produce more than they consume. The net impact of these patterns of consumption and production on per capita income through the life cycle can depend heavily on how additional births influence the investment patterns of parents. Additional births may reduce both investment in human capital (the education of each child) and physical capital or family saving. However, wealth transfers later in life and a younger population may increase productivity and saving. Increased saving implies higher investment and higher growth rates.

A key factor in determining the economic costs and benefits of children is the social institutions that affect the distribution of family income to family members. In Sub-Saharan Africa, lineage groups play an important role in determining these costs and benefits. Lineage groups share in the costs of raising children. They also share in the benefits. One of these benefits is risk reduction.

Remember that lineage groups reduce risks by engaging in diversified production. The larger the lineage group, the more easily it can diversify production and hence reduce risk. Larger lineage groups may have more assets to share in order to help family members in hard times. In addition, individual members of a lineage group can specialize more as the lineage group becomes larger.

The existence of lineage groups might help in part to explain high fertility in preindustrial Africa because they share in the costs of raising a child. In nuclear families, the costs of child rearing falls mostly on the child's parents and, in many such societies, on the mother of the child. Extended families in lineage groups share in the costs of child rearing and consequently help support larger families.

The most dominant theory drawing on this insight is the theory of the demographic transition. Transition theory divides societal processes into four separate phases. Phase I is a static society with high birth and death rates. It covers most societies throughout history. In this phase, high fertility is required to offset high mortality. Any viable society develops social norms, social mores, and social institutions to promote high fertility. Shared child rearing plays a dominant role in the discussion of phase I. In phase II, the death rate begins to fall. This decline begins because of better nutrition and health caused by rising prosperity, later augmented by medical-technology improvements. Births, however, remain high because social norms, mores, and institutions supporting high fertility are firmly in place and are slow to change. In phase III, births begin to decline as social norms, mores, and institutions evolve partly in response to society's new needs and partly as a direct response to the forces that caused mortality to decline in the first place. Finally, in phase IV, births and deaths are roughly in balance.

Transition theory has to be dramatically modified if it is to be of use in describing what has happened in any given country or region. In sub-Saharan Africa, and many other parts of the globe, the onset of industrialization brought about a rise in fertility, though it has lately started to fall in much of the world. In much of Sub-Saharan Africa, however, fertility has fallen little, if at all. The reasons for this are likely to have something to do with the course of development in Africa and the resilience of traditional, rural social institutions.

When industrialization or modernization began in Africa, the introduction of market-oriented production in a modern sector may have made it easier for lineage groups to diversify in order to reduce risk. Young adults could move to the modern sector to seek modern-sector employment. The returns to this employment served three purposes. First, and most obviously, the young adult might earn more income in a higher-paying job. Second, the worker might be paid in cash and not subsistence goods. Recall that taxes must be paid in cash and that modern-sector employment would be a source of cash income for both the worker's family and his or her group. Third, risk could be reduced for the lineage group. Recall that risk is reduced to the extent that sources of income are uncorrelated. The modern-sector employment is typically not in agriculture, may be export oriented, in mining or the urban service sector, and, consequently, is not likely to be highly correlated with the weather. Hence, modern-sector income employment is not likely to be highly correlated with income in the traditional, rural economy.

The growth in the modern sector presents opportunities for large families to reduce risk as long as there are wealth transfers within each lineage group (Caldwell 1982). The increase in the number of occupations and of jobs in the modern sector both create an incentive to having larger families because larger families can reduce risk in two ways. They reduce risk by taking modern-sector employment and by choosing a diverse number of careers. Hence, it might be expected that fertility would rise with modernization.

In modified transition theory, fertility will initially rise with modernization. Eventually fertility will still decline because the bonds tying members of a kinship group together will begin to weaken. These bonds will weaken partly because they depend on physical proximity. In order to take modern-sector jobs, workers must move to key urban centers. The bonds stay strong for a considerable time after moving, but eventually they start to weaken. They may lose much of their strength and their rationale for the next generation of urban workers. Consequently, in modified transition theory, it is thought that fertility will begin to fall.

Migration in Africa is in many ways different from migration in this theory. For one, much of the migration is often temporary, whereas in modified transition theory migration is permanent. Workers often leave their birth location, where their kinship group lives, and only take employment for limited periods. Because they do return, the subsequent decline in bonds to their kinship group does not occur. Hence, the expected decline in fertility does not occur for many workers and their families.

There are other reasons why fertility might fall. Fertility depends on the status of women. As women achieve more status, they are able to achieve better education and have more control over birth decisions. More of the costs of child rearing are pushed onto the male. The status of women may not matter much in these decisions if the extended family takes on many of the responsibilities of child rearing. Consequently, the continued need for kinship groups to provide protection against risk has kept fertility rates high.

Perhaps the best way to reduce fertility in Africa would be to provide a better system of social security for families in the traditional economy. This proposition is often misunderstood. Old-age pensions are not the type of social security that will do much to reduce fertility. Wealth transfers in the lineage group replace many types of insurance available in more-developed economies. A system of financial and insurance institutions where families could safely save could increase families' ability to deal with risk. Lineage groups would not then be the major source of security. The incentives for large families would thereby be reduced. In addition, as explained earlier, production would become more efficient and population growth rates would fall.

As discussed previously, population growth rates are also determined by mortality. A dark cloud has recently emerged over Africa concerning population. HIV/AIDS has reached frightening proportions in the population with estimates for some countries ranging up to 35 percent of the population aged fifteen to forty-nine having been infected. Temporary migration patterns in Africa, where males move away from proximity to their lineage group, may be partly responsible for this alarming spread of HIV/AIDS. Denial by governments and failure to take early action is also a source of the spread. There are encouraging signs that countries are finally taking rigorous action. Furthermore, the infection rate for those between the age of fifteen and forty-nine is still fairly low in many African countries, such as Nigeria (5 percent), with an average infection rate for Sub-Saharan Africa of about 10 percent.

The future of Africa's population size is uncertain. There are dramatic demographic events that are shaping that future. Due to past population growth, a high percentage of Africa's population is below the age of twenty. They will have to find answers to forces causing high fertility and high mortality. These answers will partly involve a way of developing the traditional, rural economy. Security and investment in creating market opportunities in the rural economy could play an important role in reducing fertility and mortality and in increasing economic growth rates.

The Failed State

The difficulties and problems discussed above are made all the more difficult by the phenomenon of "failed" or "collapsed states." It is generally assumed that the centralized state controlled by the ruling elite has a monopoly on violence within the boundaries of the state. However, there are a number of states and regions in Africa in which the ruling elite no longer has a monopoly over violence. More specifically, the influence of the central state ends quickly and may not extend much beyond the boundaries of the capital city. Various rebel groups often claim control over various parts of nations, thus contesting the monopoly over violence of the ruling elite.

While not purely an African phenomenon, failed states are an all too common phenomenon in the region. Over the last forty years, nearly twenty African countries, or about 40 percent of Sub-Saharan Africa, have experienced at least one civil war. "It is estimated that 20 percent of [Sub-Saharan Africa's] population now lives in countries which are formally at war and low intensity conflict has become endemic to many other African states" (Elbadawi and Sambanis 2000, 244). This violence is often characterized by ethnic conflicts, pitting one group against another.

The phenomenon of failed or collapsed states is not particularly surprising. Within the context of patron-client politics, the persistent search for mechanisms to generate rent flows, which can then be allocated to reward supporters and punish foes creates an atmosphere of ever-increasing economic distortion. If the reader will recall, by short-circuiting markets the ruling elite can create scarcities of critical outputs and inputs and then use its power to decide who gets access to these inputs and goods. However, creating these distortions leads to increasing economic losses: a shrinking of the economic pie. One would expect that, taken to the extreme, these sorts of policies would weaken the power of the existing ruling elite and thus result in a loss of the monopoly over violence.

One might wonder why a ruling elite would continue to engage in policies that devastate the economy and eventually undermine their monopoly over violence. Of course, miscalculation on the part of the ruling elite can result in just such a situation. However, there may be some additional factors at work.

First, most of the states in Sub-Saharan Africa were colonized by European states, which, in turn, constructed state institutions whose main purpose was to extract resources and/or wealth from the region. Thus, the institutional structures resulted in the colonial states being dependent on only a small sector of the economy, the enclave export sector, to provide the revenue necessary to support the state. Thus the rest of the economy and its participants were not actively involved in the production process. Tax schemes did not penetrate deeply into the social fabric, and government organization and penetration of the society was limited. An indigenous elite then inherited these institutional structures with independence. The implication, as discussed earlier, was that most of the new ruling elite in these countries was only loosely tied to the bulk of their populations and economies. As a result, most of these states remained extracting and illegitimate, and thus weak.

Second, there were changes in the production structure for generating violence. It has generally been argued by many scholars that this production process was subject to significant economies of scale. That is, the cost of producing power (i.e., violence) declines with the size of the economy, population, and society. To field large numbers of armed forces requires significant capability to generate the resources necessary for armament. In other words, the production of power is subject to significant fixed costs. Once these are undertaken, larger operations reduce per unit costs. If there are significant increasing returns, then whichever elite group is able to expand their activity rapidly enough can then lay claim to a monopoly over the means of violence.

However, the growth in the international arms industry and technological innovation in the production of weapons and power has reduced the fixed costs in the establishment and projection of power. In other words, there are fewer economies of scale, and it becomes much easier for competitors to set up operations and contest control of the countryside.

In earlier chapters, it was argued that threats to a ruling elite could spur them to become more responsive to the needs of their citizens. However, this relationship is not linear in nature. If the threats become extreme so that the probability of survival of the ruling elite's position becomes low, then the elite are likely to become even more predatory.

Thus, collapsed states within the African region would seem to be the result of three factors. The state apparatus inherited from the colonial powers was predatory in nature. These states, when they became independent, lacked legitimacy and were therefore weak. The indigenous ruling elite maintained this structure and policies were based on patron-client relationships. In order to maintain a hold on power, the ruling elite increasingly distorted their economies by utilizing policies whose purpose was to generate artificial rents, which could then be distributed to supporters. The economic decline was augmented given that small rebel groups now could gain access to large quantities of arms, and the monopoly over violence by the ruling elite ceased. All of these factors have resulted in the phenomenon of the failed state.

Botswana: A Success Story

To this point, the picture painted of the development process in Sub-Saharan Africa is quite bleak. However, that is not entirely accurate. There are a few African success stories, and this section will briefly look at one, Botswana.

In the past thirty-five years, no country has performed as economically well as Botswana. Botswana in 1998 had a real income per capita (adjusted for PPP) of $5,796, almost four times the African average. Between 1965 and 1998, Botswana's economy grew at an annual rate of 7.7 percent. These are truly astounding achievements, especially given the conditions that existed at independence. When the British granted independence, there were only twelve kilometers of paved road in the country. There were only 22 Botswana citizens who had graduated from a university and only 100 from secondary school. The country is predominately tropical and is landlocked. While Botswana is blessed with deposits of diamonds, they currently account for around 40 percent of the country's output (such natural resources have been a curse for almost all other Sub-Saharan African countries).

The question that naturally comes to mind is how did Botswana achieve this success? The answer would seem to be that the government tended to follow good policy, and those policies flowed out of an institutional structure that was conducive to economic growth. These institutions created an atmosphere in which property rights were respected by both the population and the ruling elite. In other words, the ruling elite in Botswana seems to have been able to solve the commitment problem. The ruling elite has promised entrepreneurs that they will be able to keep the fruits of their investment and savings, while not engaging in predatory behavior which would have given the elite the greatest gain in the short run. Thus, good economics seems to have come out of good politics.

One might initially think that the success of Botswana might have been the result of following a laissez-faire approach. However, Botswana has been characterized by significant government intervention in the economy—central-government expenditure is around 40 percent of GDP. The state has played an important role in the economy.

Acemoglu, Johnson, and Robinson (2000b) attribute Botswana's success to the establishment of an effective set of institutions of private property. There are two aspects to this. "First, institutions should provide secure property rights, so that those with productive opportunities expect to receive returns from their investments. The second requirement is embedded in our emphasis on 'a broad cross-section of the society' having the opportunity to invest. A society in which a very small fraction of the population, for example a class of landowners, holds all the wealth and political power may not be the ideal environment for investment, even if the property rights of this elite are secure" (ibid. 5).

How did Botswana establish this institutional structure? One can only understand this by taking a short look at its history. (Much of the following comes from Acemoglu, Johnson, and Robinson 2000b.) The dominant tribe in the region was the Tswana (eight main subgroups), which migrated into the area of modern Botswana in the eighteenth century. In these societies, the chief was the dominant individual who allocated land for grazing, crops, and housing. Authority was expressed through a hierarchy of officials. However, public forums also existed, composed of all adult males, which, in turn, discussed issues of interest to the tribe. Those provided an effective mechanism to achieve the policies of the chief and for the chief to gain information as to the issues before his people. These also acted as effective constraints on arbitrary rule by the chief. This type of organization was quite rare in precolonial African societies.

Eventually, the Tswana tribes were incorporated into the British Empire. However, colonial institutional organizations did not penetrate deeply into Tswana society because the region was not deemed terribly important. The British ignored this area for fifty years, and it was not until 1934 that any attempt was made to establish authority over the chiefs there. However, World War II and the ensuing independence movements throughout Africa short-circuited these attempts.

After independence, the Botswana Democratic Party (BDP), led by

Seretse Khama, came to dominate politically. This party easily won the first election and has won every election since. Although this party has ruled continuously, there is considerable evidence that it has been responsive to threats to its power (i.e., electoral threats). For example, in the late 1960s and early 1970s, the electoral threat of lost power spurred the government to carry out the Accelerated Rural Development Programme, involving extensive investment in infrastructure in the rural areas.

Under the constitution, there is a national assembly, with thirty-one elected members and four specially appointed by the president. Executive power resides with the president, who is chosen by the National Assembly. A House of Chiefs was also created, but it has little power.

At first, the Botswana government had few assets on which to draw. Initial development plans were focused on the rural sector, in particular cattle ranching, which predominated. "Building infrastructure and developing infrastructure was entirely in the interests of the BDP political elite. Specifically 2/3 of the members of the National Assembly in the early years were large or medium sized cattle owners" (ibid.18). In addition, the Botswana Meat Commission was founded. It was a marketing board that would purchase cattle from ranchers, process them, and then sell the products on regional and world markets. It was controlled by the cattle interests and thus was not used as a mechanism to tax agriculture, but instead it has served to develop the sector. Mining companies were also encouraged to explore the country. In order to stimulate industry, the government introduced the Botswana Development Corporation. In 1982, a policy was utilized to subsidize industrial ventures.

One additional point should be made. Botswana has long been a member of the Southern Africa Customs Union. This meant that Botswana has had no independent trade policy, as goods circulated freely between it and the countries of Southern Africa. The government gets a share of the customs revenue collected by South Africa, the custodian of the union's revenue pool. What is important here is that Botswana's government officials had no day-to-day control over this revenue. Nor did they have the ability to interfere with the flow of goods through Southern Africa. Perhaps the essential thing is that producers in urban areas knew this. Lobbying policy makers for favorable trade policies was thus useless. Therefore, as no urban-based lobby could expect to have influence, the incentives to exercising power in nonproductive ways was reduced.

Let us summarize the experience of Botswana. It has not engaged in laissez-faire policies, but it has engaged with the international system through international trade and foreign investment. Instead of engaging in policies characterized by urban bias, initial efforts were made to invest in and heavily develop the rural, agricultural sector. Multiparty political democracy exists and functions fairly well. Much of the export revenue generated comes from the export of diamonds, but much of this revenue has been invested back into the economy. The result is that economic growth has been rapid. Corruption exists, but its extent is quite limited by the standards of the region.

How does one explain this exception to the dismal experience of Africa? The definitive answer to this is unknowable. However, a number of factors seem to be important. First, the precolonial political system placed constraints on the power of chiefs. The colonization process did not destroy these practices. Thus, with independence, the new institutions reflected the precolonial experience. The ruling elite and the institutional structure were thus viewed as being legitimate by a large part of the population.

Those whose economic interests lay within the agricultural sector dominated the governing elite. Initial investment and development efforts were aimed at the development of the agricultural sector; urban bias did not characterize the policy choices made by the rural-based elite.

Although the elite were subject to electoral threats to their positions, these threats were not extreme. To lose political power was not the path to extinction. As a result, electoral threats stimulated the ruling elite to engage in economic policies that provided growth. In this way, then, the elite could strengthen their political hold.

Of course, there is a threat to all of this success, the threat of HIV/AIDS. This disease has staggered this nation, with approximately 30 percent of the adult population infected by the virus. This disease attacks and kills people in the working ages, thus having a devastating effect on production and economic activity. If the rapid economic expansion of Botswana is to continue, then it must come rapidly to grips with this problem.

Botswana is an exception to the dismal economic experience of much of Africa. This is certainly partly the result of certain accidental factors. First, the colonial experience was much more benign in Botswana compared with much of the rest of Africa. The newly independent state was thus viewed with greater legitimacy. Second, large deposits of diamonds were found and served as a reliable source of export revenue. In addition to the exogenous factors, the ruling elite also made policy choices that were necessary for rapid growth. The rural sector was not neglected. Significant investment was made to raise overall productivity. The political survival of the elite was dependent on providing rapid economic growth.

What We Have Learned

So, what have we learned from the African experience that is similar to what has been learned from examining other regions? It would seem that, once again, the agricultural sector is a key factor in explaining the overall success or failure in economic development. It appears that much of the failure in Africa is the result of policies deliberately aimed at impoverishing its most important sector. The major exception to the dismal experience in Africa, Botswana, seems to support the overall conclusion that initially significant investment must be made in agriculture, that this is a key to long-run development.

The distinguishing characteristic of this region would seem to be the impact of colonialism. The colonial states and their borders were arbitrarily established. Given that these colonies were not heavily settled by Europeans, the institutional structure established was aimed at extracting resources from narrow sectors of the indigenous economy (e.g., minerals, primary products). Few institutions aimed at broad economic development were created. At independence, indigenous elites merely took over the process of extraction from colonial officials. Thus, the new, indigenous elite did not have to "earn" their revenue, and few mechanisms for restraining the predatory impulses of the ruling elite evolved.

The colonial inheritance resulted in the newly independent regimes lacking legitimacy, which in turn resulted in a patron-client type or style of politics. Given the structure of the economics in this region, this resulted in an urban bias in policy making that devastated the agricultural sectors of the region. This posed an insurmountable barrier to future economic development.

The experience of Botswana was quite different. Its precolonial history was of a tribal structure that had evolved popular constraints on the behavior of chiefs. British colonialism had only a light presence in the region, meaning that the traditional structure was not destroyed and replaced with a set of extracting institutions. With independence, a rural-based elite invested in the most important sector of the economy, agriculture. A functioning multiparty democracy evolved, constraining the actions of the ruling elite.

It would seem that the future of Africa is dependent on two important factors, one economic and the other political, and they are interlinked. First, there must be a significant investment in rural development and the physical infrastructure necessary to support that development. Second, a political-institutional structure constraining the ruling elite must be established. This system need not necessarily be democratic, but it must be pluralistic. That is, the ruling elite must be subject to political competition such that the pursuit of economic development is perceived as the best means toward maintaining authority.

Key Terms

African Efflorescences	Todaro Paradox
Predatory Colony	Lineage Groups
Developmental Colony	Risk
Patron-Client Politics	Consumption Smoothing
Legitimacy	Fertility Rate
Public Infrastructure	Demographic Transition
Urban Bias	Failed State
Protectionist Policies	HIV/AIDS
Migration	

References

Acemoglu, Daron, Simon Johnson, and James A. Robinson. 2000a. "The Colonial Origins of Comparative Development: An Empirical Investigation." Massachusetts Institute of Technology, Department of Economics.

———. 2000b. "An African Success Story: Botswana." Centre for Economic Policy Research. 1–53.

Bates, Robert H., and William P. Rogerson. 1980. "Agriculture in Development: A Coalitional Analysis." *Public Choice* 35: 513–27.

Caldwell, John C. 1982. *Theory of Fertility Decline.* New York: Academic Press.

Compson, Raymond. 2001. "Africa Backgrounder: History U.S. Policy, Principal Congressional Actions." CRS Report RL30029. Washington, DC: Library of Congress.

Davidson, Basil. 1992. *The Black Man's Burden: Africa and the Curse of the Nation-State.* New York: Times Books.

Elbadawi, Ibrahim, and Nicholas Sambanis. 2000. "Why are There So Many Civil Wars in Africa? Understanding and Preventing Violent Conflict." *Journal of African Economies* 9 (October): 244–69.

Harris, John R., and Michael P. Todaro. 1970. "Migration, Unemployment, and Development: A Two-Sector Analysis." *American Economic Review* 60 (March): 126–42.

Kurer, Oskar. 1996. "The Political Foundations of Economic Development Policies." *Journal of Development Studies* 32 (June): 645–68.

Lipton, Michael. 1977. *Why Poor People Stay Poor.* Cambridge, MA: Harvard University Press.

Moore, Mick. 2001. "Political Underdevelopment: What Causes Bad Governance." Working Paper, Institute of Development Studies, March.

North, Douglass. 1990. *Institutions, Institutional Change and Economic Performance.* Cambridge: Cambridge University Press.

Oliver, Roland, and Anthony Atmore. 1994. *Africa Since 1800.* Cambridge, UK: Cambridge University Press.

Olson, Mancur. 1971. *The Logic of Collective Action: Public Goods and the Theory of Groups.* Cambridge, MA: Harvard University Press.

Rodrik, Dani. 1998. "Trade Policy and Economic Performance in Sub-Saharan Africa." Working Paper 6562. National Bureau of Economic Research, Cambridge, Massachusetts.

World Bank. 2000. "Can Africa Claim the 21st Century?" Washington, DC.

The World Resources Institute. 1996. *World Resources 1996–97.* New York: Oxford University Press.

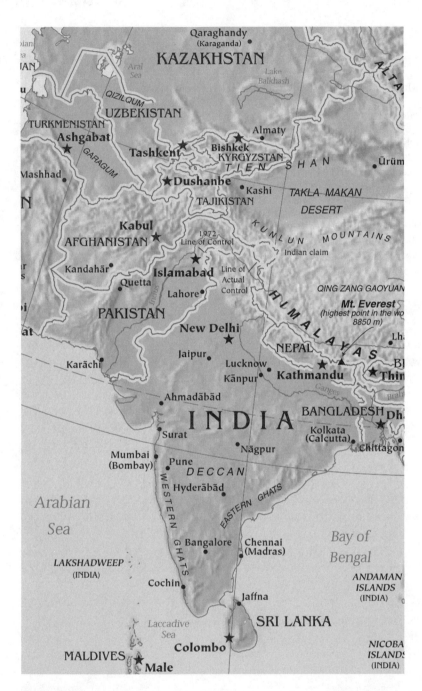

South Asia

5

South Asia

According to the *Encarta*, South Asia comprises the countries of Afghanistan, Bangladesh, Bhutan, India, Maldives, Nepal, Pakistan, and Sri Lanka. While this chapter will throw some light on the region of South Asia as a whole, the discussion will concentrate more specifically on India since it is the largest democracy within this region and, perhaps more importantly, India plays a major role in the current global economic environment. The South Asian region, home to 1.4 billion people, is rich in history and cultural heritage. The countries of the region are unique in various aspects, but they also share several common elements other than geographical proximity. For the past decade, South Asia has been the second fastest growing region in the world, after East Asia, with an average annual growth rate of 5.3 percent. Yet 45 percent of its population lives below the international poverty line of $1 a day, comprising about 40 percent of the world's poor. Rapid population growth and a high density of population pose serious threats to the economies comprising South Asia. Disguised unemployment is a direct consequence of the "population explosion" this region has experienced.

Being in the same geographical area, the countries of South Asia share a typical monsoon-type climate. These countries are dependent on the monsoon rains for the success of their crop yields. This has a direct impact on the economic performance of the countries since most of their economies are dominated by the agricultural sector, which is mostly traditional and labor intensive in technology. Though one might find this hard to understand, especially for a country such as India since its "green revolution" has been much talked about, the economy is still heavily dependent on the uncertain monsoon rains for its agricultural sector, which has usually accounted for two-thirds of its gross domestic product (GDP).

Sociocultural similarities include the important role of diverse religions in shaping the societies, the culture, and history of South Asia. Three main religions, Hinduism, Buddhism, and Islam dominate the region, but a host of other religions also find their home in this region. The countries comprising South Asia share some common social practices, such as the caste system, extended or joint family, and intracaste arranged marriages. The region is characterized by different ethnic and cultural groups associated with language, common ancestry, locality, and/or customs and beliefs. Additionally, the region also houses various different tribes characterized by unique tribal cultures.

Politically, too, the countries of South Asia share some common history. Other than Nepal, the countries were prior colonies of Great Britain and achieved independence in the mid- to late twentieth century. India was partitioned in 1947 and two sovereign states were created: India and Pakistan. Bangladesh, the eastern wing of Pakistan, gained its independence in 1971.

The countries of the region, with the exception of Sri Lanka, show similar trends in their economic, social, and human-development indicators in the past five decades. The countries have been plagued with many perils of underdevelopment, such as excessive dependence on an agricultural sector that was technologically inefficient and dependent on vacillating weather, low labor productivity, high rates of unemployment and underemployment, lack of infrastructure, population explosion, low per capita income, low rates of economic growth, rampant poverty, inequality of income distribution, high levels of illiteracy, extreme gender bias, low life expectancy, and high child mortality.

The postindependence development strategies practiced by the countries have also been similar, such as a reliance on industrialization based on import-substitution policies and the dominant role of the state in the economic reform and growth process. Recently, however, there have been several changes in this region that may have enabled it to break away from the vicious cycle it had been trapped in for decades. From a position of stagnancy and chronic poverty and underdevelopment, India became the world's fifth-largest economy in 1995, after the United States, Japan, China, and Germany, based on gross national product (GNP) (PPP). One major reason for the size of the economy is the country's population, at over 1 billion. However, with the economic reforms put in place in 1991, which stimulated economic dynamism, the growth of the information-technology sector, and consistent economic growth, India in particular and the region overall has the rest of the world closely watching it as an emergent economic force.

Due to the importance of India in South Asia, much of this chapter will concentrate on examining its developmental experience. Later on, an attempt is made to broaden the perspective so as to consider other areas in South Asia.

The first two sections will look at the experience of precolonial, colonial, and postindependence India. The third section will try to create a theoretical framework in order to understand India's post–World War II experience and evaluate its sustainability. The remainder of the chapter will present an overview of India in the areas of population, poverty, agriculture, religion, caste, gender bias, and education.

Preindependence India

In analyzing both pre- and postindependence India, it will be very helpful again to make use of the dualistic model of economic development. If the reader will recall, in this model the economy is divided into a rural, traditional sector and an urban, modern sector. The traditional sector is often characterized by surplus labor, labor that could be withdrawn from the sector without any significant fall in output. Land is a factor of production specific to this sector (no capital is utilized).

The modern sector is usually thought to utilize labor and capital, which is specific to that particular sector. Expansion here is dependent on savings, which leads to capital accumulation, which in turn draws labor out of the traditional sector. Economic development is seen to occur as the modern sector expands, pulls surplus labor out of the traditional sector, and eventually the traditional sector shrinks in size.

The dualistic model was modified in Chapter 2 to analyze the early development of Europe. Instead of a modern sector, there was a sector producing nonagricultural goods in small scale, household or putting out sorts of operations. These sorts of activities generally utilized handicraft types of technologies and were located in rural areas as well as towns. One might label this protoindustrial activity.

From the perspective of the model outlined above, one can visualize economic development as proceeding in three stages. First, subsistence agriculture dominates production, with the bulk of resources involved in food production with little specialization. Second, protoindustrialization takes place as a result of a process of specialization in production driven by commercialization and the growth of markets. Finally, protoindustrial, small-scale technologies are replaced by large-scale, factory production. One should note that there is nothing inevitable in the movement from one stage to another.

The model has a number of implications. Similar to the discussion of the European experience, the extent to which protoindustrialization could occur was certainly limited by the productivity of the agricultural sector. That is, surplus labor could be mobilized for the production of nonagricultural goods without threatening food production. However, once surplus labor is exhausted, any further expansion of nonagricultural production would reduce food availability and push up the cost of food, which in turn would force up wages. With the profitability of nonagricultural production reduced, the expansion of this sector would be halted. Thus, significant expansion of protoindustrial production would be limited by the productivity of domestic agriculture. This is especially true if there is little opportunity to import food through international trade.

One would thus expect economic efflorescences to occur with increases in agricultural productivity. The increased agricultural productivity would release labor for nonagricultural production, while also providing demand for nonagricultural production. During periods of agricultural productivity growth, one would expect increased demand for nonagricultural production and the shift of labor to nonagricultural production.

India, before colonization, has sometimes been viewed as a region in which lack of economic development meant that subsistence represented the general standard of living and that stagnation characterized economic activities and technology in general. That is, India represented a region caught in the traditional Malthusian trap in which rapid population growth kept India locked into a low-level equilibrium, wherein the bulk of its population merely subsisted.

The above characterization of India before British colonization could not be further from the truth. India had gone through several periods of economic and political efflorescences. According to historian Angus Maddison (2001), India had the world's largest economy between the first and fifteenth centuries, from a 32.9 percent share of the world GDP in the first century to 24.5 percent in 1500. In 1700, India's share of the world's income was 24.4 percent, relative to Europe's 23.3 percent. Before the middle of the eighteenth century, the south of India was a very dynamic place. Specifically, increases in agricultural productivity had made grain prices very low, meaning that low nominal wages did not imply low living standards. However, the low nominal wages meant that Indian cotton textiles were a major export. These textiles were produced mainly through an Indian form of the putting-out system. Significant networks of merchants provided materials and orders to producers and arranged for the marketing of the textiles. Increased agricultural productivity thus allowed for the specialization and division of labor to occur, resulting in extensive protoindustrialization (Parthasarathi 2001).

For centuries, cloth and textiles represented the most important nonagricultural items in world trade. Before the Industrial Revolution, South Asia, not Europe, dominated this trade. In 1750, according to the economic historian Paul Bairoch, the Indian subcontinent accounted for a quarter of world manufacturing output (as cited in Parthasarathi 1998).

Therefore, the notion that Europe in the eighteenth century was uniquely dynamic must be rejected. The commercialization and proto-industrialization of Europe in the seventeenth and eighteenth centuries also occurred in South Asia and, as discussed in this book, in other places in the world. "The expansion of markets, the extension of money use, the growth of manufacturers and the rise of non-bureaucratized state forms were found not only in Europe, but also in South and Southeast Asia, China, and West Africa. By 1700, these changes had progressed very far in several parts of South Asia, among them South India, with the development of sophisticated financial networks, a thriving export trade in cotton cloth, a vibrant internal commerce in cotton and yarn, foodstuffs and metal goods, and a diffusion of coinage to even the lowest strata of society" (ibid., 106).

How is one to explain the development of protoindustrial production and commercialization in India? The dualistic model implies that this sort of growth and development must be fueled by increases in agricultural productivity. Indeed, agricultural productivity seems to have achieved high levels in India in the seventeenth century. It seems that the Mughal Empire had provided a significant degree of political unity. Centralized administration, a uniform revenue policy, a network of inland trade fostered by Mughal peace, as well as significant investments in agricul-tural infrastructure resulted in, from a historical perspective, significant increases in agricultural productivity. This agricultural growth fueled specialization and commercialization, and the significant development of protoindustrial production.

Thus, developments in South Asia and England were very similar. However, with the nineteenth century, science came to be increasingly applied to the production process in England. Machinery was applied to the production process. This did not occur in India or any other place for that matter. Indian nationalist writers have argued that the colonization of India by England disrupted an evolutionary process by which India would have transformed itself via an industrialization process. This has been labeled deindustrialization. The argument here is that England disrupted Indian exports of textiles via the introduction of machine-produced goods and displaced Indian producers from international markets. The production of textiles via protoindustrial processes in India thus declined and deindustrialization occurred (Dutt 1969).

The process discussed above seems to be more complicated, however. According to recent work by Clingingsmith and Williamson (2004), the deindustrialization of India had begun before the transformation of industrial production began in England. The latter is thought to have begun in the early nineteenth century and certainly had a negative impact on the structure of the Indian economy—employment in manufacturing declined as a percent of total employment. This occurred as a result of the terms of trade shock resulting from the significant increase in manufacturing productivity (particularly in textiles) in England. This productivity shock drove down the relative price of manufactured textiles in India, thus the industry declined, as did employment. However, it appears that the deindustrialization process in India had begun much earlier, perhaps even before 1750.

The earlier deindustrialization process was driven by a different source. In the eighteenth century, the Mughal Empire was in steady and deep decline. This decline had a significantly negative impact on agricultural production in India. This resulted from the rapid spread of revenue farming, which resulted in the rapid increase in rents. In addition, war and political instability dramatically increased uncertainty and thus suppressed the incentive to accumulate and innovate. Specialization declined, agricultural productivity fell, and protoindustrial production was greatly reduced.

The rising price of grain that resulted from the above forces pushed up nominal wages. This in turn made it increasingly difficulty for Indian textile exports to remain competitive in international markets. This meant that English-produced textiles were already beginning to push Indian textiles out of international markets even before the productivity surge resulting from the industrialization of production processes in England (Clingingsmith and Williamson 2004).

In summary, India underwent deindustrialization during the late eighteenth and nineteenth centuries. This deindustrialization occurred in two stages. In the first stage, the collapse of the Mughal Empire drove down grain productivity, pushing up nominal wages and hurting India's competitiveness in terms of manufactured textiles. In the second stage, productivity advances stemming from the adoption of the factory system in England drove down the price of textiles, causing further deindustrialization in India.

While displacement of Indian producers did indeed occur, there is little evidence that the Smithian growth experienced in southern India would have resulted in an industrial revolution. It was pure Smithian growth with little use of fixed capital or machinery. There was little application of science to the production process. In other words, it does not seem that industrialization would have been the natural result of Smithian growth based on protoindustrial practices. Therefore, while colonization certainly disrupted the Indian economy, it does not seem sensible to conclude that it halted an industrialization process.

An alternative view is provided in the work of Morris (1963). This perspective sees colonization as a dramatic break with the past. However, this disruption was positive in nature since it provided the foundation for Westernization and modernization. That is, British rule brought law, peace, roads, railroads, and other infrastructure. However, it seems that there was little increase in the standard of living for most Indians, and thus little progress in terms of per capita GDP.

However one views the colonial process, it is clear that at the end of the colonization process India was a very poor country. Industrial development was limited and the country did seem to be caught in a low-level equilibrium trap in which increases in population were enough to offset any increases in GDP.

India After Independence

India, led by Mahatma Gandhi, gained its independence from British rule in 1947. The nation saw it as the victory of the Gandhian strategy of nonviolence. The fruits of independence were bittersweet since the freedom was tied with the partition of India (into India and Pakistan) along communal lines. Large-scale communal riots broke out in both countries following independence. Another tragic event that followed India's independence was the assassination of Gandhi at the hands of a Hindu fanatic. This marked the end of an era of unity and idealism in Indian political history. Thereafter, Bhimrao Ambedkar framed the constitution in 1950 and the Republic of India was created on January 26, 1950. The constitution created a parliament, home to the representatives of the one of the world's largest electorates, comprising two houses: the Rajya Sabha, or the Council of States, and the Lok Sabha, or the House of the People.

At the time of independence, Indian per capita yearly income was very low (U.S.$95 in 1974 prices). According to Maddison, India's share of the world's income fell from 24.4 percent in 1700 to 3.8 percent in 1952. Achieving economic growth following independence was a priority for political leaders such as Gandhi and Jawaharlal Nehru, though their opinions on how to achieve such growth were quite different. Nehru was the first prime minister of independent India, and under his leadership the state played a dominant role in economic development and in building institutions. Under his auspices, a planning commission inaugurated the first five-year plan, which targeted raising the savings rate as a means to achieve economic growth.

Nehru's main objective was the creation of a developmental state that could establish an industrial structure, raise India's rate of saving, promote rapid growth, eventually reduce poverty, and move India into the modern world. The dominant ideas concerning these issues were influenced by the seeming success of the Soviet Union in transforming itself into an industrial and military powerhouse. As such, there was reluctance in India to rely on private entrepreneurship and the unfettered operation of markets. After all, how could newly established industries in India hope to be able to compete with established industries in the rest of the world? This, of course, is the infant-industry argument, which has been referred to in earlier chapters.

The strategy of development utilized by Nehru has been called import substitution. This involves using tariffs and quotas to protect new domestic industry. Domestic industry will thus expand to replace imports. The state in India also played a key role in allocating available investment funds through the issuance of licenses and the utilization of contracts. Because imported capital was critical, foreign exchange controls were used to try to prevent the importation of consumer goods and encourage the importation of capital. This often resulted in an overvalued exchange rate. In addition, large parts of heavy industry were under state owner-ship and control. The net result was to raise the return to production for the domestic market, while lowering the relative return for production for international markets. Thus, exports grew increasingly sluggish and India's share in world trade fell dramatically, from 1.4 percent between 1951 and 1960 to 0.5 percent between 1981 and 1990.

One can think of this strategy within the context of the dual-economy model developed above. The third stage of development in that model involved a shift from the small-scale manufacturing based on handicraft or cottage technology to large-scale, factory production. The difficulty was in terms of how to promote such a shift. Import-substitution strate-gies attempt to provide the stimulus for such a shift by dramatically increasing the incentives for production for the domestic market by protecting domestic production from foreign competition. The hoped-for result is that domestic manufacturing firms would grow, learning by doing would occur, and that they would become efficient producers. Domestic industry would expand, per capita income would rapidly increase, poverty would fall, and India would become an important and influential nation.

In some sense the strategy was successful. India did establish a growing industrial base, savings rose from 10 to 25 percent of GDP, and between 1950 and 1980 growth rates for real GDP and per capita GDP were 3.7 percent and 1.5 percent, respectively (DeLong 2003). This growth was in dramatic contrast with the colonial period. However, when compared with the economic performance in East Asia, the growth rates achieved by India seemed anemic at best. In addition, the new industries that were created did not become efficient. Instead, increased subsidies were re-quired to keep many in operation. Corruption of political officials at both the state and national levels became an increasing drag on the growth process. Balance-of-payments crises also arose as exports declined rela-tive to imports. The developmental state constructed after independence became increasingly inept, corrupt, and ineffective.

During the early years following independence, significant other po-litical issues emerged, specifically, the different languages spoken and differences in culture within the country led to internal political conflicts. Ultimately, Nehru had to concede to the demands of reshaping India's internal boundaries along linguistic lines. Thus, in 1960, the former state of Bombay was made into Maharashtra, Gujarat, and Karnataka, and in 1966 the states of Punjab and Haryana were created out of Punjab. In spite of these concessions, language continued to remain a volatile political issue in India. Even though Hindi was constitutionally recognized as the national language, the government had to allow the use of English as an official language for states that were inclined to use it (English is spoken as a second language by more than 10 million Indians and there are fifteen officially recognized Indian languages, though there are as many as 850 languages spoken).

Nehru was unsuccessful in resolving the hostility between India and Pakistan, which grew with the partition of India. The main dispute was over the borders of the states of Jammu and Kashmir, with each country claiming some common territory as their own. Moreover, India entered into conflict with China during the 1950s over land in the northeast, in the state of Arunachal Pradesh, and in northeastern Jammu and Kashmir. The dispute escalated into a full-fledged attack by Chinese forces in 1962, and came to an end with a Chinese declaration of a ceasefire only after India appealed to the western world, particularly the United States, under John F. Kennedy, for involvement and military aid.

Nehru, who died in 1964, was succeeded by Lal Bahadur Shastri. India and Pakistan soon clashed over border disputes in 1965. This time, the former Soviet Union intervened to end hostilities in 1966. Shastri died soon after the ceasefire. He was followed by Nehru's daughter, Indira Gandhi, who was the leader of the Indian Congress Party and who had served as a member of parliament since 1955. The Congress Party whom she represented was, however, defeated in the 1967 elections. In the midst of the political crisis that engulfed the country (along with an economic crisis following severe drought and an economic strategy dominated by the public sector), Gandhi nationalized the largest banks.

In the 1970s, some dramatic changes were taking place in India's countryside. The import-substitution strategy generally followed at this time resulted in significant urban bias. As for other regions discussed in earlier chapters, the relative price of manufactured goods rose relative to agricultural goods, much of the infrastructure investment was concentrated in urban areas, and the costs to farmers of critical inputs were often very high. Thus, agricultural growth was quite slow. However, in the 1970s new seed varieties were developed through international research efforts. Some of these varieties were adapted for use in India. These high-yield seed varieties were very responsive to increased applications of fertilizers combined with controlled applications of water via irrigation. The result was a significant increase in food-grain production such that India became self-sufficient in these grains. This tremendous growth has been called a green revolution (Hayami and Ruttan 1985).

However, there were a number of difficulties. First, the green-revolution techniques were only effective within certain regions in India, specifically the Punjab and Harayana. Much of the rest of rural India was not dramatically affected. Regional disparities thus increased. In addition, the oil crisis of 1973 created inflationary pressures as well as balance-of-payment difficulties. About the same time, allegations of corruption associated with the 1971 national elections led to growing resentment against Indira Gandhi. Gandhi reacted to this unrest by ultimately declaring a state of emergency in 1975. Initially, the emergency rule seemed to work, but opposition to Gandhi's rule increased. In 1977, Gandhi was defeated by the Janata Party. The Congress Party was split and the faction loyal to Gandhi was named the Congress (I) Party—the "I" signifying Indira. Morarji Desai of the Janata Party became prime minister of India, but he remained in office for only two years, after which his government collapsed.

Indira Gandhi came back to power after winning elections in 1980. The 1980s saw a shift in attitude toward private enterprise. Instead of viewing businesses as groups to be confronted or regulated, they were to be encouraged in their activities. Gandhi involved her son Rajiv, an airline pilot, in politics following the tragic death of her younger son, who had held political aspirations. Soon after assuming office, the country was faced with major political crises. In the state of Assam, a nationalist movement was underway against immigrants from West Bengal, and in Punjab, a terrorist group was fighting for an independent Sikh state. In 1984, Gandhi sent troops into Punjab to tackle the terrorists who were housed in the Golden Temple in Amritsar. The skirmish took many lives and caused much damage and destruction. This enraged the Sikh population in the country. On October 31, 1984, while taking a walk within her housing complex, Sikh members of her security guards gunned down Indira Gandhi.

After Indira Gandhi's death, Rajiv Gandhi was elected as prime minister. He too continued the economic reforms initiated by his mother (Rodrik and Subramaniam 2004). Economic reform under Rajiv Gandhi's government had three primary objectives: promote exports, rationalize the tax system, and liberalize government regulation of private industry. Quantitative controls on the import of many varieties of industrial machinery were eliminated. In addition, customs duties on imported capital goods were slashed. Export incentives were enhanced by exempting the first 50 percent of export profits from taxation. In addition, export subsidies were increased and the value of the Indian currency was allowed to decline against other major currencies. Income tax rates were reduced by some 20 to 30 percent depending on the tax bracket. Other reforms reduced, somewhat, the regulation of private business.

The economic effects were somewhat mixed. From 1985 to 1990, India's real GDP growth rate rose to 5.6 percent. The dollar value of exports increased 14 percent annually. However, India's fiscal deficit reached 12 percent of GDP and its current-account deficit, as a share of GDP, expanded from 1.7 to 3 percent in the latter part of the 1980s. These macroeconomic problems were occurring at a time of escalating unrest in different parts of the country, internally, and increased tension with Pakistan. Gandhi's government was accused of large-scale corruption in 1989 elections, which they lost.

In analyzing this period, there is significant disagreement as to the source of the more rapid economic growth. Rodrik and Subramaniam (2004) argue that there was an attitudinal shift of the Indira Gandhi government, and later the Rajiv Gandhi government, to a "pro-business" orientation instead of a "pro-market" orientation. A probusiness orientation concentrates on improving the existing businesses in a country and eases restrictions to enable this, instead of trade liberalization, which is generally promarket. In other words, it was not that the reforms eliminated restrictions and freed markets, but that the regulatory status of the state was reoriented. Instead of being aimed at production for the domestic market (import substitution), reforms were targeted to promote export production. This view is also argued by DeLong (2003), but it is contested by Panagariya (2004). Panagariya argues that it was fundamental reform aimed at freeing markets that promoted growth. Both sides agree that the growth in the 1980s was fragile and mainly funded by internal and international borrowing. This created a fiscal crisis such that, by 1991, India was on the verge of bankruptcy.

These attempts at reform can be seen as attempts to shift the basis for the transformation of the Indian economy. Initially, import substitution was used to raise the rate of return to investment in factory production for the domestic market. This initially met with some success, but inefficiency and corruption prevented these industries from rapid industrial growth. The reforms were aimed at raising the relative rate of return on investment for manufacturing production for export. The hope was that this would continue the shift to factory production, but on a basis that would allow for efficient long-term growth. However, the initial reforms were limited and the growth achieved was indeed quite fragile.

Rajiv Gandhi was succeeded by a coalition led V.P. Singh, but his National Front Coalition soon collapsed. He was replaced by Chandra Shekhar, but his government was toppled by the Congress (I) Party in 1991. In May 1991, however, Rajiv Gandhi was assassinated by a Sri Lankan Tamil terrorist and the elections had to thereby be postponed until the next month, when P.V. Narasimha Rao, the then leader of Congress (I), won the elections and became prime minister. The country witnessed some sweeping economic changes during the 1990s under Rao's leadership. By July of that year, the government, under the prime ministership of Rao and with Manmohan Singh as the finance minister (currently the prime minister of India), began a radical liberalization policy. Export-led growth was seen as the preferred course for the economy, along with increased foreign direct investments, to reduce its trade deficits. At about the same time, the decline of the Soviet Union and the collapse of communism in Eastern Europe led to declining trade with these markets. India thus had no choice but to enter the world market.

The reforms under Rao were aimed at deregulating industry and liberalizing trade in both goods and services. Specifically, investment licensing was eliminated (for the most part), greatly increasing freedom of entry into production. Public-sector monopolies in a variety of sectors were also eliminated, and a policy toward the automatic approval of foreign investment (up to 51 percent of foreign equity investment) was instituted. As to trade in goods, import licensing on virtually all intermediate inputs and capital was done away with. Later, import licensing on consumer goods was also eliminated. In addition, tariff rates were reduced. Exchange controls were lifted and the exchange rate unified and kept flexible. As to services, public-sector monopolies in areas such as insurance, banking, and telecommunications have been eliminated or significantly weakened in many areas. All these actions led to the remarkable growth of exports and annual average growth rates of real GDP and GDP per capita, of 6.24 and 4.4 percent, respectively, for the 1990s. However, many restrictions remain, especially in agriculture and in consumer-goods industries.

However, while the country flourished economically, the political situation took a turn for the worse. Religious tensions, which had always existed between Hindus and Muslims, escalated over the Babri Masjid mosque in Ayodhya, a town considered sacred by Hindus. This issue led to several Hindu-Muslim riots and thousands lost their lives. Several other similar incidents took place, such as the bombing of the Bombay Stock Exchange, where again hundreds of bystanders lost their lives. All these incidents increased the seats held by the opposition Hindu Nationalist Party, the BJP, in the 1993 elections. However, the party fared considerably better in the 1996 elections after they had considerably toned down the Hindu fundamentalist aspect of their beliefs. During this time separatist movements continued in several Indian states, and conflict continued between India and Pakistan.

The political situation described above led to an unstable economic environment especially for foreign investors. The Congress (I) Party lost its majority and Rao resigned as prime minister. He and a host of other politicians were also indicted on charges of corruption in 1997. The BJP, with a minority in parliament, formed a government on the invitation of the president of the country. Atal Bihari Vajpayee became the new prime minister, but resigned after thirteen days. In a span of two years, from 1996 to 1998, the prime minister's office was held by a succession of individuals, thereby adding to the political instability of the country.

The BJP won the 1998 elections and Vajpayee became prime minister again under a coalition government. The new government began its reign by declaring India as a nuclear power, leading first to Pakistan becoming a nuclear power, and second to much suspicion (and disapproval) from the rest of the world regarding India's nuclear intentions. In April of 1999 the BJP government lost its majority, but in the next election, held in October of the same year, the BJP won a majority and Vajpayee was again prime minister. Tension between India and Pakistan over a border dispute escalated in 2001 and 2002, but was diffused after international authorities became involved in the process. The relations between the two countries have been much improved since 2003. During the BJP's rule, India continued on its path of economic growth and reform following the path of trade liberalization ushered in during Narasimha Rao's leadership. India's information-technology (IT) industry made huge leaps into the world market, earning India millions of dollars due to the outsourcing of jobs related to the field of IT. India's foreign-exchange reserves also grew at a rapid rate and crossed $100 billion by 2004. The economy as a whole grew at rates of 5.2 and 4.6 percent for 2001 and 2002 (per capita GDP grew at 3.5 and 3.0 percent, respectively).

The Indian economy witnessed large-scale economic reforms and growth under the BJP government. The BJP, confident of victory, called an early election in May of 2004 but was defeated in a surprise upset by the Congress (I) Party. The current prime minister of India is Mamohan Singh, who had served as finance minister during Rao's regime and who ushered in large-scale economic reforms in the country.

A Theoretical Framework

The chapter on East Asia illustrated the important role played by a developmental state in promoting overall growth in Japan, Taiwan, and South Korea. The lack of effective states in much of sub-Saharan Africa was seen to be one of the major obstacles to economic progress. After independence, India sought to construct a developmental state, one that could establish an industrial state, promote rapid structural change, and achieve rapid rates of growth and poverty reduction. As was seen in the above discussion, the Indian state did succeed in establishing an industrial sector and did raise the growth rates of real GDP and real GDP per capita. However, in comparison with East Asia, the growth rates were generally much lower.

More importantly, the state became enmeshed in a patron-client system of politics. This style of politics has been discussed in detail in Chapter 4 on Sub-Saharan Africa, thus only a brief review of this style of politics is presented here. In this form of politics, the patrons (or political elite) seek to maintain their political position by providing benefits to their clients. In return, the latter provides political support for the former. Benefits are exchanged for support. Governance in such a system is hierarchical in nature, with a pyramiding of patron client ties via networks of relationships.

The political elite in such a system favor policies that short-circuit the operation of markets and create shortages for key commodities. In this context, the ruling patrons can use the powers of the state to determine who gets access to these scarce commodities. These political patrons will reward their supporters by allowing them access and punish their foes by denying such.

Corruption is rampant in this style of politics. Officials cease to make decisions based on rules and results and instead become dispensers of favors. They will misallocate resources and underfund public goods. Thus, efficiency will decline, trade will be taxed, and much of the resources of the state will be pilfered.

Indian society reflected this style of politics in that it was and is hier-archically constituted, with ultimate power held by a few individuals and groups of individuals who reside at the top of the power pyramid. This hegemony was perpetuated at various levels in the hierarchical structure. This led to a patron-client aspect in social relationships through the distri-bution of power and loyalties. The Indian bureaucracy was and is fraught with extensive corruption and an underground (i.e., "black") economy. The patron-client nature of the system prevents political expression of class-based interests.

It would thus seem that the attempt to construct a developmental state after independence failed. An effective developmental state is cohesive enough to formulate and implement policy in a coherent fashion, while extracting high performance standards from firms in exchange for sub-sidies (Chibber 2003). The Indian state seems to have evolved into an entity that could do neither effectively.

Why did this happen? Chibber argues that the establishment of an effective developmental state depends on the critical conflicts that occur between the state and societal actors. The argument is that the critical factor is the orientation of the business class toward the state. Specifically, in the case of East Asia and in particular South Korea, the capitalist/ business groups allied themselves with the political elite with the goal being overall development. Alternatively, in the Indian case, the agenda of the ruling elite (after independence) was frustrated by the domestic capitalist group. The latter refused to accept a state with strong regulatory and interventionist powers. Specifically, it resisted attempts by the state to discipline firms who received government subsidies. In South Korea, the capitalist class allowed itself to be disciplined; it did not resist.

Of course, this kind of explanation immediately leads to a second question. Why did capitalist groups react differently in the two regions (East Asia, South Asia)? Chibber argues that it was the choice of de-velopment strategy by the ruling elite. In India, the ruling elite chose an import-substitution strategy of economic development, while in South Korea the ruling elite focused on an export-based strategy. With an export-based strategy of development, firms can become increas-ingly successful only by becoming increasingly productive. Thus, the South Korean state's threats and action directed at disciplining firms was aimed at productivity enhancement, which is the long-term key to export success. Alternatively, in an inward-oriented strategy, firms are not interested in specializing to become productive in a selected line of products; instead, the incentive is for firms to diversify into an expanding variety of products, each requiring protection from competition. Thus, it was the development strategy chosen by the ruling elite that was crucial in determining how the incentive structure, guiding the behavior of capitalist/business groups, evolved.

These ideas capture at least part of the contrast between these two regions. However, the idea that it was the choice of development strategy that was key has a weakness. Both regions initially embarked on import-substitution strategies within which incentives were created for the expansion of production for the domestic market. In the East Asian case, this initial phase was followed by subsidies aimed at promoting production for foreign markets (i.e., export based). South Asia (India) is only just now beginning to make this shift and it remains to be seen whether it will follow through. So why was there a difference in policy between the two regions?

Chibber argues that the difference in policy choices stemmed from a difference in opportunity. Japanese firms were moving up the technological ladder in the late 1960s and early 1970s, moving from labor-intensive manufactured goods to more technologically complex goods. This meant that an opportunity to export the former to the large U.S. market was opening up. Foreign investment by Japanese firms in South Korea provided the expertise and marketing to allow South Korean firms to take advantage of these opportunities. The potential for rapid export growth presented itself. Those opportunities did not become available to India. While important, this explanation does not address why India could not create opportunities for itself in other markets as the Japanese did right after World War II.

There are probably several reasons why that was problematic. A clue to one of these answers lies in looking at the character of the economies in these two regions prior to independence. In East Asia, as discussed in Chapter 3, colonialism had resulted in the establishment of agricultural sectors that were highly productive and had significant potential for rapid future productivity growth. Thus, with independence, the ruling elite applied import-substitution policies within the context of dynamic rural economies. In addition, the level of human capital in rural areas was quite high by historical standards. Alternatively, in India's case, an import-substitution policy was applied within the context of a rural sector that was not dynamic and in which the potential for rapid productivity growth had not been developed.

This difference between the two regions had the following effects. It is assumed that the nationalist leaders who assumed power in the two regions (East Asia and India) were sincere in their desires to promote rapid growth. However, there are more selfish desires that also motivate decision making within the political elite—for example, the desire to enhance one's wealth through manipulating the power of public office. These two sets of desires can be reconciled by examining North's (1990) view of individual decision making. He sees individual behavior as being constrained by a number of factors, both formal and informal. There are also self-imposed moral codes of behavior. Individuals are willing to express themselves through these codes of behavior if the cost of doing so is relatively low. Thus, there is a tradeoff between choices based on pure self-interest and those based on self-imposed moral codes. One can think of a demand curve in which the lower the cost of expressing one's convictions, the more important will be the convictions as a determinant of choice.

Members of the political elite that took power in South and East Asia likely had codes of behavior that dictated that they should engage in policies that would be aimed at wealth enhancement for the well-being of their people. They were willing to set the good of the group above that of the ruling elite, up to a point. In other words, the willingness of the political elite to sacrifice self-interest for their nation's interests was a direct function of the costliness (to the elite) of doing so. The costliness would seem to depend on the probability of the success of a wealth-enhancement strategy. If the likelihood of success was high, and benefits would be generated quickly, then the cost to the political elite of sacrificing their self-interest would be low and thus the probability that the elite would engage in wealth-enhancement policies would be high. Alternatively, if the probability of success was low, then the cost to the elite of pursuing wealth enhancement for society would be high and the elite would be more likely to pursue strategies aimed to meet their own, narrow self-interest. That is, they are more likely to construct patron-client networks that allow them to use the resources of the state to enhance their own wealth and the wealth of their supporters, and reduce the wealth of their political opponents. The policies that result are likely to harm overall growth (Grabowski and Shields 1996).

With this argument in mind, recall the comparison of South and East Asia. In the latter, dynamic agricultural sectors already existed, within which significant amounts of human capital (education and skills) had already been accumulated. Strategies of wealth enhancement followed by export promotion were thus more likely to succeed. Alternatively, India had a stagnant rural sector in which levels of education and skill accumulation were very low. The probability that wealth enhancement, via import substitution and then export promotion, would work was low. Policy making by the political elite quickly degenerated into rent seeking, corruption, and patron-client politics.

There are variations on the above argument that can also be made. Infant-industry protection (i.e., import substitution) is likely to result in rapid increases in productivity and efficiency for the firms involved only if they can learn by doing (by producing) very rapidly. If the domestic market is growing rapidly, firms learn rapidly and become capable of competing internationally. Alternatively, if the domestic market is growing slowly, then newly established firms will grow slowly and learn slowly; they will not likely become competitive enough to begin exporting. In East Asia, the dynamic rural sector meant that there was rapid growth in the domestic market. It was therefore relatively easy to switch to an export-oriented strategy (from an import-substitution one). Alternatively, the stagnant rural economy of India meant that it was difficult to shift to an outward-oriented strategy, export promotion.

Do the policy reforms of the 1980s and 1990s imply that the Indian state (i.e., the Indian political elite) is becoming more developmental? Is the current economic expansion likely to be sustainable? If so, how was this change brought about? Globalization may have caused the political elite in India to become more developmental via a number of avenues. First, the rapid growth of China represents something of a threat to India. A rapidly growing China has also been a China that has become an increasingly powerful factor in the region. China and India have already clashed once in the postwar period. This potential threat may have focused the ruling elite on economic policies aimed at wealth enhancement.

India may also be looking to China as a role model. The latter has acted as a magnet for foreign investment and this investment is part of why China has grown so rapidly. India's ruling elite modified their policies to provide a more hospitable environment for foreign investment. A simple perspective here is that, in a global financial system, those countries that threaten foreign investors will find capital fleeing to regions where the environment is more hospitable. Bad policy is punished, good policy rewarded.

Another factor may have been the success of the green-revolution technologies. The rapid growth in grain production allowed India to solve its food problem. Parts of the rural sector of India became quite dynamic. This likely made it easier for the rural sector to release resources for export promotion. However, this also points to the fragility of the Indian growth experience. A large segment of the rural area is not dynamic, and therefore productivity is not growing rapidly. In addition, levels of education and skill (i.e., human capital) are still low throughout much of rural India. Further, severe drought and rural distress still have significant potential for derailing the growth process. The rural sector is not broadly dynamic. Can industrialization and export promotion proceed with a stagnant rural economy? If not, India's current economic success may be quite fragile.

A further reason why the Indian growth experience may be fragile has to do with the structure of the political system. As was argued above, Indian politics is of the patron-client variety. The restraints on the political behavior of the elite are rather limited. Rent-seeking behavior and corruption abound. This contrasts with India's formal institutional structure. According to its constitution, India is a parliamentary democracy and there are many formal rules that, in effect, should place constraints on the ruling elite. Thus, the formal sets of institutional rules place checks and balances on the exercise of power, while the informal rules allow the ruling elite to get around these rules by manipulating its clients (political supporters). The *de jure* institutional structure is much different from the *de facto* institutional structure.

This divergence implies that the commitment problem is not entirely resolved. As the reader will recall, a state strong enough to protect property rights is a state strong enough to take them away. How is the state to credibly commit to wealth-enhancing policies? It was argued in earlier chapters that credibility in commitment could only occur as the result of a struggle between the ruling elite and the bulk of society. If the ruling elite is dependent on society in general for the resources necessary to maintain their position, then they will have to design institutional mechanisms that penetrate society to allow for the extraction of those resources. The members of society will stubbornly resist those efforts unless they are provided with the services and resources that they need. It is out of this struggle that institutional rules arise that allow for the solution of the commitment problem.

India has not yet undergone this process, and thus the commitment problem has yet to be resolved. However, the situation seems right for this process to unfold. India's recent economic success has been impressive. However, as Kalkar (2001) has pointed out, there is enormous fiscal stress on the central and state governments. The combined fiscal deficits of these two layers of government have reached 10 percent of GDP. This is one of the highest ratios in the world. The national debt is as much as 82 percent of GNP and is rapidly increasing. This has resulted from the massive borrowing undertaken by both state governments as well as the central government. Tax capabilities must be developed as part of the solution. Specifically, there will need to be an increase in the tax-to-GDP ratio through improved tax administration. In order to accomplish this, a struggle must occur within which firms and households will demand adequate services in return. The struggle that ensues will create an informal set of rules that will eventually become the *de jure* constraints on government behavior. It is through this mechanism that the commitment problem can be resolved.

A part of the above solution is likely to be the creation of a system of fiscal federalism, or what Montinola, Qian, and Weingast (1995) have called "market-preserving federalism." Such a system is characterized by a hierarchy of governments with a delineated scope of authority in which the subnational governments have primary authority over the economy. In these schemes, the national government has the authority to police the common market. Revenue sharing among governments is restricted and thus all levels of government face a hard budget constraint. This structure must have an institutionalized degree of durability.

Such federalism allows state governments to experiment with a variety of economic strategies. Those that succeed will enhance the prosperity of their particular state and this will allow the state government to collect additional tax revenue. Those experiments that fail will reduce the revenue of the state government. Economic competition among the state governments will reward economic success and punish failure. This will act to restrain government choices, predatory state behavior will decline, and the commitment problem is resolved. More will be said about this later, when the recent experience of China is discussed. For now it is only being argued that through the process of conflict and struggle discussed above a market-enhancing fiscal form of federalism may be the result.

The most glaring weakness in the notion that India has now become developmental is still connected with weaknesses in the agricultural sector. In a study utilizing pooled state-level data for India for the period 1957–91, Datt and Ravallion (1998) found that progress in raising rural living standards has been quite diverse across Indian states. Differences in trend rates of poverty reduction seem to be strongly linked to trend growth rates in average farm yields (productivity growth). Differences in trend rates of growth in nonagricultural production were found, but were not linked to differences in the rates of poverty reduction. Also, higher irrigation intensity, higher literacy, and lower infant morality all contributed to higher long-term rates of poverty reduction.

In more recent empirical work by Datt and Ravallion (2002), the more rapid growth of India in the 1990s does not seem to have resulted in a more rapid rate of poverty reduction. In addition, states with relatively low levels of initial rural development and human-capital development were not well suited to reduce poverty in response to economic growth.

Having examined the historical development of the Indian economy, attention will now turn to presenting an overview of India's current situation in terms of population, poverty, agriculture, religion, caste, gender bias, and education. This will then be followed by an analysis of what has been learned.

Population Growth and Unemployment

Population growth is and has been a chronic problem for the region of South Asia. This region experienced rapid economic and social development during the 1990s. While it has been among the world's fastest-growing regions, improving the health and education of its people and reducing poverty rates, it remains a region enormously challenged to improve the quality of life for all its 1.4 billion citizens. During 1950–60 and 1960–70, while GNP increased by 3.5 and 4.1 percent, per capita income grew only by 1.4 and 1.8 percent, respectively (Uppal 1977). Population growth has been perceived as a serious threat to economic development in this region. The decades following 1941 onward found Bangladesh, India, Sri Lanka, and Pakistan all experiencing annual population growth rates of 2 percent and above. This growth has been associated with the phase of the demographic transition associated with a fall in mortality rates not accompanied by a comparative fall in birth rates.

The past decade saw India exceed 1 billion in its population. India was the first among the South Asian countries to incorporate population planning into its economic plans, starting in 1951. According to an Indian planning-commission report, the recent ninth of the five-year plans in India, projects a decline in the population growth rate to 1.59

percent per annum by the end of the Ninth Plan (2002–07), down from over 2 percent in the last three decades. However, it expects the growth rate of the labor force to reach a peak level of 2.54 percent per annum over this period, the highest it has ever been and is ever likely to attain. This has resulted from the change in age structure, with the highest growth occurring in the age group fifteen to nineteen years in the Ninth Plan period.

The addition to the labor force during the Ninth Plan period is estimated to be 53 million. The acceleration in the economy's growth rate to 7 percent per annum, with special emphasis on the agriculture sector, is expected to help in creating 54 million work opportunities over the period. This would lead to a reduction in the open unemployment rate, from 1.9 percent during 1996–97 to 1.47 percent by 2007. According to the planning commission, the states which face the prospect of increased unemployment in the post–Ninth Plan period are Bihar, Rajasthan, Uttar Pradesh, Kerala, and Punjab.

The Indian economy is characterized by significant underemployment, wherein people are hired at jobs for which they are over qualified. In 1993 and 1994, open unemployment was only 2 percent, while the incidence of underemployment and unemployment taken together was as much as 10 percent. Low levels of education, human capital, and gender bias characterize the Indian labor force. Table 5.1 shows that the majority of the labor force has primary-level education.

The gender bias in employment is also clear from Table 5.2. It can be seen that females are highly underrepresented in full-time employment (main workers), though one sees more females in part-time employment (marginal workers), which is typically underpaid and more insecure. One consequence is the higher percentage of unemployed females compared with males. Moreover, if one looked deeper into the different categories of employment, one can again see gender bias in the form of men being employed typically in higher-paid jobs, with higher responsibility and status compared with women. This is linked to the gender bias in education and sociocultural expectations and practices.

The majority of the labor force in India is employed in the "unorganized sector," that is, sectors that do not provide workers with social security and other benefits of employment. In the rural areas, agricultural workers form the bulk of the unorganized sector. In urban India, contract, subcontract, and migratory agricultural laborers make up most of the unorganized labor force. The unorganized sector is made up of

Table 5.1

Education by Gender

State/Union territory	Total/Rural/Urban	Sex	Number of main workers	Proportion of workers with educational level (in percent)					
				Illiterate	Below primary	Primary but below middle	Middle but below matriculate	Matriculate but below graduate	Graduate and above
India*	Total	P	285,932,493	51.0	7.8	13.9	10.9	11.9	4.4
		M	221,658,584	43.3	8.7	15.8	13.0	14.2	5.0
		F	64,273,909	77.8	4.8	7.3	3.7	3.9	2.5
	Rural	P	222,289,579	58.2	8.3	13.6	9.7	8.4	1.8
		M	166,293,608	50.1	9.5	15.9	11.9	10.5	2.2
		F	55,995,971	82.3	4.7	6.9	3.3	2.2	0.5
	Urban	P	63,642,914	26.0	6.3	14.7	15.0	24.2	13.7
		M	55,364,976	22.8	6.4	15.5	16.3	25.5	13.4
		F	8,277,938	47.0	5.3	9.5	6.7	15.6	15.9

Source: Census of India (1991).

Note: P = persons, M = males, F = females.

* Jammu and Kashmir were excluded due to lack of available data.

Table 5.2

Employment by Gender

State/Union Territory	Sex	Population	Main workers	Marginal workers	Nonworkers
				%	
1	2	3	4	5	6
India*	Persons	838,567,936	34.1	3.4	62.5
	Males	435,208,158	50.9	0.6	48.4
	Females	403,359,778	15.9	6.3	77.7

Source: Census of India (1991).
*Jammu and Kashmir were excluded due to lack of available data.

jobs to which minimum wage is rarely extended. Moreover, laborers do not have job protection through membership in labor unions. These features combine to create overwhelming levels of poverty, both rural and urban.

Last but not least, child labor remains and continues to be a pervasive problem in India in particular and in South Asia in general. Some of the reasons given for the existence of child labor are poverty, lack of education, the caste system, an absence of extensive social-welfare schemes, a lack of access to loans, the attitudes of parents, and lower wages. All the South Asian countries have enacted legislation that addresses some aspects of child labor, such as bonded labor or the employment of children in hazardous industries, and have implemented some innovative projects in child-labor pockets, such as the ready-made garment industry in Bangladesh and the "carpet belt" in India. The rates of child labor tend to be higher among boys and in rural areas since girls work in informal sectors, such as within the home or as domestics (which is harder to capture in the statistics). India is home to the largest concentration of child laborers in the world, in spite of initiatives designed to reduce child labor dating back to British rule and since independence. In 1987, India devised a new child-labor policy under the Rao government to acknowledge and address the problem and reduce child labor on a large scale. However, child labor continues to remain a pervasive problem in the country. The 1981 Indian census estimated 13.6 million child laborers.

Poverty

For the past decade, South Asia has been the second fastest-growing region in the world, after East Asia. In spite of the economic progress, more than one-third of the people in the region (530 million) live in extreme poverty, surviving on less than $1 a day (according to the United Nations Development Programme). South Asia's pervasive poverty is both a cause and consequence of its low level of human development. Despite improvements in education and health services, the region still has the world's highest illiteracy rate. South Asia also has one of the highest maternal mortality ratios in the world and, in addition, is home to millions of malnourished children. Environmental degradation, inadequate infrastructure, and social exclusion are among the other numerous obstacles to growth and poverty reduction.

The economic success of the region has resulted in a significant drop in poverty rates in the recent decade, however. Estimates for India in the late 1970s put the number of people who lived in poverty at 300 million, or nearly 50 percent of the population at the time. Poverty was reduced during the 1980s, and in 1989 it was estimated that about 26 percent of the population, or 220 million people, lived below the poverty line. Slower economic growth and higher inflation in 1990 and 1991 reversed this trend. In 1991, it was estimated that 332 million people, or 38 percent of the population, lived below the poverty line. Estimates for 1999 and 2000 showed that there had been a 10 percent drop in poverty between 1993–94 and 1999–2000. However, it was later found that a national sample survey of consumption conducted in 1999 and 2000 to estimate the number of poor had introduced major changes in the survey design, making the new estimates incomparable with previous ones. The new survey led to an overestimation of consumption, thus showing a sharper reduction in poverty than actually occurred. Researchers at the Jawaharlal Nehru University in New Delhi made the necessary corrections to the new survey to make it comparable and showed that the poverty ratio had declined by only 2.8 percent between 1993–94 and 1999–2000, and that there was an increase in the number of poor by some 5 to 6 million. In spite of these mistakes, it is obvious that the country has been experiencing declining trends in poverty since the late 1980s and through the 1990s.

The poverty rates in India have varied between regions and between Indian states. According to Deaton and Drèze (2002), regional disparities in poverty increased in the 1990s, with the southern and western regions doing much better than the northern and eastern regions. Moreover, economic inequality also increased within states, especially within urban areas, and between urban and rural areas. The poverty rankings of the different Indian states in 1990 were very different from those in 1960, suggesting that the states had different levels of success in dealing with the problem. According to Datt and Ravaillion (1998), infrastructure and improved human resources in some states lowered long-term poverty rates, while deviations from these trends were caused by inflation and shocks to farm yields.

Several steps are being taken to tackle the problem of poverty. The World Bank–sponsored Poverty Reduction Strategy Papers (PRSPs) is one such example. Pakistan completed its interim PRSP in December 2001. Sri Lanka's PRSP, *Regaining Sri Lanka,* was discussed by a joint World Bank/International Monetary Fund board in February 2003. PRSPs for Bangladesh, Nepal, Bhutan, and Maldives are also underway. Though there is much debate among economists in terms of the real gains to a country from foreign aid, South Asia is the largest regional recipient of concessional lending from the International Development Association, the World Bank affiliate that provides interest-free loans to the world's poorest countries. India is the largest single cumulative recipient of World Bank assistance, with lending totaling over $59 billion at the end of 2003. Substantial amounts have also been received by Pakistan, with around $13 billion, and Bangladesh, with around $10 billion in cumulative lending.

Dependence on Agriculture

The Indian economy has been dominated by the agricultural sector, with 70 percent of the Indian population depending on this sector for its livelihood at the time of independence and with agriculture accounting for 50 percent of its GDP (Heitsman and Worden 1996). Agriculture in the immediate postindependence period suffered due to droughts and famines. Agricultural technology in India has been primarily labor intensive and traditional in nature, characterized by dependence on the irregular monsoon rains. One of the unique features of the Indian subcontinent is how almost its entire rainfall is concentrated in the few monsoon months. Only a small percentage of Indian farmers enjoy the luxury of natural irrigation. Thus, all through history Indian agriculture has been linked with effective water-management practices. The green revolution in the

1960s was a first step in raising productivity levels through better irrigation and use of better technology, such as high-yielding seeds, even though it may have increased income inequality between rich and poor farmers and between states that were more advanced in irrigation and agriculture technology compared with others.

Following independence, the Congress (I) Party conducted a contradictory policy with respect to Indian agriculture. While it attempted to reduce problems in the Indian countryside by investing in irrigation, agroresearch, agromodernization, and mechanization, these efforts were restricted by its reluctance to hurt the interests of the feudal and mercantile intermediaries. Over time, a combination of peasant uprisings and the gradual expansion of industrial capitalism has brought about significant changes in rural India. Today one can identify three categories of Indian farmers: those who have become rich capitalist farmers; a large middle layer, who sometimes profit in good agricultural years; and the poorest farmers, who are barely able to survive, even in "good" years. A fourth group includes seasonal laborers, who are mainly landless and who work for the first and second category of farmers, usually as sharecroppers.

Traditional agriculture could not keep up with population growth. However, government support of the green revolution, which encouraged the use of high-yielding crops, fertilizers, and managed irrigation in the northern Punjab region of India in the 1970s, allowed India to gain self-sufficiency in food production by the mid-1980s. However, the green revolution also left behind states that, unlike the Punjab region, were not endowed with irrigation and fertile soil. Moreover, even within the Punjab region, wealthier farmers were able to take advantage of the green revolution by investing in new technology, which increased their productivity dramatically, but also increased the disparity between them and the poorer farmers, who were unable to invest. Moreover, the government followed a policy of urban bias by artificially keeping down food prices while pushing up industrial prices through tariff barriers. Finally, agricultural trade was restricted by regulations and "canalizing agencies" that controlled agricultural exports. These policies led to distortions in prices in both agricultural and industrial sectors of the economy, and to the misallocation of resources.

One of the areas targeted by the economic reforms of 1991 was the urban bias in policy. Industrial tariffs were thus gradually reduced. In 1994, controls on agriculture were also reduced, although some restrictions remain in place. Devaluation of the currency, the rupee, further added to the competitiveness of Indian agriculture. Subsequent to these reforms, agricultural growth has been, on average, 3 percent between 1991–92 and 1995–96 (Gulati 1998). According to the World Bank (1997), the growth would have been higher but for the liberalization of input prices, such as fertilizers and high-yielding seeds, whose prices rose dramatically and negatively, affecting Indian farmers. Moreover, the reforms often did not reach small- and medium-scale farmers, who neither benefit from economies of scale in production nor low-interest loans.

One of the main limitations for India's competitiveness in the world market and in its own domestic market is its poor infrastructure. The government is taking steps to improve this by building state and interstate highways that will connect all major cities, business centers, and ports. However, these are expensive and time-consuming undertakings, and the economy pays the price while it waits for their completion. India's regional disparities in agricultural productivity and growth can be partially traced to differences in levels of public investment in infrastructure for agriculture, particularly investments in irrigation technologies and rural credit (Rao 1994, Datt and Ravallion 1998, Gulati and Kelley 1999).

Agriculture's share in India's GDP has declined in recent years, thus marking a structural shift in the composition of the GDP. Agriculture's share in the GDP was only 32 percent by the mid-1980s, alongside an increasing share of the manufacturing and service sector. A falling share of agricultural sector in the GDP and an increase in production shows that total factor productivity in agriculture has improved over time, with a growth in annual average value added in agriculture being 3.1 percent from 1980 to 1990 (Krueger and Chinoy 2002).

Religion and Caste

The main religions practiced are Hinduism, Buddhism, and Islam, but there are also Christians, Sikhs, Jains, Zoroastrians, and some Jews. These religions are quite distinct from one another and the countries in this region have seen several instances of violence associated with religious differences. A number of the South Asian religions, such as Hinduism, Islam, and Sikhism, have significant common roots and share certain social practices (such as the extended-family system), marriage practices (endogamy in marriage in southern India and among Muslims), and certain rituals (such as saint worship).

Hinduism, unlike most others, has no formal founder or formal church.

It can be traced back roughly to ancient Aryan beliefs and practices. Hinduism defines much of Indian culture and tradition and is practiced by the majority of Indians. The principle religious texts of Hinduism include the Vedas, the Upanishads, and the two famous epics called the *Ramayana* and the *Mahabharata*. Islam is one of the most widely followed religions in the world. The Prophet Muhammad founded it and its religious text is the Koran. Buddhism was developed by Prince Siddhartha, later known, on reaching enlightenment, as the Buddha. Though Buddhism does not follow any particular religious text, it teaches its followers to believe in the "four noble truths," to follow the "eightfold path" of virtues to attain "nirvana," which is enlightenment. Buddhism is an important and influential religion of South Asia and has many followers all over the world. Sikhism is one of the newest major religions of the world. If was founded by Guru Nanak, who was born a high-caste Hindu in India. The major religious text of Sikhism is the Adi Granth or the Guru Granth Sahib. Jainism was founded by Mahavira in the sixth century BC. It is similar to Buddhism in its teachings. The Zoroastrians are also called Parsis in India. It was founded by Zoroaster and follows the Avesta as its principle text.

Before the spread of colonialism, the common roots shared by the different religions formed a bond between the diverse traditions within South Asia. However, with the spread of colonialism and the introduction of protestant Christianity, significant changes were introduced into the preexisting religious traditions. Some of these included an increased attention to textual content resulting in the increasing importance of certain upper castes within society who had mastery over the religious texts, a greater division within groups, efforts to create personal and family laws related to religions (such as the Hindu Undivided Family Act, inheritance, marriage, etc.), and a greater importance of caste through its inclusion in electoral politics.

The caste system, which was originally associated with the division of labor within Hinduism, today has permeated into almost all religions in the Indian subcontinent. The caste (or varna) system dates back thousands of years. Traditionally, there were three main castes: Brahmins, Khashatriyas, and the Vaishyas. The Brahmins were the teachers and conductors of religious services; the Khashtriyas were the warriors, and the Vaishyas the traders. This hierarchical structure associated with the Aryan people did not include the untouchables, also called the Dalits, or Sudras, though they have over time become a fourth caste within the system.

Hindus were believed to be born into a certain caste. In other words, caste was a predetermined aspect of one's life, except in the case of an intercaste marriage (traditionally shunned) where the bride automatically gave up her caste and got inducted into the husband's caste upon marriage. Though the caste system has been considerably weakened, in terms of being associated with particular professions it continues to dominate the subcontinent's society.

By allowing caste to enter into electoral politics, caste has gained in importance. According to Osborne (2001), the large role played by the government in India has influenced how the caste system has evolved there. Analysis of recent Indian elections confirms that caste has grown in importance in national and state politics in India. Thus, it seems odd that while caste has become less important in economics, it has become more important in politics. Osborne argues that this has happened due to the criteria the Indian government has chosen for reservations, treated as a special class. In most other countries, the disadvantaged classes are identified on economic principles, but in India they have been identified based on their membership into the lowest castes. This has made the task of identification easier for the Indian government since caste is a preexisting condition. Data show that the proportion of Indians qualifying for such reservations has grown dramatically since independence. Thus, government distribution of rents based on caste and ethnicity has led to the expansion and firmness of the caste system, though this might not have been the intended consequence.

Gender Bias

Gender bias has been a part of almost every aspect of life in South Asia and has been extensively documented. Promoting gender equality and empowerment of women is one of the "Millennium Development Goals" of the World Bank. The most common areas of gender bias are evident in the labor market, in education, and within the household. As a region, South Asia has both the lowest literacy rates and the largest gap between the rates of male and female literacy. According to the 1971 census, only 46 percent of males and 22 percent of females were literate. By 1991, the literacy rates were 64.1 percent for males versus 39.29 percent for females. The numbers vary by age group and place (urban versus rural). According to the annual report *Human Development in South Asia* (Haq 2000), while South Asian women make up about 21 percent of the world's female population, 44 percent of the world's illiterate women are South Asian.

In South Asia, men and women have about the same life expectancies, whereas everywhere else females have a longer life expectancy than men. Hence, South Asia is the only region in the world where there are more men than women—where the natural ratio of women to men is severely distorted. In the late 1980s, the Indian economist Amartya Sen coined the term "missing women" to describe the great numbers of women in the world who are literally not alive due to discrimination. According to 1991 Bangladeshi census figures, for every 1,000 men, there were only 945 women. This number for India was 927 women for every 1,000 men, while the ratio worldwide is 1,060 women for every 1,000 men. The sex ratio is even more greatly distorted in some regions of India. In part of the states of Bihar and Rajasthan, the female-male ratio is 600 to 1,000. Sen estimated that, worldwide, there are 100 million missing women. More recent estimates suggest that there are 50 million missing women in India alone.

The condition of women's health has far-reaching consequences. It has been established that women in poor health are more likely to give birth to low-birth-weight babies and would be less likely to provide adequate care for their children. Moreover, the health of the female head of household also affects the economic well-being of the family. Women of South Asia face serious health concerns, including concerns about reproductive health, violence, nutrition, and HIV/AIDS. Many of the health problems are related to high levels of fertility. It has been found that place of residence, education, and religion are strongly related to both fertility and contraceptive use in India. Maternal mortality and morbidity are two direct consequences of high levels of fertility (Velkoff and Adlakha 1998). The spread of HIV/AIDS is a more recent but urgent issue facing South Asia. According to UNAIDS, over 7.4 million people in Asia are living with HIV/AIDS, comprising nearly one-fifth of the world's HIV infections. Almost two-thirds of those infected are living in India. Other countries in the region, such as Bangladesh, Pakistan, and Nepal, are characterized by a low prevalence among the general population, but have significantly higher rates among certain subpopulations.

Women of South Asia in general and India in particular face bias in education (see earlier discussion), in spite of the government's pledge of education for all. The consequences of women's illiteracy are not just economic, since studies have shown that uneducated women typically have high levels of fertility and mortality. Additionally, a mother's lack of education has adverse consequences for her children as well. The 1951 census, taken just after India's independence, showed that 9 percent of the female population and 27 percent of males were literate. By 1971, only 22 percent of women and 46 percent of men were literate, and by 1991, 40 percent of women and 64 percent of men were literate. Unfortunately, of the literate women, a majority has only primary-level education, which may not necessarily be enough education to improve their economic status. Large disparities in education level and a gender gap continues to exist among the Indian states. Some of the reasons for such disparities are poverty, parental education and attitude, societal norms, lack of adequate school facilities, lack of access, lack of teachers, and so on.

The labor-market participation of women in this region is markedly lower compared with the rest of the world. Moreover, women are mostly working in the informal and agricultural sectors of the economy and in unpaid jobs, which easily go unnoticed. According to World Bank estimates, as late as 2001 only 14 percent of the women in South Asia worked in the nonagricultural sector. The reason behind the discrimination lies to some extent on the supply side due to a mismatch between the costs of educating daughters and the returns to such education. Education comes with various explicit costs (of books, tuition) and implicit costs (opportunity cost of loss of earning from child labor or helping with household work, psychic cost of societal attitudes toward female education), and as long as the returns to education do not match or overcome these costs, parents have no incentive to educate daughters. On average, South Asian women work at least ten to twelve hours a day, while men, on an average, work two to four hours less, and still, in rural areas, females earn one-third that of their male counterparts. Poverty is a related consequence of labor-market discrimination—so much so that the world is witness to what is termed the "feminization of poverty." With reduced participation in the labor market and relatively lower wages, women become increasingly economically dependent and victim to further discrimination.

At the household level, there is documented evidence of gender discrimination in intra-household allocation of resources. Further, the extended-family system means that sons are perceived as the caregivers of parents in their old age, while daughters are married and take care of their in-laws. This increases the reliance of parents on sons, especially given that the state does not provide any mandated social security after retirement age. Another major bias against daughters comes from the practice of dowry, which is the payment made by parents of the bride to the parents of the son-in-law at the time of marriage. (The payment from the groom's family to the bride's is called bride-price.) Dowry is interpreted by some as the premortem inheritance of the bride, passed to her at the time of her marriage. Hindu custom historically prohibited women from inheriting land, particularly when there were male heirs and dowry was seen as an avenue for parents to leave a bequest for their daughters. However, over time, dowry has changed in tenor and has become an expected price to be paid by parents of daughters at the time of marriage. Dowry payments have become an unwelcome ritual, have inflated over time (Rao 1994), and have been associated with much violence against women. The National Crime Records Bureau of India quotes that there were 6,917 dowry deaths in India during 1998, though the real numbers were probably much higher. Moreover, though the dowry was traditionally associated with Hindus, it is widely practiced among different religious sects within India as well as in Pakistan and Bangladesh. Just as a daughter's marriage imposes a direct dowry cost on parents, a son, on the other hand, is a source of income since the dowry is earned from the daughter-in-law's family.

Because of gender bias, parents make higher human-capital investments for sons than for daughters. Average enrollment rates for South Asia for the period 1966 to 1996 were about 59 percent for females and 89 percent for males at the primary level and 23 and 37 percent at the secondary level (Self and Grabowski 2002). Thus girls are caught in a vicious cycle of bias. Daughters are educated less because they are not seen as a potential source of income and security for parents in their old age. Moreover, daughters impose a cost by way of a dowry and therefore there is no incentive to further increase the cost of daughters by paying for their education, even if one accepts that parents derive genuine pleasure from educating both sons and daughters. If the only alternative to education is child labor, it appears to be economically logical to educate the sons and use daughters for child labor. Though documented evidence suggests larger numbers for boys in child labor, this does not necessarily reflect the true scenario, since girls work in the informal sector, such as within homes and households, which is harder to identify statistically. Due to lack of education, girls lose their bargaining position in the labor market, which increases their economic reliance on male members within the household.

It seems strange, therefore, when one notices that in spite of such clear indications and examples of gender bias in society, there are numerous examples of females in leadership roles in the political arena in India in particular and in South Asia as a region. Some prominent examples are Indira Gandhi and Sonia Gandhi of India; Fatima Jinnah, Benazir Bhutto, and Nusrat Bhutto of Pakistan; Sheikh Hasina Wajed and Begum Khaleda Zia of Bangladesh; Sirimavo Bandaranaike of Sri Lanka; and Aung San Suu Kyi of Burma. One can find examples of prominent women political leaders elsewhere in the world, too, but there appears to be a concentration of them in this part of the world, so well known for its bias against the female gender. However, if one looks deeper, one will see that the women of South Asia have come to power following dramatic circumstances, such as an assassination of a spouse or father, sudden death of the previous leader, coups, or by moving to the forefront of the opposition against nondemocratic forces (Richter 1991). Moreover, Richter adds, these women leaders generally lack an institutional base, a regional constituency, an administrative track record, or military niche. The key variables in female leadership in this region of the world have been the ideology of patriarchy, familial ties, martyrdom, social class, female lifestyles, historical context, prison experiences, and electoral arrangements. Thus, Richter concludes that opportunities for female leadership have not brought about political liberalism and gender equality remains elusive in spite of so many glowing examples of female leaders in these countries.

Education

According to human-development reports (Haq 1997, Haq and Haq 1998), South Asia contains about half of the world's nonliterate population. Ironically, this region has experienced robust economic progress, but a lack of political commitment, at least in some of the countries, has left the region in an abysmal situation. As early as 1960, while Sri Lanka allocated 4 percent of its GNP to educational expenditure, India's allocation was less than 2.5 percent, and Bangladesh's and Pakistan's allocation was even lower (Rampal 2000). Moreover, education in this region has typically been of inferior quality. The reports on "Basic Education for the Empowerment of the Poor" (UNESCO 1998) found that primary education is plagued with lack of relevance and poor quality in almost all countries in South Asia. Over and above dealing with the abject poverty of students, schools suffer from a lack of teachers, unqualified teachers, a lack of adequate facilities, a lack of adequate funds, a lack of textbooks, irrelevant curricula, and so forth (Rampal 2000). Most of the countries in South Asia have realized that the existing highly centralized system has been responsible for the poor quality of education. The countries have now decided to move toward a decentralized system in education, but there is no mechanism in place to achieve this decentralization. Ironically, however, one needs to keep in mind that decentralization has the potential of becoming a political ploy for national governments to appease regional governments with little done by way of implementation (Weiler 1983).

Taking an in-depth look at education for a particular country such as India, one sees that education did not make much progress under British rule. It was geared toward the elite who could help administer the country. At the time of independence, India inherited an educational system that was characterized by imbalance between regions as well as within regions. The literacy rate in 1947 was a mere 11 percent. Some of the typical features of the economy leading to educational imbalance were economic inequality, gender disparity, and rigid social stratification. Upon gaining independence, the government resolved to provide free education to all up to the age of fourteen by 1960. However, there were clear inconsistencies between goals and actions. The goal set in the constitution was repeatedly revised, but the policies that were implemented to achieve these goals were short lived or failed. A breakthrough in improving literacy was achieved with the National Literacy Mission in 1988. The success of experiments conducted in Kottayam and Ernakulam in the state of Kerala added to the momentum of this campaign. For the first time, literacy was perceived as a tool for achieving social change, a big part of which consists of gender equality.

The last decade has seen the most remarkable progress made in education so far, though the level of success was not evenly distributed between the states. The 2001 Indian census claimed that, overall for the country, the male literacy rate stood at 75.85 percent, the female at 54.16 percent. Moreover, according to the 2001 census, most states had achieved 60 percent literacy rate for males and 50 percent literacy rate for females. Table 5.3 (see page 190) illustrates the distribution of literacy rates in the Indian states and the improvements that have been made since 1991.

According to Kingdom et al. (2004), the demand-side factors responsible for the increasing trends seen above are the lowered poverty rate and fertility rate and increased returns to education. On the supply side, the factors are centrally and externally funded education projects, improved management through decentralization, use of "para-[professional] teachers," and the spread of private education.

India has experienced some progress in its education in recent decades. The "District Primary Education Project I, II and III" of the World Bank (1999) found that from 1995 to 1998 there was an average increase in enrollment in all districts surveyed. Moreover, an analysis of forty districts reported that the average number of years taken to complete five years of primary education dropped from 7.9 to 6.4 years. The midterm assessment study reported an increase in student learning achievement in both mathematics and language, especially from grades one to two. In addition, the gender gap in learning achievement had been reduced to less than five percentage points. These are all encouraging trends for the Indian economy.

In spite of recent progress, one of the serious problems facing education in India has been its growing population. Even though birth rates have been declining steadily, the total population has been increasing and has surpassed 1 billion people. The distribution of the growing population has been different in the different states of India. According to Kingdom et al., the states of Bihar, Madhya Pradesh, Uttar Pradesh, and Rajasthan have experienced an increase in the school-age population, while in the others the school-age population has remained steady or declined. The levels and trends in public expenditure on education is another problem facing the country, and the distribution of the existing expenditure is worrisome. Kingdom et al. reports that the bulk of the existing expenditure goes toward increasing teachers' salaries instead of areas in greater need of funding. Enrollments have seen upward trends in recent decades, but the country is nowhere near achieving universal education. Moreover, a gender gap continues to exist at all levels of education, class sizes are too large, pupil-to-teacher ratios are high, dropout rates are extremely high, and stark inequalities exist in terms of access, attainment, caste, rural and urban levels, and across states and districts (ibid.).

What We Have Learned

The South Asian experience has been quite interesting. It is a region of great diversity in terms of ethnic groups, religion, language, and culture. Concentrating on India, stagnation and subsistence did not predominate in the precolonial period. Instead, Smithian growth did occur, trade expanded greatly, and protoindustrial manufacturing reached a high level

Table 5.3

Literacy Rates by Indian State/Union Territory

State	Literacy rate (2001 Census, in percent)			Literacy rate (1991)	Change in literacy rate (1991–2001)
	Persons	Males	Females		
India 1	65.38	75.96	54.28	51.63	13.75
Andhra Pradesh	61.11	70.85	51.17	44.09	17.02
Arunachal Pradesh	54.74	64.07	44.24	41.59	13.15
Assam	64.28	71.93	56.03	52.89	11.52
Bihar	47.53	60.32	33.57	37.49	10.04
Chhatisgarh	65.18	77.86	52.40	42.91	22.27
Goa	82.32	88.88	75.51	75.51	6.81
Gujarat	69.97	80.50	58.60	61.29	8.68
Haryana	68.59	79.25	56.31	55.85	12.74
Himachal Pradesh	77.13	86.02	68.08	63.86	13.27
Jharkhand	54.13	67.94	39.38	41.39	12.74
Karnataka	67.04	76.29	57.45	56.04	11.00
Kerala	90.92	94.20	87.86	89.81	1.11
Madhya Pradesh	64.11	76.80	50.28	44.67	19.41
Maharashtra	77.27	86.27	67.51	64.87	12.39
Manipur	68.87	77.87	59.70	59.89	8.97
Meghalaya	63.31	66.14	60.41	49.10	14.21
Mizoram	88.49	90.69	86.13	82.27	6.22
Nagaland	67.11	71.77	61.92	61.65	5.45
Orissa	63.61	75.95	50.97	49.09	14.52
Punjab	69.95	75.63	63.55	58.51	11.45
Rajasthan	61.03	76.46	44.34	38.55	22.48
Sikkim	69.68	76.73	61.46	56.94	12.61

Punjab	69.95	75.63	63.55	58.51	11.45
Rajasthan	61.03	76.46	44.34	38.55	22.48
Sikkim	69.68	76.73	61.46	56.94	12.61
Tamil Nadu	73.47	82.33	64.55	62.66	10.81
Tripura	73.66	81.47	65.41	60.44	13.22
Uttar Pradesh	57.36	70.23	42.98	40.71	16.65
Uttaranchal	72.28	84.01	60.26	57.75	14.53
West Bengal	69.22	77.58	60.22	57.70	11.52
Union territory					
Pondicherry*	81.49	88.89	74.13	74.74	6.74
Lakshadweep *	87.52	93.15	81.56	81.78	5.74
Daman and Diu*	81.09	88.40	70.37	71.20	9.89
Delhi*	81.82	87.37	75.00	75.29	6.53
Dadra and Nagar Haveli*	60.03	73.32	42.99	40.71	19.33
Chandigargh*	81.76	85.65	76.65	77.81	3.94
Andaman and Nicobar Island*	81.18	86.07	75.29	73.02	8.17

Source: Census of India, 1991, 2001.

* Jammu and Kashmir were excluded due to lack of available data.

of sophistication. However, the widespread application of machinery to production did not occur. A machine-based economy utilizing fossil fuels was not widespread.

Colonization certainly brought railroads, English common law, and other forms of social and physical infrastructure, but economic development in the form of rapidly rising per capita income failed to occur. India at independence was highly dependent on agriculture, split with linguistic, ethnic, and religious differences, and was burdened by a rapidly growing rural population, caste and gender bias, and extreme poverty.

Independence brought a ruling elite who sought to establish a developmental state and this state did achieve a significant structural change, and growth did begin to occur, but deterioration set in and patron-client politics resulted in significant growth slowing and ineffectiveness. Recent attempts at reform to promote outward-oriented growth have succeeded, but India's growth process appears to be fragile.

Agriculture would seem to be the key to stabilizing the Indian growth experience to accelerate the reduction of poverty. This theme echoes throughout this book. Solution of the commitment problem is essential if a state is to move from a patron-client style of politics to a developmental state. This process will involve a struggle between the ruling elite and the economically successful groups in society. If broad-based rural development occurs, this struggle is likely to evolve into a sort of market-enhancing form of fiscal federalism that allows for economic experimentation, rewarding good policy and punishing bad. Finally, the outward orientation of the Indian economy seems certainly to be a necessary condition (but not sufficient) for long-term Indian prosperity.

Key Terms

Surplus Labor	Market Preserving Federalism
Stages of Development	Unemployment
Malthusian Trap	Gender Discrimination
Deindustrialization	Child Bias
Import Substitution	Caste System
Green Revolution	Human Capital
Economic Reform	Feminization of Poverty
Corruption	Dowry
Infant Industry Protection	

References

Bangladesh Population Census. 1991. Vol. 1. Bangladesh.

Brasted, H.V. 1997. "Child Labour in India." *Child Labour in Asia: Some Perspectives on Selected Countries Canberra.* In M.E. Falkus et al. Aust Govt Printing Service.

Census of India. 1951. 1971. 1981. 1991. 2001. Registrar General and Census Commissioner. India.

Chatterjee, Bhaskar, *Indian Perspectives.* www.meadev.nic.in/photogallery/perspec/ind-spl/literacy.htm.

Chibber, Vivek. 2003. *Locked in Place: State Building and Late Industrialization in India.* Princeton, NJ: Princeton University Press.

Clingingsmith, David, and J. Williamson. 2004. "India's Deindustrialization Under British Rule: New Ideas, New Evidence." NBER Working Paper 10586. National Bureau of Economic Research, Cambridge, Massachusetts.

Datt, Gaurav, and Martin Ravallion. 1998. "Why Have Some Indian States Done Better than Others at Reducing Rural Poverty?" *Economica* 65: 17–38.

———. 2002. "Is India's Economic Growth Leaving the Poor Behind?" *Journal of Economic Perspectives* 16 (summer): 89–108.

Deaton, Angus, and Jean Drèze. 2002. "Poverty and Inequality in India: A Reexamination." Centre for Development Economics, Working Paper No. 107. Delhi School of Economics, New Delhi, India.

DeLong, Bradford. 2003. "India Since Independence: An Analytic Growth Narrative." In *In Search of Prosperity: Analytic Narratives on Economic Growth*, ed. D. Rodrik. Princeton, NJ: Princeton University Press.

Dutt, Romesh. 1969. *The Economic History of India.* Vol. I, *Under Early British Rule.* London: Routledge.

Grabowski, Richard, and Michael P. Shields. 1996. *Development Economics.* Oxford, UK: Blackwell.

Gulati, A., and T. Kelley. 1999. *Trade Liberalization and Indian Agriculture: Cropping Pattern Changes and Efficiency Gains in Semi-Arid Tropics.* New Delhi: Oxford University Press.

———. 1998. "Indian Agriculture in an Open Economy." In *India's Economic Reforms and Development: Essays for Manmohan Singh,* ed., I.J. Ahluwalia, and I.M.D. Little. New Delhi: Oxford University Press.

Haq, M. 1997. *Human Development in South Asia 1997.* Karachi: Oxford University Press.

———. 2000. *Human Development in South Asia: The Gender Question.* Karachi: Oxford University Press.

Haq, M, and K. Haq. 1998. *Human Development in South Asia 1998.* Karachi: Oxford University Press.

Hayami, Yujiro, and Vernon Ruttan. 1985. *Agricultural Development: An International Perspective.* Baltimore, MD: Johns Hopkins University Press.

Heitsman, James, and Robert L. Worden, eds. 1996. *India: A Country Study.* 5th ed. Washington, DC: Library of Congress.

Kalkar, Vijay. 2001. "India's Reform Agenda: Micro, Meso, and Macroeconomic Reforms." Center for the Advanced Study of India, University of Pennsylvania, Philadelphia, PA.

Kingdom, Geeta, R. Cassen, K. McNay, and L. Visaria. 2004. "Education and Literacy." In *21st Century India–Population, Environment, and Human Development*, ed. T. Dyson, R. Cassen, and L. Visaria. Oxford: Oxford University Press.

Krueger, Anne, and Sajjid Chinoy. 2002. "The Indian Economy in Global Context." In *Economic Policy Reforms and the Indian Economy*, ed. Anne Krueger. New Delhi: Oxford University Press.

Maddision, Angus. 2001. *The World Economy: A Millennial Perspective*. Paris: Organisation for Economic Co-operation and Development.

Montinola, Gabriella, Yingyi Qian, and Barry Weingast. 1995. "Federalism, Chinese Style: The Political Basis for Economic Success in China." *World Politics* 48: 50–81.

Morris, M.D. 1963. "Toward a Reinterpretation of 19th Century Indian Economic History." *Journal of Economic History* 23: 606–18.

North, Douglass. 1990. *Institutions, Institutional Change and Economic Performances*. Cambridge: Cambridge University Press.

Osborne, Evan. 2001. "Culture, Development, and Government: Reservations in India." *Economic Development and Cultural Change* 49 (3): 659–85.

Panagariya, Arvind. 2004. "India in the 1980s and 1990s: A Triumph of Reforms." IMF Working Papers, No. 04/43. International Monetary Fund, Washington, DC.

Parthasarathi, Prasannan. 1998. "Rethinking Wages and Competitiveness in the Eighteenth Century: Britain and South India." *Past and Present* 58: 79–109.

———. 2001. *The Transition to a Colonial Economy: Weavers, Merchants, and Kings in South India, 1720–1800*. London: Cambridge University Press.

Patnaik, P. 1997. "The Context and Consequences of Economic Liberalization in India." *Journal of International Trade and Development* 6 (2): 165–78.

Rampal, Anita. 2000. "Education for Human Development in South Asia." *Economic and Political Weekly*, 2523–31.

Rao, C.H.H. 1994. *Agricultural Growth, Rural Poverty and Environmental Degradation in India*. New Dehli: Oxford University Press.

Registrar General and Census Commissioner. 1977. Census of India, 1971. *Social and Cultural Tables*. Series 1-India, Part II-C (ii), New Delhi, India.

———. 1993. Census of India, 1991. *Primary Population Totals: Brief Analysis of Primary Census Abstract*, Series-1, New Delhi, India.

Richter, Linda K. 1991. "Exploring Theories of Female Leadership in South and Southeast Asia." *Pacific Affairs* 63 (4): 524–40.

Rodrik, Dani, and Arvind Subramaniam. 2004. "From 'Hindu Growth' to Productivity Surge: The Mystery of the Indian Growth Transition." IMF Working Paper 04/77. International Monetary Fund, Washington, DC.

Self, Sharmistha, and Richard Grabowski. 2002. "The Economic Impact of Gender Participation by Education Level: A Time Series Analysis." *The Journal of Developing Areas* 36 (1): 57–80.

Srinivas, M.M. 1992. *On Living in a Revolution and Other Essays*. New Delhi: Oxford University Press.

UNESCO. 1998. Basic Education for the Empowerment of the Poor: Report on a regional study of literacy as a tool for empowerment of the poor. Coordinated by Victor Ordonez, Pre K. Kasaju and C. Seshadri, Bangkok, Thailand.

Uppal, Jagendar S. 1977. *Economic Development in South Asia*. New York: St. Martin's Press.

Velkoff, Victoria A., and Arjun Adlakha. 1998. "Women's Health in India." International Programs Center, U.S. Department of Commerce, Economics and Statistics Administration, Bureau of the Census, December.

Weiler, N.H. 1983. "Legislation, Expertise, and Participation: Strategies of Compensatory Legitimation in Educational Policy." *Comparative Education Review* 27 (2).

World Bank. 1997. *India: Five Years of Stabilization and Reform and the Challenges Ahead.* Washington, DC: World Bank.

World Bank. 1999. World Bank Support for Education in India. South Asia Brief. Washington, DC: World Bank.

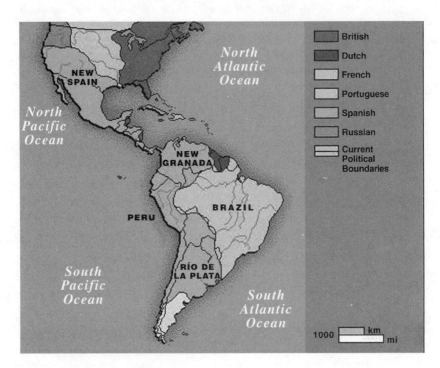

European land in the Americas

6

Latin America

Latin America underwent a much longer period as a colony than other parts of the world. Almost all the countries in Latin America were colonies for about 300 years. Like North America and unlike Asia and almost all of Africa, the colonization of Latin America was accompanied by permanent emigration from Europe. In the early years, these settlers came from Spain and Portugal. They brought with them the political, economic, and cultural institutions of their homeland. In part, the paths of economic development differed between Latin America and North America because of differences in these institutions inherited from their homelands. Hence, in studying development in Latin America, we will begin with a discussion of the Iberian Peninsula, especially Spain, around the time of Columbus.

The Emergence of Spain

Following almost five centuries of gradually eroding Moorish control, the kingdom of Spain emerged in 1479, when Castile and Aragon united, resulting in almost all of what we know as modern Spain being brought under one rule. The particular structure of the new Spanish state seems to have evolved out of, and to have been based on, the structural organization of the Roman Catholic Church. Specifically, the latter was organized into a strictly hierarchical, pyramidal structure. In theoretical analyses of the structure of firms, this type of organization is known as the U-form (or unitary type) (Maskin, Qian, and Xu 2000). The church was centrally governed by a group of cardinals, with the pope at the apex of the pyramid. The Catholic world was further divided into dioceses, each with a bishop in charge. At the bottom of the pyramid were the priests, who held religious responsibilities within the parish (Tokarev 2004).

The organization of the new Spanish state was very similar to that of the preexisting Roman Catholic Church. The Spanish monarchs, Ferdinand and Isabella, quickly established the supremacy of the state and utilized the church to strengthen their grip on power by establishing the papal judicial institution of the Inquisition under royal patronage. Jews and Muslims were perceived as threats to the goal of a strong and united Spain and were expelled from the country. The state assumed a monolithic structure similar to that of the church. In fact, the structures of these two entities were intertwined to form a sort of Spanish theocratic pyramid. Nowhere else in Europe were religious and state institutional structures as inseparable.

One can contrast this sort of pyramidal, U-form of organization with the M-form (multidivisional). M-form organizations are horizontally rather than vertically organized. That is, the organization is made up of a large number of reasonably independent groups. The advantage of the U-form of organization is that it allows for the attainment of substantial economies of scale. In addition, the resources of such an organization can be quickly mobilized to respond to emergencies. However, there are significant drawbacks to U-form institutional structures. Information must travel up and down the organizational structure. As this process unfolds, information can be easily lost, but, more importantly, it is likely to be distorted since each layer of the organization is likely to try and alter the content of the information so as to portray itself more favorably. There are no checks and balances in such an institutional structure; as a result, the structure tends to develop autocratic tendencies and there is often a lack of accountability.

The above creates a situation in which, applied to the nation-state, problems of state credibility are likely to arise. As discussed in earlier chapters, states that are strong enough to protect property rights and can provide an atmosphere conducive to investment are also states that are capable of violating such rights if it is in their interest to do so. A pyramidal, U-form institutional structure is likely to be quite powerful administratively, but with few checks or balances. Such institutional structures would likely be prone to violating rights and undermining conducive environments if it was in their interest to do so.

The newly formed Spanish state was just such an organization. It assuredly facilitated the mobilization of resources for the exploration and conquest of much of Central and South America. However, in terms of administering these new regions, the autocratic institutional structure stifled innovation. As a result, the structure of the Spanish colonies in the New World also bore this characteristic. For Spain itself, this structure offered a poor foundation for fostering economic growth. The great wealth, in terms of gold, silver, and precious gems, which Spain obtained through the conquest of the Aztec and Inca empires in the Americas had little lasting positive impact on Spain. Mercantilists argued that the wealth of a nation was enhanced via the accumulation of gold and silver through trade. However, Adam Smith and the classical economists vigorously maintained that the true wealth of a nation lies in the productivity of its economy. The productivity of the economy is in turn dependent on the amount of savings and investment that occurs, the extent of the specialization of labor, and the degree of market development.

This view that gold was irrelevant to the wealth of nations is perhaps most effectively argued with respect to the quantity theory of money, when money is tied to the gold standard. In the quantity theory of money:

$$MV = PQ,$$

where M is the quantity of money, V is the velocity of money, P is the price level, and Q is real output. By assumption, V and Q are, in the long run, independent of M. Hence, an increase in M will, in the long run, lead to an equiproportionate rise in P with no rise in Q. In other words, a doubling of the money supply will lead to a doubling of the price level.

The quantity theory of money is often explained within the context of fiat money. However, when it was developed, the gold standard governed international trade. The eighteenth-century philosopher David Hume is thought to have argued that the gold standard, through the specie-flow adjustment mechanism, would assure that there would be a balance-of-payments equilibrium, and that accumulating gold would not permanently increase consumption. The domestic money supply was a function of the domestic stock of gold. Hence, as gold entered Spain it, in effect, increased the money supply. Output does not increase in this situation because it is determined by the real forces underlying the economy (e.g., saving, investing, specialization, market development). These real forces are in turn a function of the institutional structure of the society. In the Spanish case, the autocratic institutional structure acted as an impediment to resolving the commitment problem. As a result, individuals were reluctant to take risks, save, invest, and so forth.

The Colonial Period

The structure of the economies of Latin America helped to shape the course of that region's economic development. Three key structural elements were the type of government transferred from Spain; the reliance on exporting gold, other minerals, and agricultural produce; and the shortage of local labor, which led to the forced immigration of slave labor. These three elements will be discussed in turn.

The monolithic government of Spain, dominated by the religious and military hierarchy, was transferred to the New World. Initially, conquest was a way of accumulating great wealth. The Spanish conquered and looted the ancient civilizations of the Aztecs and the Incas. From the beginning, the Spanish did not see colonization as extending Spain and the Spanish way of life to the New World. Rather, they saw colonization as an opportunity for establishing Spain as a world power. In the colonies, there was an indigenous labor force to be used for the mining of gold and silver, the cultivation of tropical fruits, and the gathering of other new goods. Government was based on the command structure of the military, with the initial leaders being primarily military men. The main positions in provincial government were filled by persons born in Spain. The Spanish-born members of the government elite were given short terms of office to ensure loyalty. They held all the military, civil, economic, and, to some extent, ecclesiastical control of the colonies. *Criollas,* or American-born descendants of "pure" Spanish blood, participated in government at the town level. They also amassed ownership of a great deal of property. Their limited access to political power, however, became a major source of grievance.

The ownership of land developed in an extremely unequal manner, with criollas accumulating large estates (*latifundio*). The land obtained by the criollas was sometimes given to them by the Spanish crown for services rendered. Often this land came from the former holdings of natives that were either decimated by the conquerors, forced to leave the land, or were forced to stay and work for the new landholders on their estates. Very small plots of land (*minifundio*), often the least desirable land, continued to be farmed by the dispossessed Indians and those of mixed Indian and European origin.

The *latifundios* differed from the feudal manors of Europe in several ways. First, there was no unifying philosophy of mutual obligations, rights, and reciprocal work. The rule of these large estates was entirely authoritarian. The prestige and power of the heads of these estates depended more on the strength of their authoritarian rule and the size of the estate than on profitability. Hence, they were not very responsive to market forces, limiting the development of entrepreneurship and market institutions.

In exploiting natural resources such as mining for gold and silver or exporting exotic fruits and produce, the economic elite did not need to attract new labor through higher wages. They forced Indians to work in these export industries and imported slaves when harsh conditions decimated the Indian population. Like the American South, the economy increasingly became a slave economy, highly dependent on exports. Hence, the development of labor markets was limited.

Another similarity with the American South was the mercantilist system imposed on the Spanish and Portuguese colonies by their European centers. However, the mercantilist restrictions on trade were much more severe in Latin America than they were in the English colonies. Any exports or imports of the English colonies with a third country had to first be shipped to England. The goods would be unloaded and, once the appropriate taxes and fees were paid, then reloaded onto English ships with an English crew. Goods traded between two English colonies, however, could be done so directly. A similar law governed the trade of the Spanish colonies with the difference that goods traded between two Spanish colonies still had to pass through Spain. The type of mercantilism practiced by England allowed colonies to specialize and export to one another. Hence, American colonies in the north were able to trade with the south as the former developed manufacturing. This type of specialization did not occur among the Spanish colonies. Hence, the Spanish colonies did not develop regional markets to the extent the English colonies did. The development of a merchant class and entrepreneurship differed between English and Spanish colonies.

The lack of specialization and division of labor resulting from the above situation meant that market development was limited and productivity growth was slow. In addition, the centralized, U-form structure of institutions transplanted from Spain failed to solve, in any real way, the commitment problem discussed earlier. Economic actors in the Spanish colonies were reluctant to make risky investments and fully engage in market production because they feared that any profits generated would be taxed away, in one manner or another, by autocratic state structures.

Independence and Trade

The independence movements in the New World were strongly influenced by the ideas of classical economics. Recall that Smith argued that increased specialization was the key to economic prosperity. Increased specialization was dependent on the size and scope of the market, which was inhibited by a mercantilist system that dramatically repressed international trade. Furthermore, Hume argued that the specie-flow adjustment mechanism would assure balance-of-payment equilibrium. Consequently, free trade was best for everyone, foreign and domestic. In other words, the mercantilist system hurt the colonies economically. Hence, independence would, according to the classical view, improve economic well-being. Of course, those with the most to gain from independence were the merchant capitalists of the colonies who were directly hurt by the mercantilist system.

The independence movement first took hold in English North American colonies. It should not be surprising that revolution first occurred where merchant capitalists had the strongest foothold in economic affairs. The resulting independence of the United States of America provided an example and inspiration for later revolutions in Latin America. These revolutions did not occur for another forty to fifty years, in part because the merchant capitalists did not develop the intracolonial trade that spurred the development of manufacturing. It was not until the Napoleonic Wars in Europe, which led to a fall in New World exports, that independence finally came to Latin America.

Initially, the newly independent economies were built around exports, as they had been before independence. The free-trade arguments of classical economics fit in well with the interests of the new ruling class that came to power with independence. However, these free-trade ideas were really more of a justification for sovereignty rather than a reflection of how the newly independent economies would operate. Land distribution, which was highly unequal because of the colonization process, became even more so as church-state conflicts allowed the latter to confiscate the former's lands and allocate them to dominate political figures. This inequality in the distribution of land ownership and control resulted in extreme inequalities in the distribution of income. What this meant was that the bulk of the population had little income to spend and thus a mass market for simple manufactured consumer goods failed to develop, as occurred in Europe, Japan, and other East Asian countries. Growth of the domestic market and production for that market developed very slowly. Most of these countries were, therefore, significantly dependent on exports, but not the export of manufactured goods. Instead, what assumed importance was the production and export of primary commodities.

The newly independent states inherited many of the characteristics of their colonial predecessor. That is, although established with the trappings of a constitution, elections, and such, they were far from being democratic. These states remained fundamentally authoritarian, pyramidal, and predatory. Political instability was an underlying feature.

Export Expansion and Growth

Once the restrictions of the mercantilist system were lifted, exports expanded rapidly for many Latin American countries during the 1800s. These expanded exports depended, as discussed earlier, on the abundant natural resources of the region. These exports were almost entirely from the mining and agricultural sectors. The chief early recipients of these freer exports were those who controlled the land. Recall that a pattern of land holding had developed during colonial times where land was divided between a few very large land holdings and many small subsistence plots. This differed from land patterns that had developed in Europe during the development of protoindustrialization and industrialization, where land was more evenly dispersed. Crops for export were grown on the large plantations, while the small plots were devoted to subsistence agriculture.

There was little linkage between the export sector and the rest of the economy. Production was export oriented and the exports were largely to Europe and, later, to the United States. Consequently, specialization of production within the region was limited. The strongest candidate for linkages with the domestic economy might have been the agricultural sector. The owners of the plantations were entirely domestic, meaning that the rent and profits went entirely to the domestic economy. These profits could positively affect development in three ways. First, they could be saved and invested, increasing capital and hence productivity. Second, they could be allocated to investment in infrastructure. Third, they could be spent on the consumption of locally produced goods and services, increasing market expansion and specialization in the local economy.

All of these avenues for profits to lead to development were limited by the economic institutions Latin America inherited from its colonial experience. The insulation of the power of landholders from markets meant that landowners were an unlikely source of either entrepreneurial activity or investment. Furthermore, their admiration of European culture meant that they would consume goods imported from Europe rather than goods produced in their own economy.

The contribution of workers toward expanding a market economy was also limited. While slavery was ended with independence in Latin America, workers participated very little in markets. They were dependent on the plantation owner for food, clothing, and shelter. They received payment in-kind and not cash for their labor.

Despite these impediments to the creation of robust domestic markets, many of the countries of Latin America achieved some prosperity in the decades following independence. By 1850, per capita income in Argentina ($874) and Brazil ($901) were, according to Engerman and Solokoff (2002), about two-thirds the U.S. level of $1,394. In comparison, Canada's per capita income ($850) was about 60 percent of that in the United States. By 1913, Brazil's per capita income fell by about 20 percent, to $700, while Argentina's per capita income nearly trebled, to $2,377, but fell in comparison with the United States. Argentina's per capita income was 49 percent of per capita U.S. income ($4,854).

Much of Latin America experienced an export boom in the latter part of the nineteenth century. This was particularly true for Argentina, whose exports grew by almost 10 percent per year between 1853 and 1873. Export growth declined during the early twentieth century but remained high. During this period, usually from about 1850 to 1930, Latin American countries are said to have had export economies.

The classical notion of laissez-faire, or minimal government, in part justified both the earlier wars of independence and the economic policy that led to this export expansion. Eventually, advocates of laissez-faire in trade lost influence for three basic reasons, capped by the experience of the Great Depression. First, the growth of exports began to slow. Second, the linkages of the export sector with the rest of the economy were perceived to be weak. Third, specialization in the export of a few primary products was perceived to introduce costs of instability of export earnings into the economy, which might not be well suited to handle this volatility. We will now turn to these arguments.

Import-Substitution Industrialization

The first reason for the decreased influence of laissez-faire was the slowing demand for the exports of the region. Prebisch (1964) argued that this decline was inevitable and, in many ways, desirable. He was pessimistic about the long-term benefits of international trade for the periphery, and believed that if developing countries were to ever truly become developed, industrialized countries, a different approach would be needed. His views are structuralist. He and other structuralists argue that because the structures of Latin American and other less-developed economies are different from rich, industrialized countries, less-developed economies respond differently to market incentives.

Prebisch divided the world into two economic zones: the center and the periphery. His ideas were similar to those of dependency theory, discussed in Chapter 1. The center consisted of highly industrialized countries, such as the United States, and the periphery consisted of the rest of the world that traded with the center. A large part of the exports of the periphery consisted of agricultural goods and raw materials. He accepted the neoclassical view that trade was mutually beneficial to both types of countries (the center and the periphery) in the short run. However, he argued that the benefits of trade went disproportionately to the center. Furthermore, he argued that the benefits of growth in the periphery were mainly felt in the center and not in the periphery.

Assumptions about income elasticity and the price elasticity of demand are key to Prebisch's argument. He argued that the demand for exports from the periphery is price inelastic. If this is the case, an increase in the production of these exports will result in a decline in total export revenue. Furthermore, he argued that rising income in the center had little impact on sales of periphery exports. Hence, very little of the growth at the center would be transferred to the periphery in terms of increased demand for periphery exports, while much of the growth at the periphery would be transferred to the center in terms of lower prices.

Prebisch described the results in terms of the long-run terms of trade (i.e., the price of exports divided by the price of imports) moving against the periphery. There are two basic reasons given for why declining long-term terms of trade might be expected. One is that much of agriculture and some natural resources are necessities. Once a critical level is reached, however, there may be little need for increased consumption. A second reason lies in the political economy of developed countries. When a country on the periphery tries to take advantage of comparative advantage by exporting labor-intensive manufactured goods, it may at first be successful. A problem with too much success is that it could result in a tariff at the center to protect its workers. This tariff could turn the terms of trade against the periphery if the center has monopoly power.

Structuralists and others began to support a strategic plan for tariffs and other trade barriers to promote industrialization via import-substitution industrialization (ISI). The plan, based on Keynesian economics, was developed by Albert Hirschman (1958). The plan supposed a strong state capable of ignoring powerful special interests and acting to enhance economic development (similar to Japan, Taiwan, South Korea). ISI is based on the notion that goods would be produced at home if domestic entrepreneurs were willing and able to take advantage of domestic opportunities. Entrepreneurship might have been weak in Latin America for numerous reasons, including its long colonial legacy that concentrated wealth among a nonproductive political elite.

In order to overcome this weak entrepreneurship, an ISI strategy was put forward. It was proposed that the state should choose imported goods to be produced at home that are currently being imported. A higher tariff should be placed on those goods to generate high profits in the domestic production of the goods and encourage entrepreneurs to undertake domestic production for the home market.

In choosing these goods, there are several factors to consider. Hirschman argued that one of the most important factors is the linkages these goods have with the rest of the economy. There are two types of linkages, as discussed in Chapter 1, forward and backward. Forward linkages refer to a supply relationship. For example, electricity is used in manufacturing many goods. A government project to build a hydroelectric dam to supply cheap electricity might encourage production of goods using a lot of electricity. Backward linkages refer to a demand relationship. Backward linkages involve the creation of demand for a final or intermediate good.

ISI plans are often divided onto two stages. In the first stage, the country seeks to promote the production of final consumer goods in which it has a potential comparative advantage, but that it is currently importing. The production process for these goods should be simple, involve domestic inputs, and be labor intensive. Examples of such goods might include textiles, footwear, or beer. A prohibitive tariff placed on these goods creates an obvious demand for domestic production and obvious profit opportunities for domestic entrepreneurs. If things go as planned, domestic resources will move into the production of these goods and domestic production will increase dramatically. Furthermore, demand will be created for intermediate inputs used in the production of these final goods.

The reason why this growth might be so rapid is the assumption that entrepreneurs need the government to act in order for them to recognize opportunities that are already there. In other words, the economy is inefficient in that investment is well below available funds. In a sense, the economy is in a state of chronic recession with unemployed labor and perhaps underutilized capital. Because the economy is at less than full employment, standard fiscal or monetary policy would move it toward full employment. However, they would not necessarily create more growth. Recall from chapters 1 and 3 that the investment rate is a possible key to growth. Fiscal and monetary policy will increase demand, but they will not necessarily increase investment. The lack of entrepreneurship may prevent investment from responding to the lower interest rates created by expansionary monetary policy. The higher investment created by ISI policies could increase growth both by expanding aggregate demand and by increasing the investment rate. Furthermore, this increase in the investment rate would not require more sacrifice via lower consumption (higher saving).

Once this process of first-stage ISI has been completed, protection can be extended to intermediate goods, such as steel production. This next phase is the second stage of import substitution. As first-stage import substitution is enacted, it increases the importation of inputs for production. Second-stage ISI protects domestic firms producing substitutes for these otherwise imported inputs, thus inducing domestic production and further industrialization.

It is not clear whether the Prebisch-Hirschman view of ISI was ever carried out. Industrialization and protection in Latin America began to occur much earlier than the post–World War II period emphasis on import substitution. Protectionism began to be important in the last two decades of the nineteenth century and the effective rates of protection were high on many final goods. These policies were motivated by pragmatic and often political reasons. Hence, protectionist policies existed well before the ISI period. The Great Depression, however, forced an unintended ISI as demand in industrialized countries fell. After World War II, increased protectionist policies were pursued and these policies were justified as being ISI policies (Haber 2006). In conclusion, for a 100-year period Latin America followed a protectionist policy with mixed success. During the last fifty years of this era, Latin America increasingly looked inward for economic growth and development.

The pattern of industrialization hampered overall economic growth in Latin America during this period. ISI was an attempt to create a modern sector that would be dynamic, generate economic growth, and would, through backward linkages, result in increased production of inputs. However, the economic sectors in many countries did not respond in sufficient magnitude to market forces to provide these inputs. Consequently, these inputs needed to be imported along with the capital equipment needed to produce the ISI goods. This need for capital imports weakened the impact of ISI tariffs.

A related difficulty with ISI comes from the notably unequal distribution of income in many Latin American countries. As we noted, this unequal distribution came from how the land and other resource wealth of Latin America were allocated during the colonial period. This unequal income distribution steered industrialization toward the production and importation of luxury consumer goods for the wealthy. These goods were often goods produced in a capital-intensive manner and absorbed little labor in their production. This led to the monopolization of manufacturing with natural-resource exports required to pay for imports. This era of inward-looking growth ended with the rapid globalization of the 1980s and 1990s.

The record during the period of ISI, in terms of growth in gross domestic product (GDP) per capita, though not spectacular was still one of achievement. GDP per capita in Latin America grew at an average annual rate of 2.7 percent between 1950 and 1980. Although this was below what was achieved in East Asia, it still represented persistent and long-term improvements. However, beginning in the 1980s, the annual GDP per capita growth rate was -0.9 percent on average (Ocampo 2004). This has often been called the lost decade in Latin America. The problems of this era are discussed in the next section.

Globalization and the International Monetary Fund

The protectionist era in Latin America ended partly as a response to financial difficulties brought on by dramatic increases in oil prices and partly because of the example provided by the success of export-oriented East Asian economies. We will consider issues and changes in the world economy that occurred subsequent to the rise in energy prices. Then we will move onto globalization and free-trade issues.

There were two dramatic spikes in oil prices. The first occurred in 1973 in response to a cut in production made by Arab exporters in response to U.S. policy on Israel. The second occurred shortly after the 1979 revolution in Iran. The reactions to these two events differed and this difference dramatically affected development in Latin America and throughout the globe.

The first oil price spike was viewed as being largely temporary. Some conservation measures were taken, but the major concern was how to finance oil imports. Latin American countries financed these imports through borrowing on the international money market. Such borrowing is not necessarily harmful to a country. Developing countries often borrow international funds to finance investment, which requires the import of capital. They also borrow to deal with short-term problems. At the time, inflation was high, partly as a response to the energy crisis. Industrialized countries followed an expansionary monetary policy because they were more concerned with unemployment than with inflation. Higher expected inflation leads to an increased spread between short- and long-term interest rates. Short-term rates were lower, so many countries borrowed short term, betting that interest rates would fall.

This precarious state of affairs was upset when a second oil-price crisis occurred. Oil prices again spiked, increasing the cost of imports. International money markets were much different this time around. Industrialized countries followed a contractionary monetary policy, being now much more concerned about inflation. Interest rates shot up to a much higher level. Hence, Latin American countries faced a double problem. They had to borrow to pay for higher oil prices if they were not to have economic difficulties. At the same time, they had to refinance a large proportion of their current debt because of past short-term borrowing. Tight money markets meant that they would need to borrow at much higher interest rates, making their financial situation even worse. Lenders were simply not willing to lend required amounts and many countries faced a severe financial crisis.

International agencies such as the International Monetary Fund (IMF) and other lenders forced dramatic changes in the economies of Latin America and many other developing economies. In order to understand the role of the IMF and the difficulties faced by international borrowers during this period, consider an analogy with bankruptcy courts for firms. Firms routinely finance expansion partly through borrowing. Hence, rising debt is not necessarily a bad thing. However, when they get into trouble, lenders lose confidence, supposing that the firm is not earning enough to carry their debt burden. They are borrowing to finance a persistent, negative cash flow. The bankruptcy court steps in at the firm's request, and the firm agrees to take the actions the court feels are needed to reverse its negative cash flow. These actions always involve reducing expenses, since the court cannot count on the firm's ability to increase revenue. When the firm agrees, the firm can once again borrow short term while taking actions to get itself out of bankruptcy.

The IMF serves a similar purpose for countries. When creditors loose confidence in a country it makes it more difficult for the country to borrow. Consequently, the country has to dip into its cash reserves. As these cash reserves fall, creditors loose even more confidence and a crisis may develop. Countries can turn to the IMF for help. Working on a banking model, the IMF will step in conditional on the country agreeing to take actions that will improve its cash flow. These actions are always of the belt-tightening variety. The IMF insists that the country decrease its need to borrow. The regimen usually involves cutting government consumption and increasing the costs of private consumption. To cut private consumption, emphasis has been placed on increasing the price of imports through currency devaluation and on reducing subsidies to consumers. Instead of a regime of protectionism supporting high exchange rates, the IMF has urged reform wherein a troubled economy becomes more open to trade, with the market determining exchange rates.

These actions are deeply unpopular for understandable reasons. People do not like having to cut their consumption. The solutions proposed by the IMF are often criticized for three basic reasons. First, a country in financial difficulty often resents that the IMF assumes that the source of the difficulty lies domestically, in the country facing difficulties. Why should it have to cut consumption as opposed to, for example, having lending countries increase their consumption? Second, the IMF assumes that such difficulty is long term, and not just a temporary disturbance. Why go through all the pain when the problem might only be temporary? Third, part of the problem is that too much reliance is placed on debt versus equity finance. Why not change this situation by having the IMF facilitate debt-for-equity swaps?

However, the problems faced by Latin America were indeed of a more fundamental, long-term nature and they could not be completely resolved by expansion of consumption or demand from the rest of the world. Neither could debt-for-equity swaps solve these underlying fundamental difficulties. One source of difficulty was in the ISI strategy itself. Prolonged use of this strategy acted as a tax on exports. Specifically, tariffs raise the price of import substitutes relative to exports. This acts to siphon resources away from export production and toward the production of import substitutes. In addition, tariffs cause the cost of critical imported inputs to rise. Thus exports that are dependent on these inputs will find it increasingly difficult to compete internationally. In addition, ISI strategy usually involved an overvalued exchange rate, allowing imported capital goods to be purchased cheaply. However, such overvalued exchange rates also raise the world price of the affected country's exports, making them less competitive. In addition, cheapening capital inputs leads to production processes that are too capital intensive, thus slowing the growth of employment.

The East Asian economies initially followed the ISI process. They engaged in the first stage, within which simple, manufactured consumer goods were protected. Thus tariffs and other protectionist tools were used to promote the domestic production of simple, labor-intensive, manufactured goods. However, after this stage was successfully completed these nations turned to export promotion, pushing their new manufacturing firms to turn outward and export. They did this by using a variety of subsidies and incentives that applied only to production for export.

Alternatively, Latin America moved on to second-stage import substitution. This involved the protection of the domestic production of capital goods. This proved to be extremely difficult, given the small size of domestic markets in Latin American nations. This also provided additional difficulties for firms interested in exporting.

One can think of the ISI process as creating international barriers to competition. That is, these barriers reduced the international competition faced by Latin America's domestic, indigenous producers. However, Latin America also created domestic barriers to competition. That is, these policies reduced the degree of domestic competition, competition among domestic, indigenous producers. These barriers included the creation of high entry costs, poorly functioning credit markets, and the creation of high costs for adjusting the workforce. Entry costs were pushed up by dramatically increasing the costs for establishing new businesses (licenses, fees, etc.). Poorly functioning capital markets made it very difficult to establish new firms. Finally, rules making it difficult to dismiss workers and impose costs on firms for dismissing workers were widespread in Latin America. All of these factors tended to reduce competition among indigenous firms in Latin America.

According to Cole et al. (2005), these barriers explain why Latin America has fallen behind East Asia and North America. Specifically, they argue that Latin America's relative stagnation is a consequence of its low labor productivity. Latin American labor productivity was 33 percent of the U.S. level in 1950 and was 30 percent of the U.S. level in 1998. The work of Cole et al. further shows that the low labor productivity in Latin America was not due to the fact that Latin American workers had less capital to work with, but instead was and is due to the lower efficiency with which they use both labor and capital (low total factor productivity).

The low total factor productivity is linked to the high international and domestic barriers to competition. "Both the breadth and the depth of Latin American barriers significantly exceeds those in Europe and other successful countries" (ibid., 87). Thus low total factor productivity is because firms in Latin America did not face the competitive pressures that drive firms to innovate or to make the most efficient use of technologies.

Thus, the financial difficulties stemming from oil prices were exacerbated by the effects of ISI. Exports grew slowly, if at all, and balance-of-payment crises became an increasingly difficult problem to deal with. This culminated in the economic stagnation of the 1980s, which in turn led Latin America to institute a series of economic reforms. These reforms included reducing tariffs and their dispersion, dismantling nontariff barriers, eliminating restrictions on foreign direct investment, phasing out foreign-exchange regulations, granting greater autonomy to central banks, reducing regulations concerning interest rates and credit allocation, and privatizing some firms and banks. Aggressive reformers like Argentina, Bolivia, Chile, and Peru carried out reforms very quickly, while more cautious countries such as Brazil, Costa Rica, Columbia, Jamaica, and Mexico took a more gradual approach. Reforms were not universally carried out in all countries; in some countries reform was limited or nonexistent (Ocampo 2004).

The economies of Latin America changed dramatically because of these changes and a changed international environment favoring globalization. Some countries, such as Mexico and Nicaragua, witnessed a dramatic increase in exports as a proportion of GDP during part of this period. The majority of Latin American countries, however, showed little increase, or in some cases, a decline in exports as a proportion of GDP. This pattern is just about opposite to the pattern in high-income Organisation for Economic Co-operation countries, where a majority saw strong increases in exports as a proportion of GDP.

In terms of per capita GDP growth, the 1980s, as pointed out earlier, has been called the lost decade. In the 1990s, growth in per capita GDP resumed, increasing at an average annual rate of 1.9 percent per year. However, in the late 1990s and in the early part of the new century, this growth rate once again became negative. The growth achieved in the 1990s, while positive, was still less than what had been achieved in the period between 1950 and 1980 (2.7 percent per year) (ibid.).

The sluggish reaction to reform discussed above may reflect a more fundamental difficulty with trying to generate rapid growth in Latin America. This more fundamental difficulty is related to the extreme inequality in the distribution of wealth and income. This inequality may present a barrier to the effectiveness of economic reform. More specifically, a high degree of inequality may dramatically reduce investment in both physical and human capital, reducing long-term prospects for economic growth. This negative impact might arise in several different ways. In a democratic system voters will be tempted to vote for those who will redistribute income in their favor. However, to do this the state will have to levy taxes. Thus, whether a particular group of voters will gain depends on what they get because of redistribution relative to what they will pay in taxes. The poor will tend to pay little tax and are thus likely to gain from redistribution. Extreme inequality in the distribution of income would imply a strong demand for redistribution and therefore a high tax. The latter would tend to discourage investment and thus slow growth (Alesina and Rodrik 1994, Persson and Tabellini 1994).

Such a model does not really capture the complexities of the situation in Latin America, in particular the limited nature of democracy there. Rodríguez (1999) has developed a more interesting model. In his model, greater inequality leads to greater rent seeking by richer individuals who give monetary contributions or bribes to politicians in exchange for favors. By this activity, those at the top of the income distribution can prevent any significant redistribution being pushed by those at the bottom of the income distribution. The resources used by the wealthy to influence the political process (rent seeking), represent resources that could have been productively invested. As a result, the growth rate of the economy is reduced. Latin America may be a good example of just such a process. High levels of inequality can have other sorts of impacts. Extreme inequality can lead groups to pursue their objectives illegally and/or through the use of violence. This is most often associated with political instability and this additional risk and uncertainty may pose significant obstacles to investment and capital accumulation.

Inequality may also have a significant impact on the accumulation of human capital. In Latin America, spending on education is skewed toward higher education, which generally benefits those at the upper end of the distribution of income and wealth. Fernandez and Rogerson (1995) argue that poorer families are unable to provide the resources necessary for their children's education. If credit markets function well, it should be possible for them to borrow to finance their children's education. If credit markets do not exist for the poor, they are effectively precluded from the accumulation of human capital unless the state makes provisions via the public provision of education. However, the wealthier groups often use the political power that stems from their wealth to bias the provision of resources toward higher education, rather than primary, secondary, and so on. This effectively precludes individuals at the bottom end of the distribution from accumulating human capital.

Thus it would seem that extreme inequality in the distribution of wealth creates certain innate difficulties in terms of promoting reform that would in turn promote rapid economic growth. Extreme inequality provides the wealthy with resources that can be used to resist reform. Alternatively, even if reforms are enacted the wealthy may be able to subvert the effects. These sorts of problems may be most clearly seen in Latin America.

Inflation

Latin America has long been known for its periodic bouts with high inflation rates. There have been many different explanations of the inflation in Latin America, three of which are considered here. The first is that inflation is the result of monetary growth. Another is that inflation is a cost-push phenomenon. Both of these explanations are commonly presented in introductory textbooks on macroeconomics. A third account was put forward by the structuralists. Structuralists accept that inflation has both monetarist and cost-push elements, but contend that emphasizing these elements often misses the point. It is their view that the optimal level of inflation will depend on the structure of the economy. In the United States, optimal inflation may well be near zero, but in Argentina it may well be substantially above zero.

Structuralists argue that inflation may be the result of sluggish supply. As an economy grows, income grows, and so does the demand for many domestically produced goods, such as food. However, bottlenecks develop for locally produced consumption goods. These bottlenecks are held to be a consequence of a domestic economic elite that achieved their position through inheritance and political power. They did not become wealthy through business and producing for the market. Consequently, they are not accustomed to looking for market opportunities and are slow to respond to opportunities occurring through growth.

Uneven growth transpires, wherein export sectors—being the more opportunistic and market-oriented sectors—grow, and the domestic economy stagnates, with growth leading to higher prices. This uneven growth is itself a cause of inflation in the structuralist point of view, and instability is both generated and exacerbated by international shocks. Consequently, inflation would not entirely be a monetary phenomenon. There might be some level of inflation that could only be reduced or eliminated through long-run growth. Because it was held that these structural problems were prevalent in Latin America, it was held that modest inflation in Latin America was both likely and desirable.

The structuralists argued that living with inflation through indexation was preferable to following what they referred to as monetarist policies. The monetarist view is that inflation is caused by large governmental deficits coupled with large money-supply growth rates. The money-supply growth is partly caused by high government deficits; that is, in an attempt to pay for spending, governments print more money.

Whatever the merits of the structuralist argument, structuralist-informed monetary policy in Latin America had its limitations. It is one thing to argue that low or even moderate inflation could be structural and necessary, quite another to claim that inflation in excess of 100 percent per year is structural and should not be addressed through monetarist remedies. Many countries in Latin America saw severe periods of high inflation in the mid-to-late 1980s, notably Argentina, Bolivia, Brazil, Nicaragua, and Peru—extending into the early 1990s in the case of Brazil. Partly because of pressure from the IMF and World Bank, and partly in a desire to open their economies to more international trade, the countries in Latin America eventually instituted monetarist policies.

The result was price stability with less disruption to the economy than the structuralists feared.

Population Growth

When Spanish and Portuguese settlers came to Latin America, they did not move into largely empty lands, as was the case in northern North America, but rather into territories with indigenous civilizations. Due to the ravages of war, slavery, and small pox, the latter of which was unknown in the Americas before the arrival of the Europeans, the native population faced a population catastrophe, losing over 90 percent of their population. With natural population growth, European settlement, and, in Brazil and much of the Caribbean, the importation of African slaves, the population recovered to the point where high population growth was perceived to be a threat to sustainable development in the twentieth century.

Before discussing population growth, we need to discuss the most useful measure of fertility when working with national data. The total fertility rate (TFR) is now the preferred measure of fertility in intercountry comparisons. The TFR is an estimate of the average number of children today's women will have on the assumption that fertility patterns are the same in the future as they are today. If TFR = 2, it means that women would each have two children. Due to mortality and that slightly more males are born than females, the population would eventually be stable if TFR were between approximately 2.06 and 2.11, depending on the mortality rate and male/female birth rate of the country.

In the 1960s, fertility in Latin America was extremely high. In 1960, four Latin American countries had a TFR of 7.25 or higher, which ranks among the highest TFRs ever recorded. Only Argentina and Uruguay had a total fertility rate below four children per woman. High and rising fertility coupled with fairly low mortality rates led to rapid population growth. Indeed, population growth rates in Latin America may have been the highest ever witnessed in the history of the world. Unlike Asia, where religious authorities were typically not opposed to state intervention to encourage family planning, the Catholic Church in Latin America was and is opposed to many types of birth control and hostile to the idea of state intervention. In addition, there has not been a sense of urgency caused by famines and other disasters, such as the Bengal famine in 1943–44 that legitimized state intervention in South Asia (Caldwell 1996).

Despite unfavorable conditions for family planning, fertility in Latin America has fallen dramatically. Recently, only five countries had a TFR of above four and many countries had fertility rates centering on replacement. In terms of the theory of the demographic transition, this decline in fertility would be expected. Latin America has undergone a considerable period of rising income, falling mortality, and industrialization accompanied by urbanization. However, the initial response of fertility to declining mortality was far from the prediction of transition theory (Dyson and Murphy 1985). Fertility initially increased as mortality fell, suggesting that the demand for births increased with the onset of the demographic transition. This rise in the demand for children might have been the result of the strong influence of the Catholic Church on values. However, despite the influence of values fostering high fertility, fertility did eventually and dramatically decline. The TFR in Latin America is still higher than in Asia, where family-planning intervention by government is widely practiced and supported, but fertility in Latin America no longer represents a considerable threat to long-term economic growth and sustainable development.

Solving the Commitment Problem

Throughout this book it has been argued that one of the primary factors in successful economic development is the solution of the commitment problem by the ruling elite of the state. For this to occur, the state must be both strong and restrained. The strength of the state comes from its ability to mobilize resources, mainly via the tax system. The restrained state is one whose policy choices are constrained so as to respect long-term promises, property rights, and so on (Borner, Bodmer, and Kobler 2004). Such a state can effectively provide an environment for rapid economic development by providing physical infrastructure, investing in human capital, and investing in agricultural research, all of which are crucial. Of course, the crucial question is how the emergence of a strong but constrained state comes about.

In previous chapters a certain process through which states evolve or develop was outlined. This analysis can be briefly summarized. The ruling elite of any state is in constant search of revenue and resources in order to maintain their strength. If the elite are broadly dependent on an agricultural sector in which the bulk of production occurs on relatively small farms, then the state will have to earn its revenue there. That is, it will have to construct an institutional apparatus that penetrates the countryside in order to extract the necessary resources. There will ensue a struggle between the elite and farmers over the agricultural surplus. In this struggle, it is likely that initially the ruling elite will behave badly by trying to extract as many resources as possible. Farmers will react by withdrawing from market production, hiding their activities, engaging in overt acts of resistance, and so on. As a result, the overall revenue raised by the ruling elite will decline. However, a dialectical learning process occurs in which the ruling elite realizes that by investing in agriculture and committing to restraint with respect to taxation, the punishment that is inflicted on them by the noncooperation of farmers will cease. As a result, the state and its ruling elite develop a reputation for sound policy and the possible loss of that reputation acts to constrain state behavior.

This sort of process has been labeled by Borner, Brunetti, and Weder (1995) as credibility gained through reputation. The state has learned to commit itself through a dialectical learning process based on having to earn its income. This process was shown to have successfully unfolded in Japan, parts of East Asia and India, and in northwestern Europe. However, in much of the world this has failed to occur, particularly in Latin America. This was likely due to the historical process that occurred with the initial colonization of Latin America. Specifically, this process created agricultural sectors characterized by extreme inequality in the ownership/control of land, with the bulk of the population marginalized. In addition, Spain did not have to earn the revenue from its colonies; certainly, it extracted large amounts of gold and silver from there, but this process did not require the creation of an institutional structure that would pervade the colony. The end result was that the bulk of the revenue was unearned and thus the Spanish colonial government felt no responsibility to provide any services in return, except to an extremely small landed elite. Thus there was no mechanism by which the bulk of the rural population could retaliate against capricious government behavior. The state and its ruling elite did not learn the lesson of commitment.

With independence and the appearance of democracy, little that was fundamentally important changed. That is, a small indigenous ruling elite replaced the Spanish. This indigenous political elite depended on a small economic elite who in turn was basically concentrated in the production of primary goods. Again, the ruling elite did not earn their revenue from a broadly based group of agrarian producers via taxation. An agrarian-based process of learning to solve the commitment problem never took place. Instead, the natural protectionism provided by high transportation costs combined with import-substitution policies created an expanding urban-based manufacturing sector, but this growth process continued to be based on an extremely unequal distribution of wealth and income. Hence the indigenous industrialization was limited by the size of existing domestic markets.

More importantly, this industrial growth occurred within an environment within which states and the ruling elite had undergone very little political development. The commitment problem had not been solved and states would periodically reform, only to renege on the reforms and seek to extract as much surplus as possible. Sustained growth could not be firmly established.

The mounting difficulties of ISI combined with oil-price increases and ensuing financial crises forced many Latin American states to engage in reform once again. However, this time the reform took place within an environment of rapid globalization. Most economists have focused on the economic effects of this globalization, as discussed earlier in this chapter. Here, the focus will be on political development. Borner, Brunetti, and Weder (1995) have suggested that states and their ruling elite can learn to solve the credibility problem through openness. The specific mechanism through which this can occur is external exit. That is, resources that are mobile may be able to inflict punishment on a ruling elite that fails to be able to commit to effective growth policies. In an open environment, such mobile resources can exit the country.

This possibility provides a powerful weapon to sanction state behavior. "If a country is open to emigration of labor and capital this limits the discretionary power of the state very directly. Every discretionary move that hurts the private sector can prompt the most valuable mobile factors to leave the country and thus reduce the tax base of the government" (ibid., 92). This mechanism may be extremely important in the context of Latin America. Given the extremes in the distribution of wealth, indigenous reform movements are never likely to be fully effective. Rent-seeking behavior on the part of the wealthy and powerful is likely to distort and limit the effects of economic and/or political reform. Thus the growing interconnection of the world via globalization, the linking of factor, goods, and services markets provides a strong disciplinary mechanism. States and the ruling elite who persistently fail to construct institutional constraints for solving commitment problems will find their growth and development prospects limited. Most importantly, their performance relative to their neighbors will suffer. Their status and international influence are likely to also suffer relative to more successful neighbors. This will act as a disciplining device on the state.

One should not think that this process would occur smoothly and without conflict and upheaval. Cohen, Brown, and Organski (1981) argue that upheaval and violence within developing nations does not just indicate political decay. In many situations it is part of political development, and the struggle involved in coming to the solution of the commitment problem. This is likely to be the case as groups within Latin America struggle to prevent reform or to reduce its effectiveness. How this process unfolds in this region has yet to be seen.

What We Have Learned

Latin America, despite tremendous natural wealth and a historic start, has lagged behind its northern neighbors in economic development. We have seen that institutions developed in a manner that was hostile toward wealth accumulation through production for the market. These institutions played important roles in slowing economic development in Latin America. Economies developed that did not respond well to market incentives in part because wealth was created and maintained through political power and not through the market. Various measures, such as ISI, were taken to counteract the slow response of the economy to market opportunities. These measures were undertaken in part because they rewarded an existing political elite. Initially ISI succeeded in promoting rapid industrialization. However, the distortions introduced by such policies resulted in mounting difficulties: sluggish export growth, balance-of-payments difficulties, fragile financial systems, overly capital-intensive manufacturing, and so on. These mounting difficulties caused an entire decade of potential growth to be lost (the 1980s). These experiences support a conclusion drawn in previous chapters. A successful process of economic development must engage the world; that is, less-developed countries must expand their export capabilities. A transition from import substitution to export promotion must occur.

Latin America in particular illustrates the difficulties associated with extreme inequality in the distribution of wealth and income. Such extremes seem to pose barriers to the accumulation of both physical and human capital and lead to extreme degrees of rent seeking and corruption. Given the historical process by which inequality evolved, the mechanisms by which political development occurred in northwestern Europe, North America, and parts of South and Southeast Asia did not operate in Latin America. Thus, Latin American states and ruling elites have failed to solve the commitment problem.

Openness and the effects of globalization may be more important for its political rather than its economic effects in Latin America. The mobility of capital and labor may provide the mechanism by which political development may occur in Latin America. However, this process is not likely to be easy and may well continue to involve upheaval and violence.

Key Terms

Total Fertility Rate
Terms of Trade
U-form
M-form
State Credibility
Quantity Theory of Money
Latifundio
Minifundio
Structuralism
Center/Periphery
Linkages
Import-Substitution Industrialization
Inflation
Debt
IMF
Economic Reform
Solutions to Commitment Problems
Specie-flow Adjustment Mechanism
Criollas

References

Alesina, A., and D. Rodrik. 1994. "Distributive Politics and Economic Growth." *Quarterly Journal of Economics* (May): 465–90.

Borner, Silvio, F. Bodmer, and Markus Kobler. 2004. *Institutional Efficiency and Its Determinants: The Role of Political Factors in Economic Growth.* Paris: Organization for Economic Co-operation and Development.

Borner, Sylvia, Aymo Brunetti, and Beatrice Weder. 1995. *Political Credibility and Economic Development.* London: Mcmillan.

Caldwell, John C. 1996. "A New Look at the Asian Fertility Transition." *Pakistan Development Review* 35 (4): 385–93.

Cohen, Youssef, B.R. Brown, and A.F.K. Organski. 1981. "The Paradoxical Nature of State Making: The Violent Creation of Order." *American Political Science Review* 75: 901–10.

Cole, Harold, Lee Ohanian, Alvaro Riascos, and James Schmitz. 2005. "Latin America in the Rearview Mirror." *Journal of Monetary Economics* 52: 69–107.

Dyson, Tim, and Mike Murphy. 1985. "The Onset of Fertility Transition." *Population and Development Review* (September): 399–440.

Engerman, Stanley, and Robert Sokoloff. 1994. "Factor Endowments, Institutions, and Differential Paths of Growth among New World Economies: A View from Economic Historians of the United States." NBER Historical Paper 66. National Bureau of Economic Research, Cambridge, Massachusetts.

Fernandez, R., and Richard Rogerson. 1995. "On the Political Economy of Education Subsidies." *Review of Economic Studies* 62: 249–62.

Franko, Patrice. 1999. *The Puzzle of Latin American Economic Development.* New York: Rowman & Littlefield Publishers.

Haber, Stephen. 2006. "It Wasn't All Prebisch's Fault: The Political Economy of Latin American Industrialization." In *The Cambridge Economic History of Latin America,* ed. Victor Bulmer-Thomas, John Coatsworth, and Roberto Cortes Conde. Cambridge: Cambridge University Press.

Hirschman, Albert O. 1958. *The Strategy of Economic Development.* New Haven, CT: Yale University Press.

Maskin, E., Y. Qian, and C. Xu. 2000. "Incentives, Information, and Organizational Form." *Review of Economic Studies* 67: 359–78.

Ocampo, José Antonio. 2004. "Latin America's Growth and Equity Frustrations During Structural Reforms." *Journal of Economic Perspectives* 18: 67–88.

Persson, T., and G. Tabellini. 1994. "Is Inequality Harmful for Growth?" *American Economic Review* 84, 600–21.

Prebisch Raul. 1964. *Towards a New Trade Policy for Development: Report by the Secretary-general of the United Nations Conference on Trade and Development.* New York: United Nations.

Rodríguez, F. 1999. "Inequality, Redistribution and Rent-Seeking." Department of Economics, University of Maryland Working Paper.

Swift, Jeannine. 1978. *Economic Development in Latin America.* New York: St. Martin's Press.

Thorp, Rosemary. 1998. *Progress, Poverty and Exclusion: An Economic History of Latin America in the 20th Century.* Washington, DC: Inter-American Development Bank/Johns Hopkins University Press.

Tokarev, Alexandar. 2004. "Evolution of Pyramidal and Decentralized Institutional Structures: Economic Impacts in Spain and England." PhD diss., Southern Illinois University Carbondale.

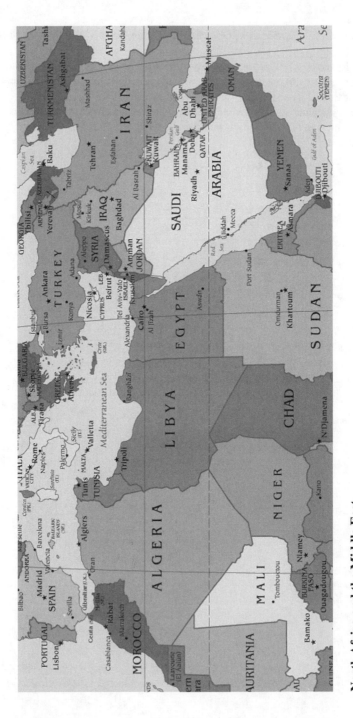

North Africa and the Middle East

7

The Middle East and North Africa

The economies of the Middle East and North Africa (MENA) have been closely tied to Islam, which spread throughout the region in the first two centuries following the death of the Prophet Muhammad. Islamic rule spread throughout MENA and in the early eighth century had reached westward to encompass most of present-day Spain. During this time, Islam developed economic institutions that differed from those of Europe's. These institutions were partly based on the Koran and early writings about Muhammad, and partly on the economy and how it evolved. Given the success of Islam in quickly spreading throughout MENA and parts of Europe, one might suppose not only that Islam had a persuasive message for people in the region but also that the economic and governmental institutions that it created were well-suited for the region at that time. For many centuries, MENA was scientifically and economically at least as advanced as Western Europe. It, however, failed to either keep up with the agricultural revolution in Europe or to later industrialize. At least part of the reason for this failure to advance has been sought in terms of explaining the slowness with which MENA's economic and social institutions adjusted to changing economic needs.

Early Economy in the Precolonial Era

Four features played a role in the development of MENA institutions in the early history of Islam. First, the early rulers came from nomadic tribes and were dependent on animals as a source of wealth and on being mobile in order to find appropriate grazing for their livestock. Second, while agriculture originated in the valleys of the Nile and the Euphrates

River systems, farming methods favored small plots of land and did not undergo the revolution that occurred in Europe and China. Third, agriculture often faced a system of double taxation. The state taxed agriculture and powerful tribes expropriated crops. Fourth, the roots of the bazaar economy were stronger in the feudalistic system of MENA than in Europe. All of these features influenced the development of economic and political systems in MENA.

The economic laws and institutions in MENA were developed largely by the end of the ninth century and continued with little change until the eighteenth century. Some of these laws were clearly set out in the Koran, such as inheritance laws, while others, such as those governing partnerships, property rights, and Islamic trusts, were not so clearly based on the Koran (Kuran 2001, 2003, 2004a). Inheritance rules are known mainly by the feature that daughters receive half as much as sons do. All daughters receive the same share of the estate, and all sons the same share. Provisions were made for other family members, including, in some cases, cousins. These inheritance rules are detailed, explicit, and comprehensive. Because they were explicitly stated in the Koran, they proved to be difficult to change in societies modeled on the teachings of Islam.

One impact of these inheritance rules was that it made it difficult to maintain concentrated wealth from one generation to the next. Contrast this to the situation in Europe, where primogenitor rules of inheritance developed, where the deceased's eldest son received the bulk of the estate. Primogenitor rules clearly helped preserve concentrations of wealth. The more egalitarian inheritance rules of MENA, coupled with partnership laws that made it difficult to form and maintain many types of partnerships, may have limited specialization and economies of scale from emerging in MENA as they did in Europe. The partnership rules that developed made it more difficult to form partnerships that could raise large quantities of funds than was the case in Europe.

The partnership laws of classical Islam were developed in the seventh through tenth centuries and continued almost unchanged until Western commercial law began to be adopted in the eighteenth century. These laws were friendly to commercial interests in part because a large proportion of Islamic scholars in this period were merchants. They legitimized prevailing merchant customs. This legitimacy helped create trust in the system and helped commerce to prosper. Unrelated individuals could overcome mistrust to form partnerships. However, some of the very rules that helped create trust made it difficult for the system to evolve. The process of protoindustrialization, which began to transform Europe in the eighteenth century, did not occur in MENA despite initial advantages. More suitable and more strongly established partnership laws in MENA may actually have hindered economic change because their greater degree of acceptance made modifications in response to a changing economic environment less likely to occur.

Consider three features of partnership laws that may have hindered protoindustrialization and its transformation into an industrial revolution. First, partnerships often required equality in monetary contributions by those making monetary contributions. A partner's contribution could exclusively be labor, but if that person also contributed some money, the monetary contribution had to be the same as the money contributed by other partners. Consequently, the vast majority of partnerships consisted of one partner exclusively contributing labor and the other partner exclusively contributing money. Second, partnerships often had to be dissolved upon the death of one of its members. Third, individual partners were often the party that was responsible for contracts they entered into and not the partnership as a whole. All three of these features made it difficult for the partnership's assets to expand and, combined with the egalitarian inheritance rules, made it difficult for partnerships to survive the death of one of its members. Few partnerships extended beyond the traditional scope developed for long-distance trade. The typical partnership consisted of a sedentary investor and a merchant who carried out a commercial mission. Requirements for equal shares, the inability of the partnership to act as an independent entity, and its likely dissolution at the death of any partner made it difficult for the partnership's assets to grow and reach the economies of scale and scope of European partnerships and corporations.

For whatever reason, the economy in MENA during the period before the nineteenth century can best be classified as a bazaar economy (Geertz 1978, Wilson 1995). Goods in a bazaar economy are highly heterogeneous. While both buyers and sellers are rational in that they are optimizing agents, they often lack critical information for making optimal purchases or sales. Information that would affect prices, such as the quantity and quality of available goods, going prices, market possibilities and production costs, is often unknown or known to different extents by seller and buyer. Strategies to both obtain and hide information are central to the bazaar economy. Bargaining skills, not production or managerial skills, are central to the accumulation of wealth.

Transactions in the bazaar economy combine elements of transactions in traditional economies with elements of highly organized market economies. In traditional economies, trust between transactors is built through repetitive transactions. Transactors know whom they are dealing with and gain confidence that they will not be cheated. A compatibility of interests develops as buyers and sellers seek to establish a reputation for fair dealing and honesty. Repetitive transactions with the same buyer or seller are also a feature of a bazaar economy. However, a compatibility of interests does not develop. Repeated transactions are by their nature adversarial. All transactors are trying to gain and hide information through a bargaining process of making and receiving offers to search for a good bargain. Bargaining searches could be extensive with many potential transactors or intensive with far fewer potential transactors. Intensive searches require that each party believes the other is serious and that the bargaining is likely to result in an actual transaction rather than in a short exchange of information. Repetitive intensive bargaining occurs as transactors gain confidence that the offers of the adversarial transactor are serious.

The Precolonial and Colonial Eras

In a sense, Western colonialism began to have a tremendous impact on MENA long before the establishment of colonies there. The Industrial Revolution resulted in a substantial increase in trade between Europe and MENA that began to transform the region's economies (Owen 1981, Isawi 1982). European powers began to compete for control of MENA economies, threatening the region's independence. During the Napoleonic Wars, the military power of European armies and the threat they posed to governments in the region became obvious. Napoleon conquered Egypt in 1798 and briefly occupied it, until 1801. This larger perceived threat resulted in a period of reform in an attempt to compete both economically and militarily with the Europeans. These reforms were respectively aimed at creating a national economy and a modern state, where the central government would become a primary source of economic and political power.

The most notable of these reforms were made in Egypt and Turkey. New military organizations were created based on conscription rather than on paid, volunteer soldiers. Conscript armies were equipped with modern weapons and trained in modern battlefield techniques. The establishment of this new military organization resulted in, and perhaps required, substantial political and economic changes. Perhaps the most important impact of a conscript army was the concentration of military and political power in the central government rather than in various tribal organizations.

Revenues for the central government had to be dramatically increased in order to support this new military. Four of the chief sources of new revenue that the central government most successfully tapped were as follows. First, the ownership of land was transferred from the tribe to individuals, who could be taxed. Second, international trade was taxed. Because tariffs were limited by treaty, only taxes on exports could be increased to generate more revenue. Third, agricultural production for the market, both domestic and international, was encouraged and taxed. Fourth, state monopolies were established for some products and an excise tax was placed on their products.

The change in land tenure from tribal to individual ownership, along with a shift from subsistence farming to farming for the market, tied farmers to the market and made them individually more vulnerable to fluctuations in market forces. This change was partly positive in that it provided farmers with incentives to improve production methods and switch to crops that are more valuable. All these changes tended to increase production. On the negative side, the individual farmer, who in the past shared risk with the tribe, would now individually bear the risk. When a crop failed, the farmer would be more likely to borrow money. This distress borrowing often led to alienation from the land. Consequently, large amounts of land, formerly tribal or village land, was transferred to what became a large landlord class. A new class of landless agricultural workers also emerged from among those who had lost their land. At the same time, much of the formerly communal land was unevenly distributed so that some wealthy tribal leaders were given control over large tracts of land, creating a landed class devoted to the state that gave them their wealth.

Many of the new cash crops were produced for export, such as cotton, tobacco, and opium. Because these crops competed with food crops for resources, there was a need to import food. For numerous reasons, a tax on food imports was viewed as being undesirable. One reason may be rooted in a long history of episodic famines. Importing as much food as possible and hoarding such food may have been viewed as being highly desirable given this history. Another reason might have been the view that a tax on exports was a tax on foreign consumers, while a tax on imports was viewed as a tax on domestic consumers. Export taxes were thereby viewed as being more desirable. This reliance on imports weakened merchants and craftsmen as a group. Domestic consumers were favored over domestic producers.

Infrastructure to bring agricultural goods to market was built and security from theft and confiscation was provided for farmers. The heaviest state investments were in transportation. A system of railroads was built to bring goods to ports for export. The construction of the Suez Canal was accomplished in 1869, which provided much quicker transportation from Europe to South Asia and linked much of MENA to a larger trade network. This new infrastructure had the impact of connecting MENA to international trade.

The state established monopolies for the production of what were viewed as key strategic items. Early state monopolies were on gunpowder, wine, and snuff. Excise taxes on these goods were an important source of revenue for the government. Much later, of course, profits on oil revenue became an important source of revenue for oil-producing MENA countries. The existence of state monopolies, particularly on gunpowder, strengthened central governments in their struggle with tribal leadership for dominance.

One result of these changes was to introduce a struggle between central government and traditional tribal rulers for control over the destiny of MENA. This struggle, to different extents, continues to this day, undermining the legitimacy of central government. This struggle undermined the ability of governments to support a modern military and thus to provide independence from Western Europe. The reforms served to make MENA more dependent on Europe through increased trade with Europe and through the adoption of many European legal and commercial institutions when it came to commerce. These reforms also increased the importance of Europeans and local non-Muslims in the economies of the era. Non-Muslims, who always had the possibility of adopting non-Islamic legal systems in commerce, were simply better able to adapt to European laws and rules of commerce (Kuran 2004b).

The colonization of MENA can be thought of as an extension of this era of reform. With the exception of Algeria, colonization did not result in emigration to the colony. Consequently, there was little creation of the political, legal, medical, educational, and other systems to make a permanent desirable home for Europeans. Consequently, colonization did not lead to economic development as it did, for example, in North America. Much of this colonization began because of the collapse of the Turkish Ottoman Empire.

The Emergence of Nation-States

MENA has long comprised many independent states, empires, and tribal regions. In a sense, the modern nation-state, with its people bound together in a national identity, is still struggling for legitimacy there. Many people in the region identify themselves first as Arabs, second by tribe, and only third by nationality. Exceptions include Turkey and Iran, with their predominantly non-Arab population, and Egypt, with its long history as a distinct nation or people. The current map of the Middle East was largely created by European colonial powers after World War I and again after World War II. The rulers of these new nations have had to struggle for legitimacy.

The class structure was largely established in the late 1800s during the reform period discussed above. The colonies and the states that emerged largely reinforced this class structure. One exception, however, was the dismantling of much of the merchant class, which had come to consist largely of foreign merchants and non-Muslims. Foreign merchants and—with the rise of tensions over Palestine—Jewish merchants were often forced to leave the region (Kuran 2004b).

Initially, royal families appointed by the colonial powers ruled most of the MENA countries. Soon, however, a number of charismatic leaders overthrew many of the royal heads and captured the imagination of their people—not only in their own countries, but also in MENA as a whole. Their governments drew inspiration from socialist ideas and established many state-controlled industries. Because they were often installed by the military and could justify a large army because of regional instability, the military became part of the political elite, especially in countries near Israel. As a percentage of their population, Syria, Jordan, and Iraq had even larger militaries than Israel. These commitments to large armies were partly a result of hostilities within the region, particularly with Israel. They were also partly a result of the illegitimacy of the state. A military that was perceived to be powerful could intimidate neighbors and could maintain central power and suppress domestic dissent. Whatever the cause, the result was that resources that could have been used to enhance economic development were used to achieve noneconomic goals.

The difficulties states had in achieving legitimacy came in part from the source of their power. Often states were installed by former colonial powers to govern regions that had largely been governed by an assortment of tribal powers. Many of these new states had been part of the Ottoman Empire, and when the empire was abolished after World War I, they became European colonies. When the colonial period ended, these fledgling states needed to develop legitimacy and their own identities. What emerged was a great deal of unrest and insecurity. This unrest and insecurity not only diverted funds to military purposes, but also increased the perceived risk of investing in the region, thereby reducing investment.

As was the case in precolonial days, central government and the military was supported by a taxation system that depended on taxing exports. The ability to raise revenue for many countries in the region was tremendously enhanced by the discovery of oil resources and their exploitation. Oil resources at once transformed the economies of oil exporters (and other countries) in the region, served as a source of revenue and, hence, strength for central governments, and introduced instability to the region in the quest to control oil wealth. In the next section, we will explore the impact of oil on oil exporters within MENA.

Petroleum Exports and the Petroleum Exporters

The discovery of huge oil reserves has brought enormous wealth to petroleum exporting countries in MENA. Oil has dramatically changed their economies in many ways. It has not brought the kind of economic growth and development that these countries had hoped to achieve. Initially, the new wealth led to dramatic changes in their economies. Countries like Saudi Arabia were transformed from largely rural societies into societies that were predominantly urban. Investment was attracted from abroad to develop oil fields. The rent from the ownership of oil went into infrastructure investment, government consumption, the establishment of armed forces, education, and so forth.

While the discovery and development of natural resources can be highly beneficial, particularly in the short run, it can also retard future economic growth. There are four basic reasons given as to why an initial increase in wealth might lead to lower economic growth after some highly beneficial short-term period. First, recall that in Chapter 1 we discussed the growth issue of convergence. Due to diminishing returns, we might expect convergence in income. That is, poorer countries would grow more rapidly than richer countries. Second, when we discussed sub-Saharan Africa the role that natural resources play in establishing a predatory state was discussed. Natural resources may be used to support the political elite to the detriment of growth and development in general. Third, the value of some resources, such as oil, might be expected to be highly volatile. Uncertainty resulting from this volatility might discourage future growth and development. Finally, there are foreign-trade issues concerning the possibility of immiserizing growth and what is called the "Dutch disease," which suggests a detrimental impact on long-term growth. We will discuss, in order, the four reasons why the discovery of large reserves of oil might have had a negative long-term impact on oil exporters in MENA.

First, convergence means that countries that are slow to develop may eventually catch up with countries that developed early. A typical way of testing for convergence was developed in Barro (1991). The method is to see if the level of per capita income in some early year, say 1960, is related to the pace of subsequent economic growth, say growth between 1960 and 2000. If countries with high 1960 income grew more rapidly than low-income countries between 1960 and 2000, then divergence occurred. Divergence means that, in a sense, the rich became richer relative to the poor. If high-income countries grew less rapidly than low-income countries, then convergence occurred. Convergence means that the poor closed part of the income gap between rich and poor. Empirical studies have typically found some convergence. Because oil-exporting MENA countries had and still have higher per capita income than other MENA countries, convergence implies that the rate of growth of oil exporters will be lower, in the long run, relative to nonoil-exporting MENA countries.

Second, oil wealth may also have resulted in institutional arrangements that retard the long-run growth rate. These arrangements were called a patron-client political system in the chapter on sub-Saharan Africa. In an attempt to gain legitimacy, the oil wealth of the political elite was used to establish a patron-client political system in the oil-exporting countries of MENA. The political elite may be traditional rulers, such as in Kuwait, the United Arab Emirates, or Saudi Arabia, or charismatic nationalist leaders, such as in Iraq. Specific benefits provided to the clients include the subsidization of consumption, the subsidization of client producers, the provision of special educational advantages, and the creation of government employment. Consumption subsidies include providing some gasoline, electricity, water, and housing either free or at low prices. In addition to inexpensive or free electricity, production subsidies may include financing and direct subsidies to some market activities. For example, Saudi Arabia heavily subsidizes wheat farming.

Perhaps the most visible sign of the patron-client relationship comes in the attempt to provide good employment for a subset of the population. Some of these subsidies are provided to the entire population, while others are only provided to a subset of the population, such as citizens. Many of the oil exporters have a considerable number of guest workers, who are not eligible for subsidies such as financing or other subsidies provided to locally owned firms. Furthermore, while in some countries guest workers have remained in the country for several decades, neither they nor their children are eligible for many social benefits. These guest workers are also prevented from owning property and becoming entrepreneurs in the business sector. As such, the economy is less efficient than it otherwise might have been, and economic growth is hampered.

Third, the value of resources such as oil, which can be sold now to generate income or stored to generate future income, may be naturally volatile. The basic decision the owner of oil reserves must make is whether to sell the oil now or leave it in the ground. As an asset, oil in the ground will gain or lose value as the price of oil rises or falls. If the owner expects the value to rise, the owner may decide to keep the oil in the ground in order to sell it in the future. Whether more can be earned by selling the oil now or in the future will depend on its rate of return as an asset in the ground versus the rate of return on its generated revenue.

The speculation that drives the price of any commodity such as oil, gold, or diamonds, which are demanded both as commodities and as assets, differs from the typical forces of supply and demand. For the typical commodity, supply is the aggregate marginal cost of producing the commodity and demand is the aggregate marginal benefit of consuming the commodity. When the commodity is held as an asset, speculation as to future production and consumption may be more important than current production and consumption in determining price.

Due to the complexity of the process by which oil is discovered, pumped from the ground, transported to refineries, refined, and marketed, the price of oil as an asset may be easier to understand by focusing on another asset, gold. Gold is demanded both as a commodity and as an asset. Gold is held as an asset because its price is expected to rise. As an asset, gold competes with other assets that yield interest and dividends, such as stocks and bonds. Investors will purchase and hold gold when they expect it will appreciate in value at a rate at least equal to the expected net returns on stocks or bonds.

To illustrate the choice between holding gold versus holding stocks or bonds, consider a two-period model. Let P be the current price of gold, P_e the expected future price, and i the interest (or dividends) that could be earned on stocks or bonds if they were held instead of gold. For simplicity, assume that there are no storage costs for either gold or the alternative asset (stocks or bonds). Risk-neutral investors will not hold gold unless its price is expected to grow at a rate as high or higher than the rate of return on other assets, i. Hence, in Equation (7.1), the investor will hold gold if:

$$P_e \geq P \bullet (1+i). \tag{7.1}$$

If investors believe that the rate of return to holding gold exceeds the rate of return on other assets, they will purchase more gold. In other words, as in Equation (7.2), they will buy gold as long as:

$$P_e > P \bullet (1+i). \tag{7.2}$$

These purchases will drive up the current price, P, until:

$$P_e = P \bullet (1+i), \tag{7.3}$$

when the returns to different assets are equalized.

In looking at Equation (7.3), it should be evident that gold prices might be volatile. A change in the expected future price will cause the current price to move in the same direction. If expected future prices are based on past current prices, this could lead to instability and the development of speculative bubbles and crashes. If investors expect the price of gold to rise, they will purchase gold, bidding up its current price. This increase in price could lead investors to expect prices to rise even more, resulting in further price increases.

Because oil, like gold, can be stored, we would expect oil prices to depend on more than the production and consumption of oil. Oil can be stored as reserves in the ground, as crude oil at refineries and as refined oil at various locations. An increase in expected oil prices will lead to more oil being stored in each of these stages in the production process in order to sell the oil in the future, when it might be more valuable. This increased storage will cause a rise in the current price through the corresponding reductions in supply. Furthermore, if an increase in the current price leads to speculation that the future price will rise, this increase in the price of oil might lead to the formation of a speculative bubble. The price of oil, therefore, depends in part on psychology and how investors feel about the future, just as the stock market depends on psychology.

High volatility of prices for natural resources has both short- and long-term effects on economic development. In the short term, swings in resource prices will lead to swings in the rate of economic growth. For example, gross domestic product (GDP) growth rates in Saudi Arabia rose to over 20 percent in early 1979, when oil prices rose, but fell close to zero or went negative for most of the 1980s and 1990s, with the exception of 1990 and 1991, when oil prices rose as a result of the Persian Gulf war. Similarly, growth rates in the oil exporting countries of MENA were lower than for the rest of the MENA countries during the 1980s and 1990s due to low and declining oil prices.

Swings in economic growth due to swings in resource prices can be detrimental to economic growth and development in the long run. Countries that rely on exports of natural resources for a large portion of their foreign exchange could face instability in their export earnings. This export instability would increase the foreign-exchange risk of investing in such a country. Investors typically require higher average returns before they will make higher risk investments. Hence, instability would lower investment not just when those earnings are low, but would lower average investment in the long run and thus would negatively affect long-term economic growth.

Fourth, the price of oil exports is also important to notions of immiserizing growth and of the Dutch disease, both of which have received attention in the trade and development literature. The possibility of immiserizing growth, introduced in Bhagwati (1969), will be considered first. Immiserizing growth would occur if increased exports of oil were to lead to a decline in real GDP for the oil exporter. For this to occur, an increase in oil exports would need to lead to a strong worsening in the terms of trade. *Ceteris paribus*, a rise in a country's exports is expected to decrease the price of those exports and, hence, worsen the terms of trade. The strength of this decline must be considerable for immiserizing growth to occur.

The possibility of immiserizing growth depends on three conditions.

First, a country must be highly oriented toward increasing its exports and changes in those exports must have a noticeable impact on world prices. This condition would seem to be met by large oil exporters, such as Saudi Arabia, Kuwait, and the United Arab Emirates. Second, the foreign demand for these exports needs to be inelastic so that a rise in exports leads to a decline in export earnings. The demand for oil is highly inelastic. By the typical estimate, a 5 percent increase in oil production will cause the price of oil to fall by half. Third, the country must be highly dependent on exports and exports must be a high proportion of gross national product (GNP). Again, the Persian Gulf countries—Kuwait, Saudi Arabia, and the United Arab Emirates—meet this condition.

While the conditions for immiserizing growth seem to exist for the oil-exporting MENA countries, it has not yet occurred. Declining oil prices in the 1980s and 1990s did result in declining real GDP, but the subsequent rapid rise in oil prices resulted in renewed growth and prosperity for these countries. Two factors make long-term immiserizing growth of major oil exporters unlikely. First, in the long term, rising demand for oil may outstrip the possibility of oil production. As petroleum reserves fall, the price of this limited resource will rise. Second, it would be foolish for any supplier to do nothing in the face of rapidly declining terms of trade. Far from being competitive suppliers with no power to control prices, the major oil exporters, individually and collectively, have considerable price control. They did not dramatically add new production when prices were low in the 1980s and 1990s in a desperate but fruitless attempt to increase declining revenues. They are now benefiting from tight oil markets.

Dutch disease concerns a different difficulty concerning the terms of trade. The theory behind this notion combines two well-established principles of development and trade. The first principle is that industrialization in the long run is the key to economic development. The second principle is known as the Rybczynski theorem. It states that growth in the domestic availability of a factor of production increases the output of goods that use that factor intensively and decreases the output of other goods. Before explaining Dutch disease, we will briefly explain the Rybczynski theorem.

Consider a country that experiences a rapid rise in the size of its labor force relative to the growth in capital or natural resources. The rise in the supply of labor will decrease the wage rate and increase the rate of return to capital and resources. The production of labor-intensive goods will become more profitable and the profitability of capital and resource-intensive goods will fall. Hence, more labor-intensive goods will be produced and the production of capital- or resource-intensive goods will fall as capital and resources are shifted toward the production of labor-intensive goods. An increase in the supply of any factor of production will have a similar effect.

Now consider the impact of the discovery and development of a new oil field. It becomes more profitable than before to produce goods, including gasoline and chemicals, for which oil is used intensively, and less profitable to produce other goods, including other manufactured goods. Consequently, resources are shifted from manufacturing to oil production and the production of oil-related goods. The profitability of the oil sector may make it difficult to industrialize without substantial subsidies to manufacturing.

This difficulty in industrializing comes specifically from the Rybczynski theorem. Dutch disease occurs when these impediments to industrialization are severe. In the story of Dutch disease, investment in the oil sector becomes more profitable through time as oil prices rise due to declining overall supply and rising demand. Resources continue to be drawn from manufacturing and the country begins and continues to deindustrialize as long as oil prices continue to rise. If the country was not industrialized in the first place, then industrialization will not occur.

There is nothing inevitable about the Dutch disease. Like the possibility of immiserizing growth, it can be prevented through appropriate policy. However, the appropriate policy is just the opposite for the two situations. With immiserizing growth, falling oil prices should be offset by policies to shift resources to manufacturing; however, if oil prices are rising, no such policy is needed. With the Dutch disease, rising prices should lead to manufacturing subsidies. If prices are falling, no subsidies are needed.

An alternative to subsidies is a policy to neutralize much of the impact of high oil revenue on the exchange rate. For example, Norway places much of its oil revenues into a rainy-day fund. This fund is held in foreign currencies. The purchase of this fund bids up the price of foreign exchange while sales of foreign exchange from the fund drive down the price of foreign exchange. In this way, Norway stabilizes the value of its currency and prevents the value of its currency from rising so high that it leads to deindustrialization. The countries of the Persian Gulf temporarily built up reserves of foreign currency, but were less successful in exchange-rate neutralization in part because they had become much more dependent on oil revenue.

The countries of the Gulf are concerned about being overly dependent on oil. One of their responses has been to build up other industries. This is particularly the case in the United Arab Emirates, where investment in manufacturing and high technology has been encouraged. Highly skilled guest workers have been employed from India and many other countries. These guest workers can stay long term as long as they have employment. However, there are restrictions on their ability to fully participate in the economy, although some of these restrictions, such as the inability to own property, may soon be removed for long-term guest workers. We will now turn to guest-worker programs and other ways in which the economies of oil-exporting MENA nations have an impact on the economies of the rest of MENA.

Petroleum and Nonpetroleum Exporters in MENA

Many of the MENA countries produce and export little petroleum. The most important of these nonpetroleum MENA countries are Egypt and Turkey. The growth rates in these countries since 1960 have been higher than in oil-exporting MENA countries, and, except for the 1980s, compare favorably with the growth rates for East Asia. In fact, during the 1970s, the rate of growth in nonoil MENA was 4.6 percent per capita, the highest in the world. It might be pointed out that this was the period when oil prices rose dramatically. One might have expected the growth rates in oil-exporting MENA countries to have been higher than the growth rates of nonoil-exporting MENA countries during this oil-boom decade, but they were not.

The growth miracle that occurred in nonoil MENA countries has been little noted. What forces created this miracle? It is as if much of the benefits of higher oil prices in the 1970s were transferred from oil producers to nonoil producers in MENA. It might be noted that a similar situation arose in Europe following the discovery of the New World. Recall from Chapter 6 on Latin America that it was Spain that first brought home the wealth of the New World. This wealth consisted of gold instead of oil. However, it was England that became wealthy, in part by increasing its own production and selling its products to Spain in return for gold. A similar thing happened in MENA. Oil initially made the oil-producing MENA countries wealthy. However, the rest of MENA has been capturing much of this wealth by increasing production and exporting to the oil producers.

Nonoil MENA countries took advantage of prosperity in the Persian Gulf and elsewhere in many ways. Some countries took advantage of this prosperity directly by supplying guest workers. Guest workers supplied savings to the country of origin, which provided much-needed foreign exchange, financed investment, and, of course, allowed the migrants to enjoy higher current and future consumption. In analyzing the economic impact of guest workers on the countries of origin and destination, it is important to understand differences between temporary and normal migration. Normal migration, was discussed in the chapter on Sub-Saharan Africa when we considered the Harris-Todaro model.

A key difference between temporary and normal migration concerns the motivation of migrants. In normal migration, a person or family moves in order to have a better life at the destination. In temporary migration, a person or family moves temporarily in order to have a better life at the point of origin. The temporary migrant saves at the destination in order to invest those savings, moves back to the point of origin, and enjoys a better lifestyle in the future.

An example of the two types of migrants can be seen by looking at guest workers in Kuwait before and after the 1991 Persian Gulf war. Before the war, Kuwait had a large number of Palestinian guest workers. Many of these stateless Palestinians did not have a country of origin. They lived, consumed, and saved in Kuwait. Their savings typically went into Kuwaiti banks. They brought their families with them and built a home. Hence, they were what we would call normal migrants even though their visas were temporary.

The Gulf war changed the status of migrants in Kuwait. Many Palestinians in Jordan and other countries openly celebrated the Iraqi invasion of Kuwait. This created bitter feelings on the part of Kuwaitis. After a U.S.-led coalition forcibly expelled Iraq from Kuwait, the Palestinians still in Kuwait were expelled and those who had fled because of the invasion were not welcomed back. Consequently, other guest migrants were recruited. A large number of these migrants came from Egypt. The Egyptian migrants fully intended to return to Egypt. Migration was an investment decision in that the migrants accumulated funds in Kuwait deposited these funds in Egyptian financial institutions with the intention of using these funds on their return to Egypt. A principle motivation was to earn enough money to purchase housing in Egypt, but other motivations, such as starting or investing in a business, were also present. The migrants often were either unmarried or did not take their families with them to Kuwait. For all these reasons, their consumption in Kuwait was and is low.

Because they have lower consumption and because their savings were transferred to their country of origin, temporary Egyptian migrants in the Gulf following the war contributed less on average to the Gulf economies than did migrants before the war. Temporary migration contributed much to the economies of their origin. It provided much-needed foreign exchange, provided savings for financing investment, and allowed the ambitious to succeed, contributing much-needed entrepreneurship to the economy of the origin.

The transfer of savings from oil-exporting MENA countries to nonoil MENA countries meant that investment could be higher in the nonoil countries than domestic saving would support. Indeed, this was the case. As a percentage of GDP, investment in the nonoil countries of MENA was almost 20 percent higher than domestic savings for the past forty years. In addition, investment in the oil exporters in the region was substantially lower than their domestic savings. This transfer of savings was partly a result of the temporary nature of Gulf migration. The availability of more opportunities for profitable investment is undoubtedly another reason.

The over achievers in Arab growth during the last four decades were Egypt, Jordan, Morocco, Oman, Syria, and Tunisia. Oman was the only one of these countries that was an oil exporter, and since Oman's oil fields were only recently developed, its growth might best be described as a characteristic of the catching-up phenomenon. One characteristic of successful MENA countries over the last four decades that distinguishes them from unsuccessful MENA countries was the growth in total factor productivity. Egypt, Morocco, and Tunisia had positive growth in total factor productivity, while the remaining Arab countries had negative total factor productivity growth.

Total factor productivity growth is the key to sustained economic development. Recall from the discussion of growth theory in Chapter 1 that technological change is the only source growth in per capita income once long-term equilibrium (steady-state equilibrium) has been reached. In a study of ninety-two developed and less-developed countries, Makdisi, Fattah, and Limam (2000) placed Egypt and Morocco tied for tenth in terms of the rate of total factor productivity growth for 1960 to 1997.

Total productivity growth means that the productivity of all factors of production is rising. Total productivity growth will, hence, directly affect the rate of growth of the economy by increasing factor productivity. Because total factor productivity growth increases the marginal products of both capital and labor, it will clearly increase GDP. It will also indirectly influence economic growth through its impact on investment. Investment funds will flow to economies that have a higher rate of return to investment, and the returns to investment will be increased by the increased marginal product of capital. Hence, higher growth in total productivity will lead to higher growth rates through its impact on the investment rate.

Total factor productivity is influenced by many factors, including exogenous technological change. Structural differences between economies may lead to differences in total factor productivity growth. Several factors may have led to the higher growth rates in nonoil-exporting versus oil-exporting MENA countries. One factor is that the former had lower growth variability than the oil producers. Other factors may have been better integration into the world economy, a more diversified economy with a larger manufacturing sector, earlier adoption of economic reforms, and a better-quality educational system that depends more on discovery than learning by rote.

One of the most striking characteristics of nonoil MENA economies concerns the relatively equal distribution of income. The Gini coefficient is a measure of inequality that provides easy comparisons between countries. Theoretically, it can range from zero, for perfect equality of family income, to one, for perfect inequality. Perfect equality means that every family receives the same income. Perfect inequality would exist if all the income went to just one family. Obviously, actual Gini coefficients for existing economies are in the middle of this zero-to-one range.

High Gini coefficients are associated with highly unequal ownership of resources, with uneven growth, and with development strategies that promote investment in capital-intensive industrialization at the expense of investment in human capital. Some representative Gini coefficients are given in Table 7.1. Latin American countries (e.g., Argentina, Brazil, Mexico) often have high Gini coefficients. One of the reasons for the high inequality in income and consumption was the early development of extremely unequal patterns of land ownership with very large estates coupled with tiny holdings. Countries with a wealth-creating natural resource (Botswana, Iran, Nigeria) also have high Gini coefficients. This inequality is partly because the exploitation of this resource created uneven growth, raising incomes for only one sector of the economy. Inequality

Table 7.1

Gini Coefficients

Country	Gini coefficient
Argentina	0.522
Botswana	0.630
Brazil	0.593
Egypt	0.344
Germany	0.283
India	0.325
Iran	0.430
Japan	0.249
Republic of Korea	0.316
Mexico	0.560
Morocco	0.395
Nigeria	0.506
Russia	0.310
Sweden	0.250
United States	0.408

Source: UNDP (2005).

in the ownership of that resource may also be a source of inequality. East Asian and South Asian countries (Japan, Korea, India), with a much more equal pattern of land ownership, developed lower Gini coefficients. High-income, industrialized countries (Germany, Japan, Sweden, the United States) and European transitional economies (Russia) have lower Gini coefficients, in part because of their emphasis on education (investment in human capital) and the equality of access to education. The higher Gini coefficient for the United States may be partly due to the uneven access to higher education, due partly to race and class.

Morocco and Egypt, two nonoil MENA countries, have fairly low Gini coefficients. Gini coefficients are not available for the oil-exporting MENA countries, with the exception of Iran. Two factors that contributed to these low Gini coefficients in Morocco and Egypt are the result of the pattern of land ownership, which is more equitable than in Latin America, and partly the diversified economy. Manufacturing exports are much larger as a percentage of total exports than is the case for oil-exporting MENA countries, where much of their exports are primary exports.

The relatively low Gini coefficients may have been one factor that led to the higher economic growth in nonoil MENA countries. However, there has been disagreement as to how inequality affects economic growth.

In the classic model, the saving rate and, hence, the investment rate is increased by shifting income from workers to capitalists (Lewis 1954, Ricardo [1817] 1965). In the classic model, capitalists save and invest while workers do not. The capitalists are driven to invest in order to earn more profits in the future. This investment is seen as being the key to growth in the classic model. The key to increasing investment is shifting income to the capitalists who save and invest.

While inequality may increase saving and investment, it may reduce the efficiency by which resources are used. Inequality may lower institutional quality and, hence, economic growth. Diversity in production and equality in family income may be a key to economic growth because it raises institutional quality. Before considering the impact of greater diversity in production and higher equality of income on institutional quality, we will first discuss what is meant by institutional quality.

The quality of institutions refers to the ability of the government to act in ways that foster economic development, meaning widespread economic growth that raises income in general and is self-sustaining. There are numerous indicators of institutional equality, of which we will consider nine. These indicators are interdependent, but will be discussed separately. Indicators of low quality are corruption, internal conflict, external conflict, risk of expropriation, and risk of government repudiation of contracts. Indicators of higher quality are a professional bureaucracy, government stability, the rule of law, and well-developed market institutions (see Hakura [2004] for a study of different growth rates in various MENA countries). We will first discuss the indicators of low-quality institutions and then the indicators of high-quality ones.

Corruption occurs when illegal payments are generally expected. Usually corruption is thought of as public corruption, involving illicit payments to government employees for government services. However, corruption involves any unlawful payment, whether to private or public persons. One type of corruption is the widespread practice of paying bribes for various licenses, such as import or export licenses. Corruption might also involve paying bribes to escape taxes and various fees, or to obtain various government favors, such as low-interest loans.

Internal or external conflict reduces the quality of institutions. They result in the destruction of capital and infrastructure, disrupted production, and wasted private and public resources. These conflicts do not need to be continuously destructive and active in order to lead to the misallocation of resources, which retards growth and development.

The risk of expropriation and governmental repudiation of contracts cannot only drive away foreign capital and expertise, but lead to the misallocation of resources. Firms and individuals undertake rent- and profit-preserving activities. They behave in a way that reduces this risk at the cost of production.

Recall that the indicators of high quality institutions were a high quality bureaucracy, a stable government, the rule of law, and a well-functioning market with clearly defined property rights. A high-quality bureaucracy is one in which its representatives and decision makers are appropriately trained. They act without showing favoritism and according to professional standards. A stable government is one in which decisions have continuity through time. A rule of law means that the law governs decisions and conflicts and does not show favoritism or prejudice. The judiciary is independent and upholds the rule of law in its decisions. The existence of clearly defined property rights and market mechanisms provides a system wherein increased production is rewarded.

There are difficulties in MENA with regard to institutional quality, such as the existence of external and internal conflict; most measures of institutional quality rank them as average for developing nations. In nonoil MENA, the diversified economy and fairly equal distribution of income have helped to enhance institutional quality. Numerous sources of income, including income repatriated by temporary migrants, have meant that MENA governments need to gain support from a large proportion of the population if they are to remain in power. This need differs sharply from the situation of the oil exporters, who only had to gain the support of the economic elite.

According to Sala-i-Martin and Subramanian (2003), concentrations of wealth and their impact on institutional quality could be the primary reason for the natural-resource curse found in some developing countries. They concluded this was the case in a study of Nigeria, for example. In addition to wasteful uses, oil revenues reduced institutional quality and, hence, reduced total factor productivity. One way in which institution quality was lessened was conflict over the division of new wealth, which led to internal strife and civil war. Sala-i-Martin and Subramanian suggest that future oil revenues from newly discovered deposits of natural gas in Nigeria should be distributed directly and equally to all adult citizens for whatever consumption or investment they wish to undertake.

This distribution would change the situation where the government has easy revenue through its ownership of natural resources and the resulting incentives for rent seeking. When the government directly receives the wealth from oil, the surest path to individual wealth becomes obtaining and using government influence. In addition, individuals might invest their windfalls in economic activities that are more in line with the factor proportions that exist in the economy. This would reduce waste, which often occurs when government leaders invest in highly capital-intensive prestige investment.

What We Have Learned

Economic institutions are to be judged not only in how well they suit the needs of the time, but in terms of how well they adapt to changing needs. Economic institutions developed differently in MENA than in Europe. These differences were partly due to differences in religion and partly due to underlying differences in the ways in which people in the two regions made a living. Europe was highly oriented toward sedentary agriculture with good land and the heavy, wheeled plough pulled by harnessed horses. Land was the source of wealth and institutions and inheritance laws emerged that consolidated control over land. MENA was highly oriented toward trade in exotic commodities brought over great distances. Institutions and inheritance laws emerged that fostered this trade within the framework of a bazaar economy. Both institutions were well-suited to the economies in which they developed, but it was European institutions that evolved more rapidly to support an industrialized economy.

The discovery of oil in parts of MENA dramatically influenced the economies. It clearly and dramatically made the oil-exporting countries of MENA much wealthier. However, in recent decades the oil-exporting economies have experienced much lower growth than the nonoil-exporting economies. This resource curse was due to instability in oil revenues, deteriorating terms of trade from 1980 until the past few years, a shift of resources from industrialization jeopardizing future growth, and the unequal income distribution that resulted, leading to poor institutional quality. The nonoil-exporting countries diversified their economies, took advantage of resources provided by temporary migrants, had a more equitable income distribution, and experienced growth partly by improving the quality of institutions.

This resource curse was both economic and political. In one sense, the political curse is the strongest because there are policies to offset the economic curse. These policies are simply hard to enact given poor institutional quality. Perhaps the greatest current political challenge in MENA concerns instability. In response to instability in the region, the military consumes a high proportion of GDP and maintains a large standing army. This diverts resources from manufacturing and other economic activities to a nonproductive use.

Key Terms

Corruption
Islamic Inheritance Rules
Partnership Laws of Classical Islam
Predatory State
Dutch Disease
Price Volatility
Immiserizing Growth
Terms of Trade
Nonpetroleum Exporters
Guest Workers
Total Factor Productivity
Gini Coefficients
Institutional Quality
Primogenitor
Bazaar Economy
Export taxes
State Legitimacy
Patron-client Relationship
Rybczynski Theorem

References

Barro, R. 1991. "Economic Growth in a Cross-Section of Countries." *Quarterly Journal of Economics* 106 (May): 407–43.

Bhagwati, J.N. 1969. "Optimal Policies and Immiserizing Growth." *American Economic Review* 59 (December): 967–70.

Geertz, C. 1978. "The Bazaar Economy: Information and Search in Peasant Marketing." *American Economic Review* 68 (May): 28–32.

Hakura, D.S. 2004. "Growth in the Middle East and North Africa." IMF Working Paper 04/56. International Monetary Fund, Washington, DC.

Isawi, C.P. 1982. *An Economic History of the Middle East and North Africa.* New York: Columbia University Press.

Kuran, T. 2001, "The Provision of Public Goods under Islamic Law: Origins, Impact, and Limitations of the Waqf System." University of Southern California, Department of Economics. Working Paper.

———. 2003. "The Islamic Commercial Crisis: Institutional Roots of Economic Underdevelopment in the Middle East." *Journal of Economic History* 63 (June): 414–46.

———. 2004a "Why the Middle East is Economically Underdeveloped: Historical Mechanisms of Institutional Stagnation." *Journal of Economic Perspectives* 18 (summer): 71–90.

———. 2004b. "The Economic Ascent of the Middle East's Religious Minorities: The Role of Islamic Legal Pluralism." *Journal of Legal Studies* 33 (June): 475–515.

Lewis, W.A. 1954, "Economic Development with Unlimited Supplies of Labour." *The Manchester School* 22 (May): 139–91.

Makdisi, S., Z. Fattah, and I. Limam. 2000. "Determinants of Growth in the MENA Countries." Arab Planning Institute Working Paper Series, No. 0301/39, Safat, Kuwait.

Owen, R. 1981. *The Middle East in the World Economy, 1800–1914.* London and New York: Metheun.

Ricardo, David. 1965 [1817]. *The Principles of Political Economy and Taxation.* London: Aldine Press.

Richards, A., and J. Waterbury. 1996. *A Political Economy of the Middle East*, 2nd ed. Boulder, CO: Westview Press.

Sala-i-Martin, X., and A. Subramanian. 2003. "Addressing the Natural Resource

Curse: An Illustration from Nigeria." IMF Working Paper 03/139. International Monetary Fund, Washington, DC.

United Nations Development Programme. 2005. *Human Development Report 2005.* New York: United Nations.

Wilson, Rodney. 1995. *Economic Development of the Middle East.* London and New York: Routledge.

China and Russia

8

Economies in Transition
Socialist to Market

The post–World War II era was one of animus between the United States and the Soviet Union. This conflict was not direct, but played itself out through a variety of indirect means. Much of the conflict revolved around the organization of the respective economic systems. The United States represented a capitalistic form of organization, while the Soviet Union represented the socialist or centralized-planning system. Actually, neither system was purely capitalist or purely socialist. They were both mixtures of capitalism and socialism, but they did represent two very different systems of organization.

Initially the leaders of the Soviet Union trumpeted to the developing world that socialism represented a pathway to industrialization and wealth that was superior and quicker—relative to the capitalist path. Initially, this did indeed seem to be the case. In the 1950s and 1960s, the Soviet Union rapidly expanded heavy industrial production and managed a series of technological achievements that stunned the world (e.g., launching the first artificial satellite into space, putting manned spacecraft into orbit). Economic growth in the Soviet Union appeared to be quite brilliant. Much of the developing world sought to imitate the Soviet Union by introducing planning mechanisms as substitutes for markets and by nationalizing parts of the indigenous economy. Of course, China's shift to socialism was probably the most obvious example. However, all of Eastern Europe joined (much of it involuntary) the socialist group as well.

However, beginning in the 1970s, but particularly in the 1980s and early 1990s, growth in the Soviet Union and much of Eastern Europe began to falter. Outward indicators of inefficiency became increasingly apparent. The economic machine powering the socialist experience seemed to be winding down. Attempts at reform were pushed forward, but with little effect. This culminated in the collapse of the communist states in Eastern Europe and of the Soviet Union itself, which was followed by strenuous attempts by new regimes and new ruling elites to transform their economies from state socialism to free-market capitalism. This involved the dismantling of state controls, the privatization of state-owned assets, and the establishment of widespread markets. For some countries, the changes were traumatic and difficult.

In terms of how the transition occurred, there are two views that have emerged. One group of countries appeared to have embraced rapid change, referred to as "shock therapy" or the "big bang." Some countries, on the other hand, preferred a more gradual change, which earned them the name "gradualists." There were some countries, such as Poland, where shock therapy was used to bring down inflation, but a more gradual approach was taken in terms of privatization. A different type of transition took place in China. The change was not just gradual in pace, but it was gradual in terms of how much of the economy was transformed. There was selective elimination of state controls, the spread of market exchange, but only limited privatization and limited development of property rights. Some have labeled this the creation of a market-based socialism. The results in China have been truly spectacular. Economic growth has been extremely rapid and poverty has been dramatically reduced. China is viewed as constituting a modern-day economic miracle.

The focus of this chapter will be on the transition economies—those attempting to move from socialism to capitalism—and the transition process. It will not be possible to look at all of these economies, so the focus will be on two: Russia and China. Some may argue that comparing Russia and China is not a fair comparison given that China's initial conditions (prior to beginning the transition process) were different from Russia's in the sense that it was more similar to those facing developing countries. Alternatively, Russia and much of Eastern Europe had already attained middle-income status. However, a comparison of these two countries will expose the reader to two highly contrasting examples of economies in transition in terms of process, degree, speed, and outcome. In this comparison, the emphasis will be on looking at those factors that may account for the phenomenal success of the Chinese economy. Are there lessons to be learned that could be usefully applied to other densely populated poor countries?

In the next section, the discussion will begin with an examination of how socialist systems were organized, followed by a look at the performance of such systems through time. The difficulties of making the transition will be discussed and alternative approaches to this process examined. Then the Russian and Chinese experience will be compared. Finally, as always, the concluding section will focus on what has been learned.

Economic Systems

All human societies have three economic questions they must answer: What is going to be produced? How are the chosen goods to be produced? Who is going to get these goods? Different forms of economic organization answer these questions in different ways. One can classify these forms into three broad categories: traditional, market, and socialist. There are no pure examples of these forms in the modern world. In fact, most real-world economic systems are mixtures of the three. However, in this chapter we will focus on these three pure forms while always keeping in mind that most nations are varying mixtures of the three.

Traditional systems of organization answer the above three questions by appealing to tradition. Tradition represents the system of beliefs and values that are inherited from the past, handed down from generation to generation through teaching within the family, written records, formal and informal training, and so on. One might think of tradition as representing a region's culture. Thus, what goods are produced are determined by what one's ancestors chose to produce, what one's religion espouses, what is important according to one's customs. How goods are produced is certainly partly dependent on the materialistic foundation of society, that is, the available technology. However, within the set of available technologies certain techniques have been utilized by preceding generations and are handed down to the current generation of producers. This is often the deciding factor in terms of the choice of technology. These technologies have been tried and tested through time and thus community experience has acted as a filter, eliminating technologies that in the past have failed. Thus, there is an objective basis to traditional technology, but it is the community and tradition that determines the technology. Finally, how goods are distributed is often significantly influenced by religion, caste, and social obligations.

One might think that with modernization this role of tradition as an organizational mechanism would disappear. However, even in advanced market economies there are areas of economic activity that are still governed by tradition. One need only think of the various Amish communities in the United States, which are dominated by tradition. However, in most industrialized economies, the fundamental mechanism of organization is the market; but what exactly is a market? All markets involve transactions involving goods, and when these markets are monetized, they involve the exchange of money for goods and goods for money. Specifically, buyers and sellers interact in markets.

Within the context of markets, a decentralized decision-making process takes place. What goods are produced is the outcome of a myriad of interactions between buyer and seller in various markets. Those markets in which net demand is positive and growing attract resources and vice versa. How goods are produced is also the result of a myriad of decentralized transactions. Producers examine the relative market costs of various inputs and choose techniques of production intensive in the use of inputs that are in relative abundance (i.e., are relatively cheap). Finally, who gains access to goods is determined by income earned by households (itself the outcome of market transactions).

Most market systems are based on the principle of private property. Institutional rules exist that designate who owns what and how disputes over these rights are to be resolved. Although this is typical, there are important exceptions to this. There are a number of countries where private-property rights are undeveloped and yet market exchange dominates. Perhaps the best example is provided by China. More will be said about this later in this chapter.

The final organizational form that will be discussed is socialism. Under this organizational system, decision making is highly centralized. Specifically, a small ruling elite operating through various institutional structures determines what is produced, how it is produced, and who gets the output. This usually involves a highly centralized planning process in which resources are allocated to particular industries, prices are set, and incomes determined. For the most part, such systems reject the use of markets, and thus such institutional structures are generally repressed and limited. In addition, under this organizational system property is generally owned by the state.

Of course, as stated before, pure forms of these three types are impossible to find in the real world. Instead, most economic systems are mixtures of these three types, with the exact mixture varying greatly from society to society. The great conflict of the postwar period, however, pitted the market-based economies of the West (i.e., the United States, Canada, Australia, Western Europe), including Japan, against the socialist economies of the East (i.e., the Soviet Union, Eastern Europe, China). The next section will analyze the economic performance of the group of socialist nations, with the purpose being to provide background on the environment that generated the transition process.

Economic Performance of Socialism

Before proceeding with an analysis of the actual performance of socialism, some time will be spent analyzing the motive for establishing socialist economic systems. Much of the ideological basis for socialism comes from the theories of Karl Marx. As discussed in Chapter 1, Marx was a fierce critic of the capitalist economic system (free markets combined with private-property rights). His fundamental analysis was based on the notion that capitalist profit comes as the result of the exploitation of labor by the owners of capital. The profit extracted via this exploitation was then used to finance the creation of new capital and the expansion of the capitalist system. Marx viewed capitalism as a dynamic system that would spread worldwide, destroying the old traditional systems of organization in its wake. He did not feel that there would be any obstacles to the expansion of capitalism; however, he held the system was inherently doomed.

Being driven by profit, where profit was based on exploitation, capitalism would be driven to increased levels of exploitation, resulting in increased misery for the working class. In addition, the increased exploitation of workers implied that their ability to purchase goods would be strictly limited. Production capacity would tend to outrun demand resulting in crisis, within which unemployment would rise, firms would collapse. Eventually, he argued, the capitalist system would be overthrown as the exploited workers rise up in rebellion, take over the means of production, and eliminate the capitalist class. Thus, the age of socialism would be ushered in, with private property eliminated.

According to traditional Marxist analysis, socialism would develop in any region where capitalism had become highly developed. Marx expected a communist revolution to first occur in a country like England, a highly advanced capitalist nation. However, the first communist revolution actually occurred in an economically backward nation, Russia, in

Table 8.1

Law of Diminishing Returns

Capital	Labor	Q	MP_k	AP_k
1	1	10	10	10
2	1	25	15	12.5
3	1	45	20	15
4	1	60	15	15
5	1	65	5	13
6	1	66	1	11

1917. Russia was then still predominately agrarian in nature with only a small industrial base. It was a poor, developing country. In this context, the ideas of Marx were used by the early Russian communist leaders (Lenin and Stalin) as a foundation from which to attempt to try to propel Soviet Russia along a path of rapid industrialization.

There were a number of Marxist ideas that were quite useful to the new leaders of the new Soviet Union. First, and most importantly, growth is the result of rapid capital accumulation, which in turn is the result of savings and investing. To rapidly grow, the new Soviet state would have to extract large amounts of savings in order to finance a rapid growth in the capital stock. However, control over the saving and investment process was not theirs as long as private control over resources prevailed, as long as private property dominated. Hence, part of the motivation to eliminate private property was to seize control of the nation's wealth, allowing the ruling elite to reallocate resources. Finally, as per Marxist theory, industrialization was held to be the key to both economic and political power. Industry, especially heavy industry, was to be favored.

Socialism (i.e., communism) within the Soviet Union and Eastern Europe evolved into a highly centralized command economy, with most property directly controlled by the state. China initially mimicked much of the Soviet structure, but it evolved into a much different sort of system through time. The main thrust was the rapid accumulation of industrial capital and the creation of highly concentrated, heavy industry. For the purposes of understanding the data that will be presented below, Table 8.1 provides a useful mechanism for looking at the Soviet and East European experience. There are two inputs, labor and capital, with the latter presumed variable and the former fixed. Technology is also presumed to be fixed. Output of a single, conglomerate industrial good is represented by Q, MP_k is the marginal product of capital, and AP_k is output per unit of capital. The table illustrates the operation of the law of diminishing returns. Initially, as more capital is accumulated, MP_k rises, but eventually it falls. The same hold for the productivity of capital (AP_k). Thus, a growth strategy that emphasizes capital accumulation initially achieves increasing returns, and growth rates increase. However, eventually the law of diminishing returns sets in, with the productivity of capital declining and growth falling.

Table 8.1 illustrates an important idea in a stylistic manner. Growth based on capital accumulation (i.e., not technological change) eventually slows down. Does this reflect what happened in the socialist countries, in particular the Soviet Union and Eastern Europe? Table 8.2 illustrates the growth rates for a number of socialist countries on a decade-by-decade basis. Growth rates in the period 1950 to 1960 are quite high. However, for each subsequent decade growth rates decline dramatically. The outlier or exception in this group is China. For China, growth rates in both percentage increase in gross domestic product (GDP) and percentage increase in GDP per capita seem to accelerate with each decade. For the bulk of the socialist countries, growth decelerates.

In analyzing the postwar experience of the socialist countries of the Soviet Union and Eastern Europe, Gregory and Stuart (2004) make a distinction between intensive and extensive growth. Intensive growth occurs as the result of technological change and improvement in efficiency (moving to the expanding production-possibilities curve). Extensive growth occurs because of the accumulation of a factor of production, most likely capital. The former, intensive growth is capable of generating long-run increases in output per person. The latter, extensive growth, can generate increases in per capita income in the short term, but in the long term a growing capital-to-labor ratio runs into the law of diminishing returns (*ceteris paribus*). Examining Table 8.3, in the subset of socialist countries listed, capital grew much more rapidly than labor and capital productivity declined, becoming negative in many cases, from 1960 to 1983. Table 8.3 shows that total factor productivity (a good measure of efficiency gains) also declined in this particular period.

The story told here, and seemingly supported by the data, indicates that socialism in Eastern Europe and the Soviet Union was running out of steam. The initial rapid growth stimulated by rapid capital accumulation was running into diminishing returns, with growth rates dropping off dramatically. These economic strains created intense political strains

Table 8.2

Growth Rates: Select Socialist Countries (per capita growth in parentheses)

Country	1950–60	1960–65	1965–70	1970–75	1975–80	1980–85	1985–90
Czechoslovakia	4.8 (3.9)	2.3 (1.6)	3.4 (3.2)	3.4 (2.7)	2.2 (1.5)	1.5 (1.2)	1.2 (1.2)
East Germany	5.7 (6.7)	2.7 (3.0)	3.0 (3.1)	3.4 (3.8)	2.3 (2.5)	1.8 (1.4)	1.6 (1.6)
Soviet Union	5.7 (3.9)	5.0 (3.5)	5.2 (4.2)	3.7 (2.7)	2.7 (1.8)	2.0 (1.1)	1.8 (1.1)
Poland	4.6 (2.75)	4.4 (3.2)	4.1 (3.4)	6.4 (5.4)	0.7 (0)	0.7 (-0.1)	0.2 (0.2)
Hungary	4.6 (4.0)	4.2 (3.9)	3.0 (2.7)	3.4 (2.9)	2.0 (1.9)	1.7 (1.7)	0.7 (0.7)
Romania	5.8 (4.55)	6.0 (5.3)	4.9 (3.7)	6.7 (5.8)	3.9 (3.0)	1.0 (0.8)	0.6 (0.6)
Bulgaria	6.7 (5.9)	6.7 (5.7)	5.1 (4.2)	4.6 (4.2)	0.9 (0.9)	1.2 (1.0)	0.4 (0.4)
China	7.9 (5.6)	4.0 (2.5)	7.1 (4.0)	7.0 (4.5)	6.2 (4.6)	9.3 (8.0)	8.6 (7.2)

Source: Gregory and Stuart (2004).

Table 8.3

Annual Growth Rates

Country	Years	Growth of labor	Growth of fixed capital	Capital productivity	Total productivity
Czechoslovakia	1950–60	0.7	3.5	1.3	3.4
	1960–83	1.0	4.7	−2.1	0.5
East Germany	1950–60	0.0	2.0	4.1	5.6
	1960–83	0.3	4.0	−1.2	1.4
Soviet Union	1950–60	1.2	9.4	−3.6	2.4
	1960–83	1.3	7.3	−3.7	0.8
Poland	1950–60	1.0	2.6	2.0	3.2
	1960–83	1.5	4.7	−1.4	0.8
Hungary	1950–60	1.0	3.1	1.0	2.9
	1960–83	0.3	5.0	−2.1	1.2
Romania	1950–60	1.1	NA	NA	NA
	1960–83	0.4	NA	NA	NA
Bulgaria	1950–60	0.2	NA	NA	NA
	1960–83	0.5	NA	NA	NA

Source: Gregory and Stuart (2004).

and set the stage for the political drive to make the transition process. In all of this, China appears to be a clear outlier, with growth accelerating rather than declining. We will ignore this exception for a while longer, but later in the chapter the Chinese experience will be fully addressed. The conclusion to be drawn here is that by the late 1980s, economic failure plagued much of the socialist world and the stage was set for transition. The next section of the paper will look at transition from a theoretical approach. This will be followed by a review of the actual experiences of the Soviet Union and China (the two countries that will be the focus of the discussion).

Some Analysts on Transition

Most analysts have argued that the transformation from a socialist to a market form of economic organization involves several components. For instance, property rights must be created and enforced; that is, the state must divest itself of control over the wealth of the society and transfer this control to private hands as well as providing for the protection of these new rights. Of course, the first question that arises concerns just how this transfer of property rights is to be accomplished. A related question concerns how quickly this is to be done. Two major approaches to the first question have predominated. The state enterprises can be directly sold to private individuals or groups of individuals. These individuals can be insiders or outsiders. This could involve negotiated settlements or auctions, or some combination thereof. A second possibility would involve the use of vouchers that are distributed in some manner to the population at large. These vouchers can then be used to purchase shares in the various firms to be privatized. There are many varieties of this sort of approach. The advantage is that it allows for quick privatization. However, the use of vouchers does not provide a quick source of new working capital for the newly privatized firm. In Eastern Europe in the 1990s, this was particularly crucial for many of those firms with the withdrawal of the state as a source of funding (Gregory and Stuart 2004).

Just as two major approaches have been put forward in terms of the process of transition, two major approaches predominated in terms of the speed of transition. One set of theorists promoted rapid transition. According to them, the faster the changes took place the sooner the people of these countries would be able to reap the benefits from such reforms. On the other hand, a second group of theorists believed that such a shock would fail without the institutions essential for transition. In hindsight, some countries in Eastern Europe and Russia that embarked on the big-bang reforms did not do very well. Godoy and Stiglitz (2006) find that the speed of transition had a negative impact on the growth of these countries.

Although privatization and the creation of a system of private-property rights has generally been thought to be a crucial process in the transition from socialism, there is another strand of thought that argues that this is not necessarily crucial. This notion is most often associated with the work of Oskar Lange (1938). He argued for the possibility of "market socialism." His analysis sought to meld together public ownership with market exchange. In this context, firms would still be publicly owned, but they would have to behave as competitive firms in a simulated market setting.

In this economy, households could spend their incomes for any commodity they wanted and they would have complete freedom in terms of choice of occupation. The firms would still be owned by the state, but the rules by which state managers operate would be as follows. First, firms would be free to hire as much of any input and whatever combination of inputs as they desired, but they would have to pay the existing prices for such inputs. Second, output should be expanded until the price of the output is equal to the marginal cost of producing the output. In other words, the goal of the firms should be to maximize profit. The prices of outputs and inputs would be set by a central planning board that would seek to set a price at which quantity demanded equals the quantity supplied. In theory, such a system could be just as efficient as capitalism with the additional benefit that inequality could be reduced through the redistribution of the returns to capital and the creation of public goods (Loucks and Whitney 1973). This system would still have to deal with natural monopolies, where there are high fixed costs and where production at $P = MC$ implies losses for the firm. However, this problem is not unique to capitalism or market socialism.

Over the years critics have pointed out a number of problems with market socialism. The job of a central planning board would just be too difficult to carry out—millions of prices would have to be set and changed continuously. The information necessary to carry out these operations would be enormous. However, there is no real reason for a central planning board. If a system of market exchange could be created, then publicly owned firms could utilize these markets to buy goods, services, and factors of production. Of course, what would motivate these state-owned firms to behave as competitive, privately owned firms? In Lange's scheme, the rules by which managers are evaluated require firms to behave as competitive firms. However, an alternative suggests itself. The state-owned firms may be cut off from further provisions of state funds. Thus, firms' revenues are restricted to what can be earned; that is, firms face a hard budget constraint. In this case, state-owned firms would be forced to minimize cost and maximize profit. Of course, the social dividend available to the state (via taxation) would be limited.

In some respects, the process discussed above resembles what has happened in China in its transition experience. However, the transition it has made is not from socialism to capitalism (i.e., private property and markets), but from socialism to market-based socialism. More will be said later about this when the Chinese experience is examined. The point here is that the crucial aspect in transition is the establishment of market exchange. This indeed seems to be a very difficult thing to do.

Game theory again provides insight into the difficulty of establishing a market exchange. Market exchange is very similar to a "prisoner's dilemma" game, where the two players are a potential buyer and seller. The two choices for each are either to behave honestly in any exchange agreement or to cheat. The payoffs are such that, in any single play of the game, it is to the advantage of both players to cheat, and if both do so then the market fails. Future exchanges will not be contemplated in a single play of the game.

However, this situation changes when one allows for indefinite play. With indefinite play, each player must now take into account that should he cheat, then the other player is likely to refuse to cooperate in all future plays of the game. Thus cheating by one player yields an immediate short-term gain, but this must be weighed against expected losses in the future that would stem from the retaliation of the other player. In terms of the context of buyers and sellers, a seller contemplating cheating a buyer must weigh the short-term gain against the loss as a result of the buyer never returning to buy from that seller (i.e., buyer's retaliation). If the future revenues are important (i.e., if the discount rate is not too high), then the seller is likely to refrain from cheating and market exchange will occur.

If knowledge concerning the past behavior of buyers and sellers is available to potential partners of a market exchange, this information can be used to exclude previous cheaters from future access to market-exchange opportunities. This threat can be used as a weapon to insure cooperative behavior between buyers and sellers rather than cheating. Reputation and the potential loss of such can act as a mechanism to support market exchange. This mechanism can act as a foundation supporting market exchange, reducing the transaction cost involved in such activities.

Mechanisms involving long-term interaction among the same group of individuals resulting in the development of reputations for trustworthiness can be very effective in relatively small communities and villages. Here, the same individuals interact over long periods and reputations become common knowledge. Markets within such small communities are likely to be vigorous institutions involving the whole community. Specialization of labor will occur, but this is limited by the extent of the community. More simply, as the size of the community or region involved in exchange increases, the less likely that interaction will involve individuals for whom there is a large fund of information. In larger communities, reputation is thus not likely to act as an effective mechanism for punishing cheaters and market exchange will likely break down. In larger communities, exchange tends to occur among anonymous individuals and a different sort of mechanism is necessary to insure the foundations for market exchange and to reduce transaction costs.

In large societies or communities, the rules for acceptable market behavior must be articulated and enforced by a third party. This entity punishes those buyers and sellers who cheat, thus reducing the gains from cheating and transforming the situation from one of a prisoner's dilemma to one of cooperation. The difficulty with this solution, as discussed in other chapters in different contexts, is that the third party, most likely the state, becomes a third party in the transition game. What is to prevent the government from cheating, and if it does cheat in terms of rule enforcement, then once again the market will break down and cheating will occur among all parties involved. If the government is to provide the foundation for market exchange, it must commit itself not to cheat and to punish those that do. This commitment must be believable.

The above is the essential problem in establishing market exchange. In all existing socialist nations, existing market exchange was suppressed and planning mechanisms were put into place. This central planning was characterized "by a complex set of highly specific relations between firms" (Blanchard and Kremer 1997, 1039). That is, "For many inputs, firms had or knew of only one supplier from which to buy. For many of their goods, firms had or knew of only one buyer to whom to sell" (ibid.). This relationship was protected from possible cheating by the coercive power of the state. However, in most cases (except China) transition eliminated the central planner. In the Western industrialized nations, there were many alternative buyers and sellers available and the rules of the game are enforced by the state. Alternative suppliers or buyers did not exist in many of the transition economies.

In addition to the above, transition created a great deal of uncertainty about which firms would survive and in what form. This great increase in uncertainty implied that future exchanges between buyers and sellers might not occur. Thus, the threat of effective retaliation by a buyer or seller who was cheated in a previous transaction was greatly weakened. Reputation ceased to be a disciplinary mechanism.

The result of a movement to transition by many previously socialist nations was a breakdown of economic relations. The central-planning bureaucracy ceased to be the third-party enforcer in transactions between suppliers and producers. Reputation failed as a disciplining mechanism, production broke down, and markets were not available to substitute for the planning mechanism.

The creation of such markets was immediately faced with a significant commitment problem. New ruling elites had to proceed and enforce the rules for market exchange. The new ruling elite had to effectively commit to upholding the rules; that is, potential buyers and sellers had to believe in the commitment of the new ruling elite. This was the great difficulty in replacing planning mechanisms with markets. For instance, in Russia, the transfer of property rights to individuals led to large amounts of Russian assets being exported. According to Buiter (2000), between 1995 and 1999 Russia turned into a net exporter of capital. Hoff and Stiglitz (2002) looked at the political demand for rule of law in Russia following the move toward privatization to understand why such asset stripping took place. They find that this behavior could be explained by the uncertainty associated with the legal regime in Russia following mass privatization. This uncertainty provided incentive to the players of the games to prolong the absence of the rule of law.

The Russian Experience

The actual experience of the transition process varied from country to country. It is impossible to capture all the variety of experiences. In this section, the focus will be on the experiences of Russia. The experience of China will be considered in the next section. These countries are chosen for several reasons. First, they are the biggest economies involved in the transition experience, moving from socialist to market economies. Second, the experiences of these two countries are dramatically different. This difference raises a number of very interesting questions. These questions, in turn, lead to some very interesting analyses. (Much of the discussion below concerning Russia is based on Shleifer and Tressman 2003.)

The transition that transformed the Soviet Union into Russia and assorted independent republics was truly dramatic. In 1991, Boris Yeltsin was elected president of the Russian republic of the Soviet Union. In that year, after fending off an uprising by members of the communist elite, he dissolved the Soviet Union and made Russia independent. In January 1992, most prices were liberalized and a mass privatization program was implemented. Shares of most state-owned firms were transferred to managers, workers, and the public. Thus, by 1994, approximately 70 percent of the economy was privately held.

This was not an easy process. There was resistance at every step. Economic reformers came and went within the government as Yeltsin attempted to forge a consensus. In 1996, Yeltsin was facing reelection.

As part of this campaign, he agreed to what has been known as a "loans for shares" program. In this scenario, a number of natural-resource-based firms were transferred to several already existing industrial groups in return for loans to the government. Such was the course by which business oligarchs are said to have highjacked the privatization process and gained control of much of the Russian economy.

There were other radical changes during Yeltsin's presidency. Defense purchases were reduced by 90 percent. In addition, significant reductions in Russian nuclear arms were negotiated with the United States. All of these represented dramatic changes in policy.

The outcome of the transition process was initially disappointing. It appeared that there was a dramatic drop in output, a collapse of the economy. Given the analytical considerations discussed in the previous section, an initial fall in output was likely to occur. Official estimates of the decline indicate that between 1991 and 1998 (when recovery began) output fell by 39 percent.

However, Shleifer and Tressman (2003) do not believe that the performance was as poor as indicated by the official statistics, for a number of reasons. First, one must remember that before the contractions in output (which occurred late in the Soviet era), Russia's per capita GDP was estimated at a little over $8,000, about one-third the level of the United States. Though Russia was not poor, it certainly ranked far behind the advanced industrial economies. It was, rather, a middle-income country.

Much of the output produced in the 1990s was made up of military goods and poor-quality consumer goods, for which there was little demand. With the installation of a market economy, resources would be allocated away from the production of such goods and the reduction in GDP that resulted was actually beneficial (i.e., eliminating wasteful production).

Another important factor was that the decline in the official economy in the 1990s was matched by an increase in the unofficial economy. An indirect measure of actual production is the use of electricity. While official GDP fell by 29 percent, electricity consumption fell by only 19 percent. Hence, the actual fall in output was not as sharp as implied by the official figures.

Shleifer and Tressman also provide other statistics to indicate that average living standards did not dramatically decline. "The number of Russians going abroad as tourists rose from 1.6 million in 1999 to 4.3 million in 2000. The shares of households with radios, televisions, tape recorders, refrigerators, washing machines, and electric vacuum cleaners all increased from 1991 to 2000. Private ownership of cars doubled from 1991 to 2000" (Shleifer and Tressman 2003, 10).

Of course, any such discussion must take into account the increased inequality that occurred during this period. However, there is evidence that even individuals at the bottom of the social pyramid had benefited by the late 1990s. The percentage of people with running water, access to hot water, and central heat all had increased by the end of the decade.

The point of the analysis is not to deny that output did initially fall and that there was suffering. Instead, the point is that the fall was not as steep nor the recovery as delayed as official figures would seem to indicate. Today, Russia is a typical middle-income country. A few groups dominate big business, but that is true of most middle-income, developing nations (e.g., Mexico, Brazil, Malaysia). Yes, corruption is common throughout much of Russian society, but this is also true of most middle-income, developing nations. Thus, after a traumatic period of transition, Russia has become a typical middle-income, mixed-capitalist, developing nation.

Russia's experience with the transition process was similar to much of Eastern Europe. The creation of private-property rights and the establishment of market exchange led initially to disorganization and a fall in output, but with time, recovery has occurred. The Chinese experience with transition seems, however, to have been quite different. There was no fall in output; instead, the growth rate accelerated and continues at a high level to this day. The next section of this chapter will explore the Chinese experience.

The Chinese Experience

China's experience with transition is quite different. The first thing to note is that the reform process began earlier than it did in the Soviet Union and Eastern Europe; the reforms began in the late 1970s and continue to this day. The second point is the spectacular economic result. Unlike the situation in Russia and Eastern Europe, where reform was accompanied by a drop in output, reform in China was accompanied by acceleration in the rate of growth. Thus, not only did the economic pie not decrease, it rapidly increased. As one can see from examining Table 8.4, China's performance has been impressive.

What accounts for this impressive growth? Why is China's experience so different from that of Russia and Eastern Europe? In order to begin to answer the first question, the theory of market-preserving federalism, discussed in Chapter 5, is reviewed and extended. According to Montinola,

Table 8.4

China's Performance

Year	Growth rate	Year	Growth rate
1980	7.8	1991	9.2
1981	5.2	1992	14.2
1982	9.1	1993	13.5
1983	10.9	1994	12.6
1984	15.2	1995	10.5
1985	13.5	1996	9.6
1986	8.8	1997	8.8
1987	11.6	1998	7.8
1988	11.3	1999	7.1
1989	4.1	2000	8.0
1990	3.8		

Source: Klein and Ozmucur (2002).

Qian, and Weingast (1995), market-preserving federalism is characterized by a number of conditions. First, there exists a hierarchy of governments, with each level having authority over specific and different areas. Second, the subnational governments have authority over economic activities within their jurisdiction. Third, the function of the national government is to protect the common market; that is, it needs to ensure the mobility of goods and factors of production across subnational-government borders. Fourth, all governments at all levels face hard budget constraints. Thus, revenue sharing between different levels is limited. Finally, the arrangements discussed above must be durable; that is, governments at various levels must commit themselves to the rules.

Several significant economic effects flow from the operation of market-preserving federalism. Most importantly, under such a structure competition among the various subnational-government jurisdictions occur. If one subnational jurisdiction imposes regulations that dramatically raise the costs of production, producers outside the boundaries of this jurisdiction will not be bound by these rules and costs will be lower. Firms in this latter category can thus out compete firms in the former. If factors of production are mobile across boundaries, they will tend to move from highly regulated regions to less regulated regions.

The movement of factors across boundaries dramatically affects the well-being of local and regional governments, as long as a hard budget constraint exists. Specifically, if a particular region prospers, the revenues accruing to the local/regional government will rise. Alternatively, if a region is characterized by economic decline, the local/regional government will find its revenues declining. Thus, a local/regional government will have an incentive to minimize cost. In addition, these subnational jurisdictions will have an incentive "to provide a hospitable environment for factors, typically through the provision of local public goods such as establishing a basis for secure rights of factor owners, the provision of infrastructure, utilities, access to markets, and so on. Those jurisdictions that fail to provide these goods find that factors move to other jurisdictions. Local economic activity and tax revenues decline as a consequence" (Montinola, Qian, and Weingast 1995, 58).

In addition to the above effects, such a governmental system of organization encourages economic experimentation. The revenue prospects of subnational jurisdictions are dependent on the condition of the subnational economy. Governments will have an incentive to experiment with new policies aimed at enhancing productivity and output. At any given time, one should observe a variety of policy choices and experiments. Those experiments that succeed are likely to be copied by other jurisdictions. Alternatively, those that fail are likely to be quickly dumped (Montinola, Qian, and Weingast 1995).

In order for this sort of system to operate, the central state must be strong enough to preserve the common market. If not, then local/regional governments are likely to try to restrict the flow of goods, services, and factors across jurisdictions. Both growth and productivity will suffer as a result. However, the central government must not be so powerful as to overwhelm lower-level governments, restricting the latter's ability to make economic policy at the local level. A delicate balance is necessary for this sort of system to function effectively.

Montinola, Qian, and Weingast argue that China operated as a market-preserving federalist system during its transition process. The reform process in China began in the agricultural sector. Before 1978, the commune was the institutional structure within which agricultural production took place. Land was controlled by the commune. The latter was made up of production brigades, which in turn were broken down into production teams (composed of a number of households within a village). Above the commune was the county government. Within this context, production decisions were highly centralized and output (or most of it) was sold to the state at set prices. There was little or no role for the market.

Beginning in the late 1970s, communal agriculture was dismantled and replaced with the household-responsibility system. Control of production decisions was given to farm families who were given leases for land to farm. Initially, the leases were only one to three years, but these were gradually increased. Meeting production quotas by delivering goods directly to the state was still required, but the prices paid for the delivery of production were raised. Eventually, production above the state-mandated quota was allowed to be sold by the household on the market for the market price. This resulted in a dramatic increase in agricultural production and incomes in the countryside. Between 1978 and 1984, agricultural output grew at 7 to 8 percent annually (Li and Lian 1999).

Rural-based growth significantly increased the demand for relatively simple manufactured goods. It also provided resources for investment in new manufacturing activities. Township and village enterprises (TVEs) dramatically expanded production in response to the dramatic growth in demand. These enterprises were not privately owned, neither were they owned by the central state. Instead, they were controlled by local levels of government, townships, and villages. It should be pointed out that both households and TVEs paid taxes to the local-government jurisdiction. Thus authority and tax power were decentralized.

This decentralization of authority also involved the establishment of special economic and development zones. Through this process, various regions were given greater authority to make policy while gaining access to revenue. This was combined with major fiscal reform in 1980. The basic thrust of the reform was "that a lower-level regional government contracts with an upper-level regional government on the total amount (or share) of tax and profit revenue (negative values imply a reverse flow of subsidies) to be remitted for the next several years, and the lower-level government keeps the rest" (Montinola, Qian, and Weingast 1995, 63).

It was the last part of this arrangement that was so important. If the lower-level government should earn revenue in excess of its contracted amount, it could keep it. This provided a strong tie between the resources of the local governmental unit and local economic prosperity. As long as the common market holds, local officials will have the incentive to foster local prosperity.

The agrarian reforms and fiscal decentralization fostered the increased development of the market. However, there were attempts by various local governments to restrict output and factor mobility between regions. However, the central government has been strong enough to limit the extent of internal protectionism. This, combined with hard budget constraints at lower levels of government, implied that competition across regions was intense (ibid.).

None of the initial reform efforts were aimed at direct privatization of firms owned by the central government. Lau, Qian, and Roland (2000) have characterized this process of reform as a dual-track approach to transition. They argue that a dual-track approach is an efficiency-enhancing reform process. "The basic principle of this dual-track approach is as follows. Under the plan track, economic agents are assigned rights to and obligations for fixed quantities of goods at fixed plan prices as specified in the pre-existing plan. In addition, a market track is introduced under which economic agents participate in the market at free-market prices, provided that they fulfill their obligations under the pre-existing plan" (Lau, Qian, and Roland 2000, 121). In the Chinese case, firms owned by the central state were allowed to continue to operate under a planning system, while at the same time a market track was created through which new market-oriented firms could arise and grow.

The results of this process of reform have created significant structural change within the Chinese economy. In China, firms have been organized either as state-owned enterprises, collective enterprises (TVEs), or private enterprises. Until 1993, no state-owned enterprises had been closed by the state, yet between 1978 and 1993 the share of these enterprises in total employment was down from 75 percent to less than 60 percent in urban areas and from 60 to 30 percent in rural areas. The state share of industrial output declined from 78 to 43 percent.

The reform process outlined above appears more logical and rational than it actually was. More specifically, one might think that this process unfolded as part of a well-thought-out plan carried out by the central state. In reality, much of this reform process was driven from below, at the local and regional level, via experimentation. The reforms within the agricultural sector in the 1970s initially occurred in a small number of collectives. This was first done secretly and then later with the blessing of local authorities. Initially, farmland was leased to households, and the households, after meeting the required output quota for the state, were allowed to sell the remainder of their output (ibid.). Output grew dramatically and local officials supported the changes, while other regions began to copy these institutional innovations. The central government, under Deng Xiaoping, did not lead this reform, but instead pragmatically sought to enhance its effect. The rapid growth of TVEs in China also initially occurred without the consent or support of the central state. However, a pragmatic leadership sought to amplify its effects. Zhou and White (1995) have called this the quiet politics of rural enterprise reform in China.

State-owned enterprises have remained a significant drag on the Chinese economy, however. By 1993, China still had 300,000 of these enterprises, with about 75 million employees, and they "continue to consume a great proportion of bank credit and other resources; most have excess employment and close to half are loss-makers" (Cao, Qian, and Weingast 1999, 103). It was this problem that posed significant difficulties for Russia and Eastern Europe.

In 1995, China began to try and directly privatize and restructure state-owned enterprises. According to Cao, Qian, and Weingast, this reform was aimed at three areas: privatization of smaller state-owned enterprises; layoffs of state-owned enterprise workers; and a restructuring, involving mergers and conglomerates, of the remaining state-owned enterprises. Reform has made significant progress in the first two areas. A substantial portion of smaller state-owned enterprises have been privatized and substantial layoffs of workers have occurred. Much of this drive for reform has come from local governments and these reforms have proceeded relatively smoothly.

This drive for reform can be best explained, according to Cao, Qian, and Weingast, by the principal components of market-preserving federalism. This system has provided incentives for local governments to undertake such reforms. First, additional reforms in tax, fiscal, monetary, and banking policy have further hardened the budget constraints faced by local governments. Second, the increased competition from the nonstate sector has significantly raised the competitive pressures on state-owned enterprises. As a result, local and regional governments have an incentive to privatize since the existing state-owned enterprises represent a drain of resources on local economies. This significantly reduces the resources available to lower levels of government. These levels of government have strong incentives to get resources transferred out of the hands of state-owned enterprises. Regional competition has once again resulted in local and regional experimentation in the reform process, with successful experiments being copied and unsuccessful ones dropped.

The largest state-owned enterprises remain firmly under central control. However, the same sort of forces related to competition and hard budget constraints now exist for the central state. This may spur further reform in the future.

Explanation for Different Reform Paths

China and Russia have followed very different paths to transition, with very different results. Russia followed a process of reform carried out in a top-down manner; while markets and property rights have been established, power and decision making was and is highly centralized. In China, local and regional institutions and governments played a much more important role in the reform process. How is this difference to be explained? What factors or forces can account for these dramatically different processes? This is an extremely difficult question to answer. However, a coherent explanation is now beginning to emerge.

In Chapter 6 on Latin America, the structure of the state in Spain as compared with England was linked to a distinction between M-form and U-form organizations. U-form (unitary-type) organizations are organized into a strictly hierarchical, pyramidal structure. Decision making is centralized and information flows up and down the pyramid. Alternatively, an M-form organization is a multidivisional form. The units are organized horizontally, rather than vertically, with a large number of reasonably independent groups. The advantage of the U-form is its ability to take advantage of increasing returns to size or scale, the disadvantage is its inflexibility. This disadvantage, in hindsight, seems to be the result of a lack of incentive to be successful economically at the regional or local level. Alternatively, the M-form organization is quite flexible and likely to lead to significant experimentation, but lacks the ability to take advantage of increasing returns to scale. Its advantage appears to be its ability to provide incentives to decision makers at the individual and local level to succeed economically.

Qian and Xu (1993) characterize the Russian process of reform and transition as taking place with a U-form organizational structure, whereas China's experience took place within an M-form organizational structure. What accounts for this difference in organizational structures? Qian and Xu argue that the institutional structure of the transition state in Russia was inherited from that of the Soviet Union. First, operating on a large scale to capture increasing returns was a principle subscribed to early in the foundation of the Soviet Union and applied to agricultural and industrial production. Second, when the Soviet Union established centralized control over the economy, the M-form of organization had yet to emerge. Third, there were political reasons for establishing a U-form organization. Stalin wished to establish firm control first over outlying

Soviet republics and later over newly incorporated countries in Eastern Europe. All regions became interdependent and were ultimately and completely dependent on Moscow. The historical inheritance of the transition regime was that of U-form organization, and this became the principle by which the new regime was organized.

In China, there were a number of reasons why an M-form organization evolved. First, before the communists fully took power, in 1949, the economy and military forces in regions under communist control were organized this way. This allowed the organization to survive various military shocks. Second, the poor communication and transportation structures in China gave significant advantage to a decentralized organizational structure. Third, nationalism in outlying regions has been less of a problem in China than in the Soviet Union. Fourth, Mao Zedong, the Chinese leader, was worried by the threat of either a Soviet- or U.S.-led invasion of China, and thus industry was dispersed and turned over to regional supervision.

In summary, it seems that the organizational structures of the transition regimes in the Soviet Union and China were inherited from previous political regimes. The transition in Russia was managed through an organizational structure that was U-form in nature, while China's was managed by an M-form institutional structure. The differing paths of reform seem to reflect a significant influence of the past.

Sustainable Growth

The discussion thus far has shown that transition to a market economy has been different for China and Russia. A question that has not been addressed is that of sustainability—whether transition has led to sustainable growth and whether this too shows differences between China and Russia. Sustainable development includes economic, social, and environmental improvement, along with economic growth. The idea is one of improvement in the quality of life rather than just an increase in per capita GDP. While poor environmental quality poses several problems to the overall quality of life, it becomes a more serious problem for transition economies if environmental liabilities pose serious problems in the privatization process (Bluffstone and Panayotou 2000).

One can argue that if one thinks of the social aspects of development, such as education or health, a higher income usually leads to greater degrees of these good things. Overall, evidence shows that wealthier countries have relatively higher life expectancy, higher enrollment rates at all levels of schooling, and lower child mortality, aspects that imply an improvement in social conditions. Growth brings social improvements. However, reverse causality is also at work; that is, social improvement enhances growth. In fact, reverse feedback leads to a virtuous cycle that aids in the development process. One cannot make such a clear linkage between economic growth and improvements in environmental quality, nor can one necessarily conclude that environmental improvement leads to higher growth. Questions persist about environmental quality and development, and this is critical in understanding the sustainability of development, especially for transition countries.

Broadly speaking, there are two schools of thought in terms of environmental quality and development. One believes that development has a negative impact on the environment, while the other believes that development and environmental improvement occur simultaneously. In fact, both may be true depending on a nation's stage of development. Figure 8.1 illustrates what is known as an environmental Kuznets curve. At low per capita income levels growth will worsen pollution, while at high-income levels this relationship is reversed as economic growth leads to an improvement in the environment. There is great debate as to whether such a relationship actually exists, but it illustrates the complexity of views concerning the relationship between growth, development and the environment.

In the context of transition economies, it is most important to understand the impact of liberalization on the environment. Traditionally, there are two broad viewpoints relating to economic openness (i.e., liberalization) and environmental quality. This relationship is particularly important in the present context because it relates directly to transition economies, which are characterized by a move toward a more open, market-oriented structure. These approaches are the structural and the rational approach (Shin 2004). The structural approach deals with the effects of scale (i.e., size), technology, and product composition. The scale effect typically points to a negative impact on the environment; as industries increase in size, environmental pollution increases. The technology effect is determined by the choice of technology and it can be presumed that with higher incomes there may be demand for cleaner technology. The composition effect results from the particular combination of goods produced and points to a positive impact, with higher income being associated with consumption of cleaner goods. The result-

Figure 8.1 **Pollution and GDP Per Capita**

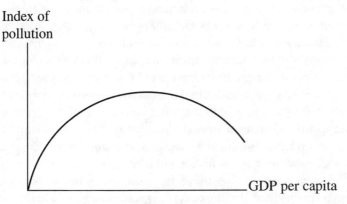

Index of pollution

GDP per capita

ing environmental quality is the net effect of these three effects, and is highly debated. The problem with the structural approach is that it does not take into account the variability of institutional structures between countries. This makes it nearly impossible to compare the impact of the components of the structural effect across countries.

The rational approach pays particular attention to the actions of firms and governments. This approach consists of two major hypotheses, the industry-flight hypothesis and the eco-dumping hypothesis. According to the former, industries that pollute choose to locate in countries/regions with fewer or weaker environmental regulations. The eco-dumping hypothesis implies that developing countries intentionally do not enforce environmental standards to give firms in these industries a competitive edge in the international market. According to the rational approach, trade liberalization will most likely have a negative impact on the environment, especially for developing countries. However, the empirical evidence seems to point to the contrary. Countries with stricter environmental regulations seem to have fared better in the international market (Smarzynska and Wei 2001). Just as in the structural approach, the rational approach also does not lead to a consensus view regarding the impact of openness or trade liberalization on the quality of the environment.

Transition economies pose interesting case studies in the context of sustainable development. The evidence suggests that socialist countries generally had poor environmental quality. This seems especially odd when, as Ferrero (1999) points out, one considers the public-good nature of the environment. One would expect that under state ownership and central planning, a public good such as the environment would have merited the same importance as other public goods, such as defense or education or health. Why did not the authorities have such an attitude toward the environment in these countries? A related question that grows out of this discussion is, following transition, where do these countries fit in terms of the environmental Kuznets curve? For instance, where would Russia fit given that it has suffered major setbacks economically following transition? If Russia belonged to the set of countries where growth was associated with environmental degradation, the downturn would imply an improvement in the environment. However, if it belonged with the group of countries where growth was associated with improved environmental quality, the setback would be detrimental for the environment. The same questions can be asked about China. Where should one place China on the environmental Kuznets curve given China's rapid economic growth? The truth is that both Russia and China had serious environmental issues when the transition process began. In Russia's case, the downturn did in fact coincide with shutting down many major polluters and led to an improvement in environmental quality, according to Hughes and Lovei (1999). In China, the initial growth spurt came with negative consequences for the environment initially, but the second phase of growth, from 1985 onward, came with a changed outlook and commitment to environmental concerns. The relationship between environment and development in the context of transition economies is highly complex.

The transition process highlighted the condition of the environment in the transition countries to the rest of the world. For example, transition revealed that less than half of Russia's population had access to safe drinking water and over 200 Russian cities' air quality exceeded Russian pollution limits. Moreover, Russia did not have adequate and efficient mechanisms to handle the disposal of solid waste, hazardous waste, or nuclear waste (National Intelligence Council 1999). Even as late as 1990 only 15 percent of Russia's population lived in areas where pollution was at acceptable levels (Feshbach 1995). Table 8.5 shows a 1994 comparison of pollution caused by sulfur and nitrogen intensities in Russia, other transition countries, and Nordic countries.

It needs to be understood that these high pollution levels in Russia were not a consequence of complete disregard for the environment by the authorities. According to Panayotou (1999), Russia, along with several other transition countries in Central and Eastern Europe, had an elaborate system of pollution charges in place. (The disaster at the

Table 8.5

Comparison of Emissions of Sulfur and Nitrogen in Selected Central and East European and Nordic Countries, 1994

Transition country	Sulfur			Nitrogen		
	Total emissions	Per capita kilogram per person	Per unit of GDP kilogram per $1,000	Total emissions	Per capita kilogram per person	Per unit of GDP kilogram per $1,000
Russia	7,197	48.4	9.8	3,401	22.9	4.6
Poland	2,605	67.6	13.7	1,105	28.7	5.8
Hungary	741	72.6	11.3	187	18.4	2.7
Denmark	155	29.8	1.1	277	53.3	1.9
Norway	34	7.9	0.3	222	51.6	2.0
Sweden	97	11.0	0.5	372	42.3	1.8

Source: Soderholm (2001).

Table 8.6

**National Pollution Abatement and Control Investment
Per Capita and as Share of GDP, 1996**

Country	Per capita (U.S.$)	Percentage of GDP
Hungary	57	0.6
Lithuania	33	0.6
Poland	72	1.1
Russia	24	0.4
Slovenia	48	0.4

Source: OECD (1999).

Chernobyl nuclear-power plant in 1986 alerted many countries to the importance of environmental issues, and most transition countries in Europe, including Russia, had a central authority in charge of environmental policy by the late 1980s.) Pollution charges were one of the solutions proposed by economists to deal with the problem posed by pollution. Pollution represents a negative spillover effect or externality resulting from the production process. Firms produce waste in the process of production and some of this waste spills over on others. This spillover reduces the costs of production to the producer, since some costs of production are borne by others external to the firm (e.g., the consumer of polluted air or water). Hence, there is too much production since producers do not bear all of the costs. A solution would be to tax the emissions of polluters, thus forcing the cost back to its source, known as "internalizing an externality." This would induce producers to reduce production and thus reduce the levels of emissions. Pollution charges were in place in Russia, but as Table 8.6 makes clear, Russia compared poorly with some other Central and East European countries in terms of investment in pollution abatement.

Russia had the lowest level of investment per capita in pollution control, as well as a share of GDP. Part of the reason for this, apart from the Russian government's preoccupation with the country's economic condition, was the outlook toward environmental policy by the officials. Success appeared to be gauged by the ability of policy in gathering revenue rather than in bringing down pollution (Soderholm 2001). The commitment, if it was there, appeared to be misplaced.

Ferrero (1999) shows that this characteristic of high investment in some public goods (defense, education, health) and lower investment in others (conservation, pollution) emerged as a rational choice in some transition economies since the burden of spending on public goods fell mainly on the wealthier people. In other words, wealthier people chose to invest in the areas that brought them higher visible returns. Moreover, the governments of these countries were more concerned about the negative impact of policies enforcing conservation and reducing pollution on economic activity. Pollution charges could not be as easily raised in these countries for fear of the reverse incentive of such measures on producers. In reality, there were different channels built into the system to make sure much of these charges were returned to producers. However, while this might have averted one channel of negative impact on business activity, it created distorted incentive structures. Moreover, even though the downturn of the 1990s reduced levels of pollution as an unintended positive consequence, the downturn drew attention away from environmental issues as governments struggled with what they considered more pressing concerns.

Soderholm (2001) gives some additional insight as to why pollution charges did not work in a country such as Russia. He argues that, in spite of transition to a market economy, Russia retained much of its communist flavor. One example of this was the pricing system of the former Soviet Union as it related to natural resources. The Soviet planners set very low prices for industry inputs throughout the 1960s. These prices did not reflect the growing scarcity situation relating to these resources and led to excessive energy consumption, which posed an additional burden on their environment. Changes were introduced only as late as the 1970s, but these did not reflect the true prices of these commodities, either. Another major problem was Russia's escalating inflation and the inability of the pollution charges to keep pace, leading to a decrease in real pollution charges throughout the 1990s. It was clear that the budget constraints put in place were soft and lacked accountability for the most part. Thus, while the new environmental policy put in place in the 1980s appeared strict on paper, it was largely ineffective both in gathering revenue and/or in bringing down pollution. For the most part, it lacked enforcement and commitment. Many studies come to similar conclusions regarding Russia's newer environmental policy (Golub and Strukova 1994, Kozeltsev and Markandya 1997).

So far, the discussion has focused mainly on the Russian economy. We will now shift our focus toward the environment in China. A slightly different perspective needs to be introduced to explain the relation between liberalization and the environment that characterized the transition process in China. Previously, two traditional theories relating to liberalization and the environment were discussed. Neither theory has clear implications for the relationship between liberalization and environment. While the structural approach has positive and negative aspects, the rational approach indicates that development would be more likely to have a negative impact on the environment, especially in the early stages of development. Shin (2004) offers an alternative framework that is particularly relevant to the context of China. According to this view, openness leads to the diffusion of global norms into the domestic economy, which, in turn, influences domestic environmental policies and helps in the restructuring and building of an institutional framework that can bring the domestic country's standards to par with global standards. The process comes through a system of learning by doing through foreign technology transfers, exposure to the environmental practices of other countries, and through the developing of new and better environmental policies. Shin cites the examples of the Shenyang and Dalian provinces to show that this has indeed been the case with China.

The argument is that China may represent a situation in which environmental concerns became endogenous to the economy. This was different from Russia, where environmental standards were determined by the authorities based on international standards, and these were exogenously imposed on the economy without making any concessions for differences in institutional structure. If environmental concerns could be endogenized, they are more likely to influence public opinion toward the importance of the environment, which in turn would affect their willingness to pay and ultimately ensure the success of environmental policy. This may be the case with China. As Chen points out, "The most important change is the penetrating awareness among the mass of the critical importance of preserving the environment" (Chen 2005, 507). Testimony of public participation and awareness toward environmental issues in China is plentiful.

China's initial economic growth, as it began its transition, came with its share of environmental problems. These problems were part of Mao's legacy. Mao's attempt to lift China economically came at the expense of the environment. Part of this was due to Mao's attitude toward the need to "capture nature" in order to achieve growth, and part of it was the existing pricing structure of natural resources. The pricing structure, similar to what was seen in Russia, kept the prices of major industrial inputs, such as natural resources, water, and electricity, artificially low and did not allow them to reflect their scarcity value. Some of the problems that China faced as a consequence were deforestation and desertification. For example, extreme deforestation caused the Yangtze River to overflow in 1998 and cause much damage and many fatalities to the Chinese people. This was only one of many pollution-related accidents that caused much damage and destruction in China. Air pollution in urban China was being caused by traffic congestion and an increasing number of cars. Air pollution was also being caused by coal-burning power stations and coal burners used in home heating. The World Bank reported that China was home to sixteen of the twenty most polluted cities in the world. Another environmental problem plaguing China was the shortage of safe drinking water as well as the shortage of clean water for irrigation.

In spite of all these problems, it seems that, since 1985, the Chinese government has made a serious commitment to environmental concerns. The commitment was affirmed at the highest levels of government with its public acknowledgement of existing problems and its commitment toward a "green GDP." Tables 8.7 and 8.8 give some idea as to China's environmental condition and achievements in the years following 1985.

Table 8.7 shows that since 1985 the number of pollution-related accidents has dropped dramatically, both in absolute terms as well as in their growth rates. Moreover, yearly investment in the treatment of pollution went up while the amount of fines and reparations on pollution cases went down. Each of these shows that in the 1980s and the 1990s there were marked improvements in environmental quality in China. Table 8.8 adds more evidence to what is learned from Table 8.7.

Table 8.8 shows that both industrial waste water and gas emissions were reduced between 1985 and 2002. In addition, the ratio of solid waste produced to utilized and solid waste produced to discharged also shows marked improvement. It needs to be noted, however, that in spite of improvements, the 2002 figures in Table 8.8 regarding industrial water discharge, gas emissions, and solid waste produced are still alarmingly high.

The importance of environmental issues is recognized by the highest authorities and by the general public in China. The Chinese government has clearly made environmental quality a priority, which is evident from its actions. In 1998, the country's environmental monitoring authority, the State Environmental Protection Administration (SEPA), was lifted to

Table 8.7

Environment in China

	Aggregate levels				Aggregate annual growth rates		
	1985	1990	1995	2001	1986–90	1991–95	1996–2001
Yearly investment (100 million yuan in implemented pollution-treatment projects)	22.2	45.4	98.7	174.5	15.4	16.8	10.0
Number of pollution accidents	2,716	3,462	1,966	1,842	5.0	−10.7	−1.1
Losses converted into cash (10,000 yuan)	NA	NA	9,938	12,272			3.6
Amount of reparations and fines (10,000 yuan) on pollution cases	NA	NA	4,260	3,264			−4.3

Source: Chen (2005).

ministerial rank, and the tenth five-year plan set environmental spending at 700 billion yuan ($85 billion) for 2001 to 2005. The country now has an established legal framework to prosecute violators, and both the president and prime minister have shifted their priority toward a balanced development (i.e., sustainable development) rather than simply economic growth. As Tables 8.7 and 8.8 show, these efforts are beginning to bear fruit as pollution levels stabilize and begin to move toward acceptable levels. The most important factor in the fight against pollution in China has been public opinion toward better environmental quality.

Some of the criticisms against SEPA have been its inability to strictly enforce regulations in the provinces given its dependence on these provinces for its revenue. However, since 1998, SEPA has been cutting its support to its affiliated organizations that are directly responsible for carrying out environmental policies. These organizations are increasingly funded by alternative sources, which have given them the freedom from provincial governments and freedom to express their views without having to worry about financial consequences. Several semi-independent organizations funded mainly through the World Bank and the United Na-

Table 8.8

Pollution Emission and Treatment in China

	1985	1990	2001	2002
Industrial waste water dis-charged (10,000 tons)	2,574,009	2,486,861	2,026,282	2,071,885
Industrial waste gas emission (100 million m³)	73,970	85,380	160,863	175,257
Industrial solid wastes pro-duced (10,000 tons), of which:	52,590	57,797	88,840	94,509
Solid wastes utilized	12,187	16,943	47,290	50,061
Solid wastes discharged	13,283	4,767	2,894	2,635

Source: Chen (2005).

tions also actively participate in carrying out environmental regulations in China (Schwartz 2003).

Certain characteristics regarding the institutional structure of Chinese environmental policy set it apart from Russia. Chinese environmental policy is characterized by an incentive structure that works from the bottom up. It works mostly through individual and firm-level networks rather than through national or international nongovernmental organizations. While all provinces in China are subject to the same environmental regulations and standards, there is a lot of variation across provinces in enforcement efforts (Schwartz 2001). The success of one province over another is seen in its relative effectiveness in enforcement of such regulations. The reward for such success has been its ability to attract foreign investors. This has created a system of competition between provinces that has resulted in an overall improvement of the environment.

Much responsibility for the success of government officials in implementing environmental policies and in their commitment to its success lies with the people of China. Schwartz (2003) points out that there are two basic components to commitment. First, there needs to be commitment from leaders, and, second, there needs to be a commitment toward those responsible for implementing policy. Both of these are critically important for the success of a policy. An additional factor that will influence enforcement is public participation. It seems as if all three conditions are being met in China.

The Chinese leadership has made it clear that cleaning up the environment is a priority, and it has shown its commitment to this cause by allocating increasing amounts of funds for implementing environmental policies. Moreover, local- and provincial-government officials have realized the importance of environmental issues if they are to attract international investors to invest in their area. Additionally, the fear that publicizing the state of the environment may turn public opinion against them for losing potential foreign investment has kept these officials alert to the conditions within their jurisdiction. Public opinion has been instrumental in putting pressure on local governments to improve environmental conditions. Public opinion is a sign of the public acknowledgement of the importance of the environment. This has acted as an incentive to promote the accountability of government officials to the people. On the other hand, public opinion has enabled the government to influence people's willingness to pay, which has generated the revenue required to implement policy. This explains how the Chinese government has been able to increase its spending on environmental issues by such large amounts. The state has recognized the importance of public participation and has increasingly delegated the responsibility of generating public opinion to nongovernmental environmental groups. The media has also played a major role in influencing public opinion in China. The media's freedom with such broadcasting is a sign in itself of the central government's support of these issues. Moreover, education programs targeted at the environment have also played an important role. Public opinion and public support have promoted the commitment of government officials to environmental concerns.

One must, however, point out that China remains susceptible to problems related to the balance of power between the center and local/regional governments. Environmental costs cross borders and allow one region to dump its costs, via pollution, on others. The state must continue to coordinate national policy such that regional and local governments have an incentive to reduce levels of pollution. Just as the central government must prevent local and regional governments from erecting barriers to the movement of goods, so the central state must create a system of incentives such that regional and local governments are not tempted to race to the bottom in terms of externalizing pollution costs. The central state must preserve the existence of the home market and it must keep local and regional governments from destroying national assets (e.g., water, air, etc.).

One also needs to realize that the government's fear of publicizing the condition of the environment has not always meant that officials have been extra conscientious and alert to the environment. In 2003, the outbreak of SARS (severe acute respiratory syndrome) in China and its rapid spread was largely blamed on an attempted cover-up on the part of the Chinese authorities. While competition between regional governments has been credited with better outcomes for all or a win-win situation through learning by doing, it has not always played out that way. There were accusations in the Chinese media that the government tried to suppress the news of a fifty-mile toxic chemical slick polluting the Songhua River following an accident at a petrochemical plant in northeastern China in November 2005. While the officials admitted to five deaths caused by the accident, they denied that there were any further consequences. This could have been partly a result of Chinese bureaucracy and partly a result of the rivalry between the provinces of Heilongjiang and Songyuan, through which the Songhua River flows. Such news instills doubt and fear regarding China's ultimate success in dealing with its environment and its ability to deal with a crisis, especially given that China has already had a few outbreaks of the dreaded avian flu.

To sum up, both Russia and China inherited severe environment-related problems as they moved into the transition process. Both countries inherited pricing structures in natural resources that did not truly reflect the scarcity of such resources and led to overuse and inefficiency. However, as things stand today, it seems that China has been more successful in getting the situation under control than Russia. Part of the story lies in the economic differences between the two countries. China is experiencing spectacular economic growth while Russia's progress is much slower. The economic situation may also explain, to some extent, the differences in allocation of funds by both countries toward implementing environmental policies. However, the main difference appears to lie in the institutional framework in each country, which influences how environmental policies are carried out. While both countries have a central authority in charge of implementing policy, it seems that the policy makers in Russia lacked commitment to environmental quality. The budget constraints were soft and did not keep up with escalating inflation. Moreover, the authorities in Russia seem to think that economic growth and environmental clean-up are opposing forces and that an increase in one will decrease the other. This has resulted in growth-promoting policies that have given the wrong incentives for pollution. However, the biggest difference between Russia and China appears to be that environmental policy in Russia is handled at the national or international level rather than at a local or provincial level, as is the case with China. As a result, a large part of China's success has come from public awareness toward environmental issues and public participation, which seems to be lacking in Russia.

It seems the differences in institutional structure regarding the environment can be traced back to the U-form in Russia and the M-form in China mentioned in the previous section. The top-down U-from structure of Russia, reminiscent of the Soviet era, did not create the appropriate incentive structure for public and local officials to get involved in dealing with the problems of pollution. The M-form structure in China, which is more of a bottom-up structure, was successful in mobilizing public opinion and public participation. This allowed the build-up of networks at individual, firm, and local levels, which, along with the message of commitment from the political leaders of the country, has been somewhat successful in moving the Chinese economy on the path of more balanced and sustainable growth.

What We Have Learned

What have we learned from examining the experience of the transition economies? The experiences of these countries have been quite diverse. China's initial conditions most resemble those found in other developing countries, especially in Asia. It would seem that the transition process was led by reform and rapid growth in agriculture. The growth in income and market relations in the countryside provided the foundation for growth in small- and medium-sized manufacturing. Although formal systems of property rights were not created, rights to income streams for farmers and TVEs were implicitly formulated and protected.

In the decentralization of power over economic policy market-preserving federalism seemed to play an important role in the process of economic reform. It provided for a process by which commitment problems could be solved. This mechanism, suitably modified to take into account local circumstances, may be usefully applied in other contexts.

The Russian experience indicates that advice to developing countries to establish an effective market system is really not much help. Establishing market systems in particular historical circumstances can be extremely difficult. It might very well involve an initial period of declining output and/or growth as the disorganization of transition makes it difficult to establish market networks. In this process, predominately agrarian developing nations, such as China, may have had an advantage over middle-income transition countries such as Russia. In China's case, the bulk of the population was still involved in agriculture, and transforming from collectivized to household production was relatively easy. Because of the network of relationships with village-based agriculture, the initial growth in markets proceeded relatively rapidly. Thus, farmers had to be liberated in order to expand production for market dramatically. In Russia, the agrarian sector was relatively small and growth was crucially dependent on a dramatic reallocation of resources. Such a reallocation was time consuming, difficult, and costly.

Finally, questions of environmental sustainability are crucial for continued growth in economies making the transition. In this context, increased flows of trade and foreign investment may play a significant positive role. The rising income from a more open economy has meant that there has been increased demand by individuals for improvements in environmental quality. International investors have brought new technologies and standards more conducive to better environmental quality. Of course, some of these investments may have promoted a downward competition leading to increased pollution as localities sought to attract foreign investment. The role of local and regional governments and the central state in this process is complex.

Key Terms

Socialism	Market-preserving federalism
Big Bang	Decentralization
Transition	Economic Experimentation
Tradition	Household Responsibility System
Market System	TVE
Productivity Slowdown	Dual-track Approach
Property Rights	M-form Organization
Market Socialism	Sustainable Growth
Prisoner's Dilemma	Environment
Middle-income Country	Environmental Kuznets Curve

References

Blanchard, Olivier, and Michael Kremer. 1997. "Disorganization." *Quarterly Journal of Economics* 12 (November): 1091–126.

Bluffstone, R.A., and T. Panayotou. 2000. "Environmental Liability in Central and Eastern Europe: Toward an Optimal Policy." *Environmental and Resource Economics* 17, 335–52.

Buiter, W. 2000. "From Predation to Accumulation? The Second Transition Decade in Russia." *Economics of Transition* 8 (3): 603–22.

Cao, Y., Y. Qian, and B.R. Weingast. 1999. "From Federalism, Chinese Style to Privatization, Chinese Style." *Economics of Transition* 7: 103–31.

Chen, Aimin. 2005. "Assessing China's Economic Performance Since 1978: Material Attainments and Beyond." *Journal of Socio-Economics* 34: 499–527.

Ferrero, Mario. 1999. "Heavy Investment and High Pollution as Rational Choice under Socialism." *European Journal of Political Economy* 15: 257–80.

Feshbach, M. 1995. *Ecological Disaster: Cleaning Up the Hidden Legacy of the Soviet Regime.* New York: Twentieth Century Fund Press.

Godoy, Sergio, and Joseph Stiglitz. 2006. "Growth, Initial Conditions, Law and Speed of Privatization in Transition Countries: 11 Years Later." NBER Working Paper 11992. National Bureau of Economic Research, Cambridge, Massachusetts.

Golub, A., and E. Strukova. 1997. "Application of a Pollution-**fee** System in Russia" In *Economic Instruments for Air Pollution Control,* ed. G. Klaassen, and F. Forsund. Dordrecht, The Netherlands: Kluwer Academic.

Gregory, Paul, and Robert Stuart. 2004. *Comparing Economic Systems in the Twenty-First Century.* Boston: Houghton Mifflin.

Hoff, Karla, and Joseph E. Stiglitz. 2002. "After the Big Bang? Obstacles to the Emergence of the Rule of Law in Post-Communist Societies." NBER Working Paper No. 9282, Cambridge, MA.

Hughes, G., and M. Lovei. 1999. "Economic Reform and Environmental Performance in Transition Economies." World Bank Technical Paper 446, Eastern Europe and Central Asia Pollution Management Series. Washington, DC: World Bank.

Klein, L.R., and S. Ozmucur. 2002. "The Estimation of China's Economic Growth Rate." *Journal of Economic Social Measurement* 28, 187–202.

Kozeltsev, M., and A. Markandya. 1997. "Pollution Charges in Russia: The Experiences of 1990–1995." In *Controlling Pollution in Transition Economies,* ed. R. Bluffstone, and B. Larson. Cheltenham, UK: Edward Elgar.

Lange, Oskar. 1938. "On the Economic Theory of Socialism." In *On the Economic System of Socialism,* ed. Benjamin Lippincott. Minneapolis, MN: University of Minnesota Press.

Lau, L., Y. Qian, and G. Roland. 2000. "Reform Without Losers: An Interpretation of China's Dual-Track Approach to Transition." *Journal of Political Economy* 102: 120–43.

Li, S., and P. Lian. 1999. "Decentralization and Coordination: China's Credible Commitment to Preserve the Market Under Authoritarianism." *China Economic Review* 10: 161–90.

Lin, Y.L., F. Cai, and Z. Li. 1996. "The Lessons of China's Transition to a Market Economy." *Cato Journal* 16 (fall): 201–31.

Loucks, William, and William Whitney. 1973. *Comparative Economic Systems.* New York: Harper and Row.

Montinola, G., Y. Qian, and B.R. Weingast. 1995. "Federalism, Chinese Style: The Political Basis for Economic Success in China." *World Politics* 48 (October): 50–81.

National Intelligence Council. 1999. "National Intelligence Estimate: The Environ-mental Outlook in Russia." Washington, DC.

Organisation for Economic Co-operation and Development (OECD). 1999. *Policy Brief: Environmental Trends in Transition Economies*. Paris: OECD.

Panayotou, T. 1999. "The Economics of Environments in Transition." *Environmental and Development Economics* 4 (1): 389.

Qian, Y., and C. Xu. 1993. "Why China's Economic Reforms Differ: The M-Form Hierarchy and Entry/Expansion of the Non-State Sector." CEP Discussion Paper No. 154, June. Centre for Economic Performance, London.

Schwartz, Jonathan. 2003. "The Impact of State Capacity on Enforcement of Envi-ronmental Policies: The Case of China." *Journal of Environment and Develop-ment* 12 (1): 50–81.

Shin, Sangbum. 2004. "Economic Globalization and the Environment in China: A Comparative Case Study of Shenyang and Dalian." *Journal of Environment and Development* 13 (3): 263–94.

Shleifer, A., and D. Tressman. 2003. "A Normal Country." Harvard Institute of Economic Research Discussion Paper No. 2019. Harvard University, Cambridge, Massachusetts.

Smarzynska, B.K., and S. Wei. 2001. "Pollution Havens and Foreign Direct Invest-ment: Dirty Secret or Popular Myth?" NBER Working Paper 8465. National Bureau of Economic Research, Cambridge, Massachusetts.

Soderholm, Patrik. 2001. "Environmental Policy in Transition Economies: Will Pollution Charges Work?" *Journal of Environment and Development* 10 (4): 365–90.

Zhou, K.X., and L.T. White. 1995. "Quiet Politics and Rural Enterprise in Reform China." *Journal of Developing Areas* 29 (July): 461–90.

9

Conclusions

What Have We Learned?

In this short, concluding chapter, an attempt will be made to summarize what has been learned through the reading and study of the previous chapters. The approach utilized in this book has emphasized three things: history, institutions, and regions. With the exception of Chapter 1, specific economic models and concepts are introduced within the regional and historical context from which they arose. As the development process was examined in each region, the initial discussion always focused on the history of the region as a whole, or a country, or a set of countries within a region. The premise was that without a historical background, it is impossible to understand how economic growth and development occurred. The historical perspective provided the initial conditions to help us understand the context or how and why economic policies were made, how and why they succeeded or failed, and what we have learned from their experience.

History and how it unfolds also shows the institutional structure of a society and how it evolves through time. This institutional structure is the skeleton of a society; it comes in formal, obvious kinds of structures, and not-so-formal, almost invisible structures. These rules, both explicit and implicit, provide the context within which economic decision making and policy making take place. That is why identical types of policies have such dramatically different impacts across regions. A good example of this is land reform. Land reform has been put forward in many different countries. In certain regions of the world land reform and enhanced productivity have gone hand in hand with economic prosperity (e.g., East Asia). However, similar reforms in other regions have failed miserably (e.g., India) and/or productivity has actually fallen (e.g., Latin America).

Given the methodology utilized, what has been learned? Experiences have been quite varied, but are there underlying similarities that permeate these diverse experiences?

Efflorescence

One often gets the impression that before the Industrial Revolution in England, the world and its history was characterized by stagnation. However, the previous chapters have argued that the world has experienced many economic efflorescences in a variety of regions throughout much of history. The analogy one can think of is of a pot of stew that has begun to boil and bubble. The world's regions are like parts of this stew, with economic activities intensifying and rising to the top in some regions only to fall and be replaced by bubbling efflorescences of economic activity in others. Historically the world has been economically dynamic, with the source of that dynamism varying from region to region through time.

The experience of Western Europe in the seventeenth and eighteenth centuries represents one of those efflorescences of economic activity. It resembled such occurrences in other parts of the world and at other times. However, in the early nineteenth century, the European experience took a different path, science was applied to the production process, and mineral sources of energy were tapped. In this way, the law of diminishing returns was overturned (at least for a substantial period of time) and a dramatic intensification of economic activity took place. Are there certain factors that explain the "rise of the West?" More likely, it was the result of a fortuitous combination of events that would likely have happened somewhere, sometime, as economic efflorescences continued to occur.

Impact of Colonization

In Europe's economic growth and industrialization, colonies and the colonization process likely played an important role. Directly, the establishment of colonies in the New World resulted in the creation of an international trading system in which primary products flowed into northwestern Europe and manufactured goods flowed out to the new colonies. This dramatic expansion in the demand for manufacturing certainly stimulated Europe's industrialization. In addition, colonization had an indirect effect in that the trade it stimulated strengthened the hand of merchants and new manufacturers, resulting in institutional and political change restricting the activities of the state (especially in England), and, instead, directing state policy toward enhancing the accumulation of wealth.

Of course, the impact of colonization on the colonies themselves was quite negative in many places. Often indigenous populations were destroyed and/or their society disrupted. In Central and South America, this resulted in the transplantation of Spanish institutions and the creation of an unequal distribution of wealth, especially concerning land. This extreme inequality in wealth posed significant barriers to economic reform in the nineteenth and twentieth centuries, and to economic growth. Africa was also significantly damaged by the colonization process. Indigenous societies were disrupted and imported institutional structures transplanted. The foundations for weak states were established while the dependence of the region on natural resources and revenue from these resources has had significant negative economic and political effects. These were colonies of extraction with little settlement by populations from the colonial powers. The main motive was to extract as much wealth as possible as quickly as possible.

However, the experience of other regions teaches that colonization was not a uniform experience, its impact varied from place to place. The most obvious case of this was the settlement of North America by the English and French. The English, in particular, brought their institutions and this combined with the predominance of small, family-farm agriculture, created the foundations for rapid future economic growth. The same can also be said concerning the colonization of Taiwan and Korea by the Japanese. The latter brought its institutions and promoted the growth of small, family-operated rice and sugar farms. This combination provided a productive foundation for the future growth of Taiwan and Korea (at least South Korea). This is not to deny that the colonization of East Asia was brutal and painful. However, here and in North America it seems that the colonial experience did provide foundations more favorable to future economic growth and development.

The spread of colonization went hand in hand with trade, investment, and the expansion of markets. As this system grew, it intruded on indigenous societies, which responded to this intrusion in a variety of ways. Much of the world was colonized, but with independence, different societies chose different paths to catch up or modernize. Some chose to isolate themselves from the expansion of the international market and sought to become self-reliant. China, after World War II, was reluctant to integrate with the international system and, also, sought to suppress markets domestically. The idea was that modernization could be achieved through the efforts of the state to mobilize available resources to achieve a great leap forward, an economic miracle. The elimination of markets proved to be a disastrous failure. Those that chose this inward-oriented path suffered significant economic damage. Integration with the world economic system and the growth of domestic markets does not guarantee the achievement of prosperity, but attempts at the suppression of such an orientation and a turn toward self-sufficiency seems to result in economic stagnation, a failure to catch up.

China, of course, represented the extreme case of turning inward. However, India and several other South Asian countries also followed paths of development aimed at substituting domestic production for trade via tariffs, licenses, and so on. These too slowed economic development, although not to the same extent as in China.

Role of the State

International trade according to the principle of comparative advantage certainly allows countries to specialize by exporting goods that they are relatively good at producing in order to import goods that they are not so good at producing. This improves the efficiency of the allocation of resources domestically and internationally and thus results in higher productivity. Trade and foreign investment also allows a nation to import the capital that it needs, and new technology is often embodied in capital. Thus trade and foreign investment can serve as conduits for new technology. Economists have often argued that it is through free trade and the free flow of investment between countries that all countries can gain and, in particular, that poor countries can catch up with the developed. However, the previous chapters have shown that few countries have engaged in free trade and the free flow of foreign investment. Most countries have regulated both trade and foreign investment. The East and Southeast Asian miracle countries sought to manage trade to accelerate the transition from low to high productivity, via learning by doing. This region has been able to rapidly move up the technological ladder. Trade and markets are necessary for the rapid creation of wealth, but free trade does not seem to be necessary.

Of course, a number of regions of the world illustrate the failures that can occur through government regulation of trade and markets. In particular, Latin America and sub-Saharan Africa certainly show how the ruling elite can use the powers of the state to greatly distort economic activities, creating significant inefficiency and, in its extreme form, destroying the economy. One should not be naïve about the state and its effectiveness. However, the previous chapters have shown that an effective state is essential to promote the rapid growth of wealth. This state must be able to protect property rights, protect its citizens, and to enforce institutional rules. Some have also argued that an effective state is necessary to coordinate the jump from low productivity equilibriums to high productivity equilibriums. An effective state is essential, but how is such a state to be brought about?

One of the fundamental themes that has run throughout this book is the importance for ruling elites to solve the commitment problem. A state strong enough to enforce property rights is a state or ruling elite strong enough to revoke them whenever it is beneficial (to the elite and its supporters) to do so. If investors sense this, they will be reluctant to invest. For rapid growth to occur, the ruling elite must be willing to commit to playing by the rules. That is, it must commit to protecting property rights for the bulk of its citizens and it must be capable of coordinating economic resources so as to generate economic growth benefiting the population at large. This commitment must be believable, and it must be credible. But here is where the difficulty lies: How to make a credible commitment?

In previous chapters, light was shed on how this might occur by utilizing the concept of earned income. Earned income requires that effort be expended by the ruling elite to collect the revenue that it needs. This has two aspects. First, the ruling elite must create a penetrating set of institutions in order to collect revenue from the bulk of the population. Second, reciprocity must be provided; that is, in order to collect revenue, services must be provided in return. Earned income evolves through a process of dialectical interaction. The ruling elite will extract revenue and then break its commitment to providing services in return. The effected population will then use various techniques to punish the ruling elite. They may move their capital elsewhere, reduce production for the market, hide their production and income, and so on. It is through this process that the state learns to reciprocate in its dealings with its citizens. The outcome of this process will be a state that keeps its promises and guarantees the promises by the sharing of power with various segments of society.

In many regions of the world, the agrarian sector has played a crucial role in this process. For example, in East Asia the ruling elite was initially significantly dependent on peasant agriculture as a source of revenue. Attempts at extracting revenue were met with significant opposition. This dialectical process of conflict resulted in the ruling elite learning to reciprocate in the provision of services for revenue and to share power as a means to effectively commit to such policies. This process also seems to have occurred in parts of Western Europe.

However, significant levels of inequality in the distribution of land ownership in some regions have acted to prevent the unfolding of such a process. The ruling elite has become dependent on a small, landed elite for its survival. As a result, the ruling elite protects the property rights of only a small proportion of the population and seeks to support the expansion of the wealth of a small proportion of the population. This results from the ruling elite becoming dependent for their revenue on a small, powerful proportion of the population. For example, in Latin America, the extreme inequality in the distribution of wealth, in particular land, has served as a stumbling block to political development.

In Sub-Saharan Africa, inequality has been augmented by the effects of colonialism and dependence on primary products to create an environment in which states are patrimonial in nature. The ruling elite has based their position on the ability to control rents that arise from the export of particular primary commodities. In addition, ethnic issues have been enhanced in order to maintain power. This, combined with the widespread availability of weapons, has led to the breakdown of the state in various regions; that is, state failure. In the long run, political and economic development in Sub-Saharan Africa will depend on productivity growth in agriculture, where the bulk of the population still earns its living, and integration into the world economic system.

In India, democracy was the established political system since independence. However, in this context, democracy became dominated by patrimonial politics in which the ruling elite established ruling coalitions that successfully protected property rights for only a small proportion of the population. The powers of the state were used to reward supporters and punish foes within the context of democratic political structures.

In the contexts that Latin America, Africa, and parts of South Asia find themselves in, the creation of effective states and the solution of the commitment problem may be fostered by the globalization process. Extractive policies by the state are likely to lead to capital flowing out, and this should act as a system of punishment. As a result, the ruling elite may be constrained from behaving in a predatory manner.

Today there is much discussion concerning the role of democracy; that is, states that engage in policies that benefit the bulk of their populations are more likely within a democratic institutional structure. Economic development is likely to be the result of the creation of democracy.

Role of Democracy

In discussing the role of democracy, there is first the challenge of actually defining this term. Because our interest here is to examine the relationship between democracy and economic growth (i.e., the creation of wealth), the definition should reflect this orientation. The definition offered by Schumpeter is that democracy is "that institutional arrangement for arriving at political decisions in which individuals acquire the power to decide by means of a competitive struggle for the people's vote" (Schumpeter 1950, 269). According to Gerring et al. (2005, 338), the real question is "whether the current in-group stands a realistic chance of becoming an out-group in the near future."

With the above in mind, how is it that democracy might promote the wealth of nations? The simplest notion here would be that a ruling elite in a truly functioning democracy would not be able to pursue policies enhancing the wealth of only a few. Nor could they engage in policies enhancing their own wealth at the expense of society. Such a state and its ruling elite would have to be responsive to the economic needs of the bulk of its citizens. This is assured via the fact that ruling elites who fail to do this are removed from office. In the long run, growth is dependent on commitments to wealth- and market-enhancing policies, and commitment to such policies is established via the diffusion of power characteristic of a well-functioning democracy. In this context, investors will have confidence in their rights to profit being protected, and innovators will feel confident that the returns to innovation will be theirs to keep.

This sort of analysis implies that the direction of causality would run from democracy to economic development. However, there is significant evidence that the direction of causality may be the reverse—that is, that rapid economic growth leads to the development of democracy. Glaeser et al. (2004) make exactly this argument. They point out that the political scientist Seymour Martin Lipset (1960) made this argument long ago. Specifically, he argued that educated people are more likely to resolve differences of opinion and conflicts via negotiating and voting than through violence. Educated specialists are necessary to run the institutions closely connected to and strongly influencing economic growth.

Glaeser et al. generalizes this argument by linking growth with the accumulation of human capital. They see growth stemming from human-capital accumulation as leading to better political and social institutions. More specifically, unconstrained political leaders make choices to promote human-capital accumulation, which in turn generates rapid growth. This in turn creates forces that lead to better institutions (constraining future leaders), in this case democracy. Thus, it is argued that democracy is a result of growth, not the other way around.

The experience of East Asia, in particular South Korea and Taiwan, would seem to support this argument. Both were led by autocrats after World War II. These dictatorial leaders chose paths that encouraged rapid accumulation of both physical and human capital. The ensuing growth eventually dispersed political power such that demands for democratic participation could not be resisted. Democracy seems thus to have evolved out of growing prosperity.

What of the alternative argument? Is there evidence that the establishment of democracy causes growth? Much of the empirical evidence over the past few decades is not supportive of this hypothesis. In fact, the net effect of democracy on growth performance seems to be zero (i.e., no net positive effect), and there is even some evidence of a negative effect on economic growth.

However, recent work by Gerring et al. would seem to provide strong support that democracy has a positive causal effect on growth. They argue that democracy's effect emerges in time. Most empirical analysis proceeds in the following manner. Measures of democracy are utilized as the independent variable and per capita gross domestic product (GDP) growth is utilized as the dependent variable. Regime type is thought to influence current and future growth rates. Regime type (e.g., a democracy) effects growth with some sort of lag. These estimations indicate that democracy has no net effect and sometimes has a negative effect on growth.

Gerring et al. gives a historical dimension to the analysis by looking backward. They attempt to measure a country's accumulated stock of democracy rather than the level (flow) of democracy at a particular period. What matters is how long a nation has been democratic, with the hypothesis being that the longer a nation has been democratic the faster the country will grow. Democracy is thus viewed as a form of political capital, similar in some respects to physical capital. The stock of the latter grows through investment over time. The level of democracy expands with years of experience, with the latter being thought of as an investment process.

How might the accumulation of democratic (i.e., political) capital foster economic growth? Consider, for a moment, economic policy and good governance. Good economic policy and well-run administrations do not automatically come with the establishment of democracy. Political elites must learn what represents good and bad policy and must learn how to construct effective bureaucracies. Voters too must learn to recognize good policy. Finally, the political elite must learn that voters have evolved and become more sophisticated and most voters must learn that ruling elites have become responsive to political demands. "More generally, democracies institute a learning process among elites and masses in which economic performance and electoral contests offer periodic corrections" (Gerring et al. 2005, 338). One would thus expect a slow transition from populist-style politics as democratic experience accumulates.

This kind of argument is similar in many aspects to the earlier arguments made in this book concerning political development and earned income. That is, a ruling elite learns by doing in trying to extract revenue from the bulk of its population. It learns that in order to extract revenue it must reciprocate with services. In order to convince producers of its commitment to do so, power must be diffused to enhance compliance. Democratic restraints on the ruling elite are just such a mechanism.

The empirical results support the above hypothesis concerning the historical impact of democracy. Accumulated democratic experience has a significant impact on economic growth and this relationship is found to be historically robust (Gerring et al. 2005). If these results are valid, then democracy can be a mechanism by which the political-commitment problem can eventually be solved, with rapid economic growth the result.

Returning to the previous discussion concerning the direction of causality, the following conclusion emerges. There is evidence to support that economic growth and human-capital accumulation cause political development, even democracy. There is also evidence that political development causes economic growth. Mutual causality seems to exist and no one should really be surprised at this conclusion. Economic growth generated by the decisions of an autocrat can increase the diffusion of power and that diffusion of power can further augment growth.

However, several things need to be kept in mind. Democracies are not created overnight. It is the accumulation of democratic experience that is the key; experience augments growth via learning. Second, it is indeed a learning process fraught with conflict. The ruling elite will initially attempt to behave in a predatory or patronizing pattern. This will involve conflict with producers, and it is through this process of conflict that learning occurs and commitment problems are solved. The path is not an easy one. Finally, political development must evolve within a nation; it cannot be imposed from the outside. Imposition from the outside tends to circumvent the learning process.

Tying It All Together

The lessons here can be boiled down to a simple set of ideas. First, good economic policy is important. That is, for many developing nations the productivity of the agricultural sector must be increased via investment in new technology. Rates of return to such investment are relatively high. In addition, urban bias must be avoided in government spending and prices must not be distorted in favor of urban dwellers. Integration with world markets must occur. However, there is likely an important role for states to play in coordinating the shift from low productive to high productive equilibriums. This would involve the use of taxes and subsidies to promote the transition to highly productive economic activities. The possible success of such policies depends on the quality of government intervention. Where political development is limited, free-trade policies would be better, although such policies were not entirely successful in Latin America in the 1800s. Investment in human capital is critical for shifting to activities that are more productive. For most developing countries, this would involve significant investment in primary levels of education.

Although the choice of economic policy is important, the political context within which policy is made is crucial. Politically underdeveloped states are not likely to be able to carry out effective economic policies. Even appropriate policies are likely to be distorted in environments in which a solution to the commitment problem has not been achieved.

Key Terms

Democracy
Wealth of Nations
Direction of Causality
Democratic Political Capital

Learning Process
Economic Policy
Political Context

References

Gerring, John, Philip Bond, William T. Barndt, and Carola Moreno. 2005. "Democracy and Economic Growth: A Historical Perspective." *World Politics* 57: 323–64.
Glaeser, Edward, Rafael La Porta, Florencio Lopez-de-Silanes, and Andrei Shleifer. 2004. "Do Institutions Cause Growth?" NBER Working Paper 10568. Bureau of Economic Research, Cambridge, Massachusetts.
Lipset, Seymour Martin. 1960. *Political Man: The Social Basis of Modern Politics.* New York: Doubleday.
Schumpeter, Joseph. 1950. *Capitalism, Socialism, and Democracy.* New York: Harper.

About the Authors

Richard Grabowski received his doctoral degree in economics from the University of Utah in 1977. He is the author of two books, *Pathways to Economic Development* and, with Michael P. Shields, *Development Economics.* His research work has been published in several journals, including *World Development, Review of Economics and Statistics,* and *Economic Letters.* This work has focused on agriculture and the process of economic development. He is currently a professor of economics at Southern Illinois University.

Sharmistha Self was born and raised in India. She received her bachelor's and master's degrees from Jadavpur University in India. She came to the United States to pursue graduate work and received her PhD in economics from Southern Illinois University in 2002. Her primary area of research is economic development, with particular focus on topics such as gender, health, and education. Much of her work focuses on Asia. She has been published in journals such as *Economics of Education Review, Journal of Asian Economics, Applied Economics, Review of Development Economics,* and *Journal of Socio-Economics.* Her experience growing up in a developing country explains much of her interest in economic development. She is currently an assistant professor of economics at Missouri State University.

Michael P. Shields received his undergraduate degree from the University of California, Berkeley, and his PhD from the University of Utah, both in economics. He has coauthored a book with Richard Grabowski and has been published in a number of journals, including *Economic*

Development and Cultural Change, Economica, World Development, Journal of Regional Science, Southern Economic Journal, and *Population Economics.* His primary research is in development economics, with an emphasis on migration and fertility. He is currently a professor of economics at Central Michigan University.

Index